Song of Saigon

Song of Saigon

Anh Vu Sawyer
and
Pam Proctor

One Woman's Journey to Freedom

Warner Faith

WARNER BOOKS

An AOL Time Warner Company

Unless otherwise noted, Scripture quotations are from the REVISED STANDARD VERSION of the Bible. Copyright © 1946, 1952, 1971, 1973 by the Division of Christian Education of the National Council of the Churches of Christ in the U.S.A. Used by permission.

Scriptures noted KJV are from THE KING JAMES VERSION.

Warner Books, Inc., 1271 Avenue of the Americas, New York, NY 10020
Visit our website at www.twbookmark.com

 An AOL Time Warner Company

Printed in the United States of America
First Warner Books Printing: February 2003

Library of Congress Cataloging-in-Publication Data

Sawyer, Anh Vu.
    Song of saigon : one woman's journey to freedom / Anh Vu Sawyer and Pam Proctor.
        p. cm.
    Includes bibliographical references.
    ISBN 0-446-52908-7
    1. Sawyer, Anh Vu—Childhood and youth. 2. Sawyer, Anh Vu—Family. 3. Vietnamese American women—Biography. 4. Vietnamese Americans—Biography. 5. Vietnamese Conflict, 1961–1975—Personal narratives, Vietnamese. 6. Vietnamese Conflict, 1961–1975—Vietnam—Ho Chi Minh City. 7. Ho Chi Minh City (Vietnam)—History 8. Ho Chi Minh City (Vietnam)—Biography. I. Proctor, Pam, 1945– II. Title.

    E184.V53 S28 2003
    959.704'3'092—dc21
    [B]   2002033062

10 9 8 7 6 5 4 3 2 1

To the women who shaped my life:

My mother, Nguyen Thi Nghia, whose strength I inherited
and
My mother-in-law, Ruth D. Sawyer, who taught
me the power of quiet faith

CONTENTS

ACKNOWLEDGMENTS

Thanks:

To all friends and strangers who told me that I had to write this book.

To friends at Christ Church, Oak Brook, Illinois; the Mustard Seed Christian Fellowship, Lawrence, Kansas; North Springs Alliance Church, Colorado Springs, Colorado; Evangelical Free Church, Naperville, Illinois; and all my students at The Classical Academy and Shepherd of the Springs Lutheran High School in Colorado Springs, who believed in me and faithfully prayed for me.

To Esther Fitzstevens; my aunts, Bac Ca, Bac Khai, and Nancy Jesudas; my brother, Phong; and Bernard, Raymond and Victor Jackson, for giving Pam and me much of their time as they recalled the rich and complicated past of Vietnam and my family history.

To my mother, for countless hours telling me of my heritage and for her courage in opening up her heart, despite the vulnerability of telling sad, hidden truths. She was more than willing to share with the world the life of a young Vietnamese woman in wartime.

To Linda Poston, director of library services at Nyack College, and Patty McGarvey, Assistant Archivist at the Christian and Missionary Alliance, for valuable research assistance; the elders of the Hanoi Protestant Church, for historical background on the church's growth in Vietnam; Isabelle Fuller, for editing French phrases; and again, Victor Jackson, who provided access to the unpublished manuscript of his mother, Hazel Jackson.

To Rolf Zettersten and Leslie Peterson of Warner Faith, for believing in the spiritual and historical significance of this story.

To Bill and Pam, for giving much of themselves to make this book happen, only because they loved me.

To Philip, Lam, James and Lena for their wonderful love and support, and for tolerating a harried mom as this book was coming to fruition. I love you!

Anh Vu Sawyer
Colorado Springs, Colorado

EXPLANATORY NOTE

In producing this manuscript, the authors have relied on first-person, eyewitness accounts of the tumultuous events during eighty years of Vietnamese history, extensive library and documentary research, and in-depth interviews involving the collective memories of family and friends. Although some names have been changed, the people and the framework of events are true. To bring to life Anh Vu Sawyer's early family history, we have inferred certain circumstances and personal encounters that address gaps in the historical record while remaining as faithful as possible to what is actually known about the personalities, experiences, and spiritual orientation of the people involved.

I call to remembrance my song
in the night.

Psalm 77:6 (KJV)

PART I

The Legacy

1

TU BIET—FAREWELL FOREVER

Do I dare tell you about the dream I had in anatomy class? If Mother knew, she would be scandalized. It just isn't the thing a well-bred Vietnamese girl fantasizes about.

Anatomy lab was right after lunch, and with my stomach full and my brain still fuzzy after a midday siesta at home, I found it impossible to keep my mind on the tedious work ahead. It was hot, stiflingly hot, as dust blew in through the open windows and onto the corpses that were stretched naked on concrete slabs around the laboratory. My nostrils burned with the pungent odor of formaldehyde, which infused the air from across the room, where eight or ten corpses were afloat in an open vat.

I was standing at my workstation and had just picked up my scalpel to slice into the thigh of a cadaver when—in my mind's eye—a handsome young man appeared just outside the door. He seemed to come out of nowhere.

He was slim and tall, with a gentle face, curly brown hair, and soft, elegant hands. He wore jeans and a loose denim shirt that appeared to have been draped carelessly over his body, giving him an air of wanton abandon. Although he looked nothing at all like the GI Joes who were everywhere in Saigon, with their buzz cuts, bulging biceps, and fatigues, I knew instantly that he was American.

The very thought of him made me blush. I had never spoken directly to an American man before. I had only heard their voices, calling to their buddies outside the bars, haggling with the aunties selling *ao dai* in the marketplace, or laughing with young women in skintight miniskirts. These Americans were loud, grasping, and self-important.

They even brought themselves so low as to walk around the streets wearing women's underwear on their heads like a trophy. To compound the shame, these young American guys would sit brazenly with their women in the front seat of a pedal-driven *cyclo*, kissing and tickling each other, as the poor old *cyclo* driver pedaled behind, trying to avert his eyes in humiliation.

"Very bad women," my mother would say when I was young, ordering me to cover my eyes as if we were walking along some kind of nude beach. I pretended not to look, but through the cracks in my fingers, I took it all in, wondering what it meant. Later on, when as a teenager I saw such things, I felt less revulsion than pity. For some reason I can't explain, I found myself overcome by a great burden to pray for their children—the mixed-race offspring of these prostitutes and their boorish Americans.

But my American lover was different. He had a tenderness about him—an inner tranquility—that was so strong and sure I was overpowered by its magnetism. When he was with me, I felt such a sense of security that nothing could harm me: not the terrifying rockets that came in the night; nor the random bombs that exploded in the markets by day; nor the salacious whispers of my friends and family; nor even the disgust of my anatomy professor, who had to keep reminding me to keep focused on my dissection.

"Ngoc Anh," he would intone, "if you intend to be a doctor, you must first get through this class."

I would apologize many times, bow very low, and pretend to be absorbed in my lab. And then, when Professor Hung wasn't looking, I would smile and cast a glance at my lover, who was still waiting for me patiently, as I knew he would be, just outside the door.

When I finally finished my work and left the classroom, he would walk me out of the building as if I were a queen. My friends were green with envy. I could see their jealous looks and hear the hushed whispers, but I didn't care.

My lover was with me, and that was all that mattered. We didn't touch, or even say a word. We simply walked quietly down the steps of Minh Duc Medical School and onto the hot, dusty street, where we hopped on our motorcycles and rode off into the evening.

Perhaps the dreams made me oblivious to what was going on in Saigon right under my nose. It was the spring of 1975, and my country was on the cusp of an historic political cataclysm. Although I was twenty years old, I hadn't the foggiest sense that a maelstrom was swirling around me.

I did notice one thing strange: I would be sitting in class one day and a messenger would come to the door, call out the name of one of the students, and he would be gone. Not just gone for the moment— but gone for good. It happened a couple of times a day. One minute a classmate like Hiep, the son of a prominent Air Force general, would be sitting next to me, and the next minute he'd be rushing out the door like the March Hare, as if he had forgotten an important appointment. We never saw him again.

These disappearances continued with increasing frequency. There was my friend Mili, the daughter of a wealthy banker, and then Bao, the son of an official attached to the American Embassy. After that came Tran, Von, and Nhan, until the class had more seats that were empty than full.

At first no one spoke of what was happening. We simply hung out with our friends as we always had, laughing at some silly joke over a bowl of noodle soup, or comparing notes on an upcoming exam. But before long, the whispers started.

"Did you notice there aren't as many Americans around?" someone said, *sotto voce*. "I hear they're all leaving."

Another confided, "I saw my cousin Duc yesterday. He was a soldier up north in Hue, and now he's home for good. He says units are retreating all over the countryside."

"How about our classmate Diep? I hear she left for Paris with her brothers and sister."

Toward the middle of April, the rumors of a North Vietnamese assault on the South were thick as a plague of grasshoppers, but we had nothing to confirm them. We tried looking through *Time* and *Newsweek*, which were readily available in Saigon, but the government regularly censored the Far East editions and decisions about the war never quite made it to their pages.

My family did have one potential source of real information: my older brother, Phong, who had graduated from California State Polytechnic Institute and was now working in San Francisco. But we hadn't heard from him in months. So we were left, like most everyone else in Saigon, to try to discern the truth of what was going on and fend for ourselves.

We had no powerful connections or financial clout to buy our way out of the country as many of my classmates did. If we hoped to leave Vietnam, we would have to find our own way.

My mother, who was always enterprising about such things, started to dig up information by talking to everyone she knew. One friend told her it might be possible for me to arrange a fake marriage license, showing that I was married to an American. With such a document, the woman said, the American Embassy would give me an exit visa.

As tempting as the idea was, other friends counseled against it. "I've heard that people end up losing their money and never get the marriage certificate," they said. "It's just a scam."

The rumors kept flying, and we kept running, first here and then there to find a shred of real information. When my mother heard that there might be some tidbit to be had at the local city hall, she sent me on my bike to hang out and listen. When I arrived there, the place was so crowded I couldn't even wedge myself inside the door. I had to wait in a field outside with hundreds of others who had obviously heard the same rumor.

All around me, people were tense and anxious. I could see them scanning the crowd for a friendly face who might give them a piece of news. But there was no news that day that could help any of us, and as the truth of our predicament began to sink in, I did what I had always done ever since I was a child: I began to pray. "If you want us to leave," I told God, "you'll have to show us how."

All my life, I had felt free to put questions to God, and in various ways he had never failed to answer. Why should I expect any less of him now? I just knew that our position at that moment appeared to be hopeless, and if indeed a way out of Vietnam existed for my family, the specific details would have to be divinely orchestrated.

❊❊❊❊❊

"*Chi* Huong, *Chi* Huong! Open the gate! It's me, open up!" Because of a twenty-four-hour curfew, which had just been imposed a few weeks earlier, we regularly kept the gate of our family compound closed and locked. Now someone was banging loudly, clamoring to get in. For some reason, he was calling out *Chi* Huong, or "elder sister Huong," the familiar name of our nanny.

"Who could it be?" asked Mother. "Don't open the door!"

Still the gate rattled, and the male voice shouted again. "*Chi* Huong—the gate—please open it!"

"It sounds like Master Phong," our nanny said.

"That's impossible," retorted my mother. "Phong's in America."

At the very mention of my brother's name, my sister, brothers, and I rushed out the door to our house and up to the gate, where my very bedraggled brother Phong was standing outside, grasping the iron bars.

Nanny opened the gate, and he quickly slipped inside the compound, where we crowded around him in awe and excitement.

I barely recognized him. When he had left Vietnam nearly eight years before, he had been a skinny teenager with a sophisticated veneer of slicked back hair, tailored designer jackets, and luxurious Pierre Cardin ties. Now he was a grown man, strikingly handsome, well fed and brimming with confidence. His hair was so long it nearly brushed his shoulders. And in his tight Levis and denim jacket, he looked every inch an American.

My mother took one look at him and almost fainted. "Why did you come home?" she asked with a look of fear in her eyes. "You were safe. You had life. Why are you here?"

"I had to come," he said. "I tried to write. I even tried to send a telegram. When I couldn't reach you, I hopped a plane to Guam and then got a lift here as a volunteer on a Red Cross helicopter."

The urgency in his eyes riveted our attention and rendered us speechless as he continued: "You must leave the country immediately," he said. "There is no hope left. The only chance you have is to get out with me, because now I'm an American citizen."

For a long while, nobody said a word. We just looked at him, unable to speak, as the enormity of what was happening to us began to sink in. Then all of a sudden, we broke into smiles and started tittering with giddy laughter.

"Yes, yes," we all agreed. We would go tomorrow to the American Embassy, as Phong had said. He was an American now, a citizen, and that meant everything would be all right. He was sure of it.

The next morning the house took on an air of celebration. It was as if someone had flicked a switch, turning the stark and scary darkness of our lives into an incredible burst of light. With Phong in our midst, we felt hopeful and safe, filled with expectation about our future life in America. Here was our hero, the bold rescuer—who had been born, appropriately, in the Year of the Tiger—who was going to bring us to the promised land.

For breakfast, our nanny spread out a feast: delicate crepes known as *banh cuon*, filled with savory meat; sticky rice with coconut milk; lemon sauces; tea; and the ubiquitous *pho*, the noodle soup that is a Vietnamese staple.

How Nanny had managed this repast, I'll never know. No shops or stores were open where she could buy such goods. Our only sources for food were the black market and whatever we could scrounge from our neighbors by bartering from house to house. But Phong was Nanny's oldest charge—she had practically raised him herself—and for her young prince, nothing but the best would do.

I gorged myself on the banquet, paying more attention to my stomach than to the serious conversation between my parents and Phong at the other end of the table. But soon breakfast was over and before I knew what was happening, Phong hustled us out the door and managed to flag down an open-air minibus to take us to the embassy.

Although it was dangerous for us or anyone else to be out in the daylight, as we traveled along I saw our friend Quang riding on a motorcycle. I waved at him happily. *We are going to life—we are going to our future*, I thought, smiling to myself.

Even after we arrived at the embassy and saw thousands of others who had gotten there ahead of us, my sense of euphoria was undiminished. We waited outside expectantly as Phong maneuvered his way inside the building to talk to an official. But when he emerged an hour later, he looked strained and defeated. "There's no way we can do it," he said, shaking his head. "They say they are only taking American citizens."

We looked at each other in astonishment, not knowing what to do next. Mother was the first to speak. Mustering every ounce of courage she had left, she gave her oldest son a direct order: "I want you to leave us," she told Phong. "Go back to your American wife. Don't waste your life for us. You've done all you can do. You have a chance to live—take it. Take it now!"

There was a finality in her voice that brooked no opposition. We all knew that voice, and whenever she was in the command mode, we knew better than to contradict her.

Phong looked at her, then at Father, and at each of my siblings, one by one. Then he looked at me. His eyes were filled with pain and yearning.

"Go, please go," I begged him, touching his shoulder lightly. Tears streamed down my cheeks, and my body heaved with sobs. Next to me, my sister Diep, eighteen, and my brothers Hai, nineteen, and Khanh, thirteen, were drowning in despair. My older sister, Tram, twenty-six, escaped this awful moment only because she was studying in Germany. Just my parents and Phong remained stoic.

When Phong could bear no more, he turned on his heels and ran into the embassy, afraid even to look back.

❖❖❖❖❖

The minute we stepped through the gate of our family compound, my mother's steely conviction drained out of her, and she became almost catatonic. With her arms crossed and gripping her body, she sat on the divan, rocking back and forth and moaning in a low, steady drone, "My son, my son."

In another room, my father, his face white as a sheet, sat slumped in a chair, chain-smoking. My sister and brothers fled to our room, where they huddled together, talking in whispers, as if something would break if they dared speak out loud.

I was beyond tears. Beyond fear. Yet I wasn't ready to surrender to some futile fate. I was consumed by a sense of urgency, an overwhelming conviction that we had to leave the country immediately. But I was also burning with an equally strong desire to wait for a little while and pray. It was almost as if a sturdy hand had been placed on my shoulder to steady me, to calm me, and to keep my mind focused.

Instinctively, I began to speak to God. I wandered from room to room with no particular destination or purpose. There really wasn't much else for me to do. In those anxious years of war, with few activities to occupy us, we either read or just sat doing nothing.

I know now that's why I daydreamed a lot, and why prayer had become a regular habit. We spent so much of our spare time worrying that, for a respite, I found my spirit yearning to be in God's presence.

Something inside of me—beyond my will, beyond my conscious mind—craved a constant connection.

I could be in the middle of some small task, such as helping *Chi* Huong prepare dinner, and I would catch myself talking to God. I wasn't even aware that I was praying, but I was. Sometimes, when I was lying in bed waiting to fall asleep, the wail of rockets overhead testing my tranquility, I would engage him in conversation. "Are you really real?" I asked. "Would you show me, then?"

Before I knew it, I was drifting off to sleep, feeling securely enfolded in the protection of everlasting arms.

Of course, these conversations weren't proof of God's existence in a visible way. But over the years, our conversations had taken on a life of their own as I had come to know that God was always there for me and his love was very real. To me, that was all the proof I needed. It was only natural, then, that as my family faced the biggest crisis of our lives, my soul drifted back to God. Over and over like a mantra, words came flooding out of my mouth. "Lord, have mercy. God, have mercy."

For what seemed like hours, I whispered my petitions, humbly beseeching God to pour out his compassion upon me and my family and permit us to leave. I knew that we didn't deserve such favor any more than the Nguyen family next door or the Duongs down the street. Nonetheless, I believed with all my heart that God had the power to pluck us out from among millions of people if he chose to, and that to such an awesome God, even my small voice was not too insignificant to be heard.

"God, you are merciful," I said simply. "Please be gracious to us."

The longer I prayed, the more I was buoyed by an unwavering sense of assurance. Nothing in our circumstances had changed: my mother was still moaning, my father was still smoking, and my siblings were still holed up in their room. Yet a stillness welled up inside of me, a gentle calm that made me feel as if I were a paper flower, a bougainvillea, floating down a meandering stream. Like that paper flower, I was being carried along by a force that was not of my own strength to a destination not of my own choosing. And as I bobbed along on the sparkling water, I remained vibrant and intact—with bright fuchsia petals that sent a message of joy and hope.

"Anh, wake up," my mother said, tugging at my sleeve the next morning. "We've decided to go to the American church. I remembered someone telling me a few weeks ago that if we get to the church, the American pastor will help us."

Over breakfast, we started talking animatedly among ourselves, weighing this new option. We lived in Gia Dinh, a suburb of Saigon that was a half-hour's motorcycle ride to the church. The problem was, we didn't have enough motorcycles for the entire family. A quick peek out on the street—where not a soul stirred—confirmed that our chances of finding a minibus, as we had the day before, were slim.

Even if we did have transportation, the thought of buzzing around the streets in broad daylight, with armed Vietnamese soldiers ready to enforce the curfew, was unnerving. Even more questionable was the idea of finding refuge at the American church itself. Allying ourselves so openly with Americans as their power was disintegrating seemed foolhardy at best.

Yet at that moment, the American church was the only plan we had. But the problem remained: how would we get there? As the debate and discussion swirled around me, I withdrew into myself.

A voice seemed to whisper in my ear: "O taste and see that the Lord is good! Happy is the man who takes refuge in him!"

It sounded just like Mr. Titus, the soft-spoken Mennonite missionary who had been our teacher at Vacation Bible School many years before.

I remembered the platter piled high with cinnamon toast that he had passed among us at snack time each day. I could almost taste the rich sweetness of the cinnamon-sugar, the saltiness of melted butter, and the crunch of toasted bread. It was an almost sinfully extravagant luxury that dissolved in my mouth and made me feel as though I were at a king's banquet.

All of a sudden, I heard a commotion and looked up to see one of my cousins rushing in the door.

"We have motorcycles," he said, "we have bikes. Where can we take you?"

"To the American church!" my mother exclaimed, pushing us out the door. Into each of our pockets, she stuffed a stack of *dong*, the

Vietnamese dollars we could use to bribe the Vietnamese soldiers if they stopped us.

The six of us hopped on the backs of the bikes and cycles with my cousins, and like some ragtag caravan, found our way to the church.

By late afternoon, the American church, which earlier had been filled to overflowing, was empty. We watched silently as one by one, frightened families had sized up the terrible truth and fled for some other haven. A few headed for the harbor, where it was said a Korean ship was welcoming people aboard. Others like *Chi* Huong, who had stopped by the church briefly to bring us lunch, were going home to take their chances with the Communists. Even my uncle and his family had finally given up and, saying a last tearful good-bye, had taken their leave of us on their bikes and cycles.

Now, my family was the only one left.

When we had arrived at the church around noon, the place had been humming with expectation. Hundreds of Vietnamese from all over the city were pressed together, sitting in the pews, huddling on their haunches in the aisles, scrunching into the choir loft, and leaning on the altar. People were eating lunches they had brought and chattering with their neighbors, as they waited for the pastor to appear and for something to happen.

But from the moment we had arrived, my mother had sensed intuitively that nothing was going to happen—for us anyway. "There's no way we're getting out of the country with so many people," she said, sounding defeated.

"Go ahead, tell her about your vision." The voice was urging me on, nudging me to respond to her fears. But how could I, *Be Tu*, or "Little Number Four," as everyone called me, have the courage to speak out?

Never in my life had I challenged my mother or even questioned her opinion. Even though I was twenty years old, I still felt like a young girl, hardly capable of opening my mouth. Yet again, I heard the whisper. "Tell her what you know."

"Mother," I said, with a firmness in my voice that surprised even me, "God gave us motorcycles and bicycles to get to the church, and soon he will send a flying machine to take us out of here."

"You don't know what you're talking about," my mother snapped, turning her head away in rebuke.

But I did know—much more than I could ever explain. During those long hours wandering around the house praying, I had received a picture in my mind of a "flying machine." Whether the machine was an airplane, a big balloon, or something else wasn't clear. What *was* clear was that sometime very soon, this flying machine would scoop us up like a mother bird and carry us off into the heavens.

Despite my mother's rebuff, I could see her shoulders relax and her body soften, as the hope of a *deus ex machina*, as improbable as it seemed, grabbed hold of her. Even as the shadows began to lengthen and the crowd began to thin out, she held onto the vision God had given me. And so we waited.

***

"Let's take a walk," I told my family. It was apparent to each of us that as dangerous as it was to be on the streets—where trigger-happy soldiers could mow us down on a whim—we couldn't stay at the American church a moment longer.

Just a few hours earlier, as we had huddled over a shortwave radio with others in the church, we had heard reports that the Communists were poised to enter Saigon at nightfall. For all we knew, they could be on the church's doorstep at this very moment, and if we wanted to distance ourselves from the Americans, we sensed that now was the time to do it.

It was nearly five o'clock when we set foot outside the church and sized up our surroundings. Although we hadn't noticed it before, the church was in a lovely residential area, with streets lined with trees. The feared soldiers—South Vietnamese or otherwise—were nowhere to be seen. In fact, no one else was around at all. We picked a direction that seemed safe and started walking.

Oddly enough, as our little family of six ambled down the street, it was almost as if we were out for a late afternoon stroll. We had no idea where we were going. We simply plodded along for a few blocks until we heard a muffled sound, like the roar of the ocean. Turning a corner, we came upon a mob of people, pressing against a building that looked strangely familiar.

"What's going on?" I shouted above the din to a bystander.

"It's the back of the American Embassy," he said. "There are heli-copters inside—everyone's trying to escape."

Yesterday the embassy had been swarming with people like us, who were waiting patiently for information. Today it was total chaos. Thousands of people were surging against a wide metal gate, trying to get inside the embassy compound. On either side of the gate stood two concrete guard booths, topped with small platforms ringed with concertina wire, about six feet off the ground. Astride the two plat-forms, U.S. Marines were pushing men and women away with the butts of their rifles.

Nothing deterred the mob. Children, grannies, and teenagers alike were climbing, shoving, clawing, elbowing—anything to find a means of escape. They were fighting to survive, desperate to be one of the lucky ones to slip over the gate through the Marines' grasp.

Before we knew what was happening, we were swept up in the frenzy. I could see my brother Hai's head a few yards in front of me. Off to the left were my mother and father, along with my sister Diep and younger brother Khanh. Without even trying, we were being carried closer and closer to the gate.

All of a sudden, the crowd seemed to open up, and in the next blink I spotted Hai on one of the platforms. He was pulling up Khanh and Diep. Then came my mother and me. We grabbed Hai's hand and scrambled up the gate and onto the platform, oblivious to the barbed wire that was stripping the clothes from our backs and punc-turing our skin.

To the right and the left of us, Marines were punching people in the face, kicking them with their shoes, and muscling them away from the platform. Yet no one laid a hand on us.

Down below me, still on the ground, my father struggled to climb up. With a burst of assertiveness, I turned to the Marine next to me—he was olive-skinned, Hispanic, with kind, compassionate eyes—and implored, "Please, could you help my father? I'll give you anything you want."

The Marine reached down, grabbed my father's hand, and pulled him onto the platform alongside me. With that, we turned our backs on the frenzied mob and hurled ourselves onto the grass inside the American Embassy compound.

Just as I started to pick myself up from the ground, I looked up to see a short, balding American civilian holding a pistol to my father's temple. He said something in English I didn't understand. But we understood the language of fear well enough to raise our hands high above our heads, as if we were criminals.

Out of the corner of my eye, I saw my mother brazenly waving two pieces of paper at the man. One was a letter from Phong's professor at Cal Poly and the other was from his inlaws vouching for our family's connections in America.

With the pistol still pointed at my father's head, the man looked at the letters, mumbled something under his breath, and shooed us on to a passageway that led farther inside the compound.

By now we were not only feeling incredibly scared and vulnerable but also embarrassed by our near-nakedness. The barbed wire had torn our clothes to shreds, our shoes had disappeared from our feet, and our arms and legs were oozing blood from the scrapes and gashes we had sustained. Luckily, as we scurried through the passageway, we came across piles of suitcases that others had tossed to the side in their haste to escape. Like scavengers, we rummaged through the luggage, grabbed some clothes, and threw them on.

When we emerged from the passageway, my heart sank. There, far in the distance, was yet another locked gate engulfed by a sea of people. I saw Americans, Koreans, Germans, and Frenchmen. Some, with cameras, appeared to be journalists. Others, with children in tow, seemed to be diplomats or embassy personnel. Still others were Vietnamese who were either connected to the Americans in some way or, like us, had slipped over the gate and into this privileged inner circle.

We had no choice but to stand in line like everyone else, and wait. We stood there for what seemed like hours, not even knowing exactly what we were waiting for. But we weren't idle. Everyone was jostling for position, some moving closer toward the front of the line, some dropping behind.

As darkness fell, we found ourselves halfway up to the gate and next to a huge pool that was right in the center of the embassy grounds. I could hear music playing in the background, and although

I found it somewhat odd, I also thought it was very kind of the Americans to give us this little bit of cheer.

Despite our desperate situation, I felt a strange calm. I wasn't the least bit nervous because the image of the flying machine kept coming back to me. In fact, I couldn't get it out of my mind. With each passing minute, I felt more and more certain that God was about to act.

Suddenly, in the midst of the crowd and the confusion and the darkness, I saw everything around me with luminous clarity. It was as if I had tunnel vision, where objects appeared larger than life and seconds seemed to last forever. The first thing I saw was that most of the Americans and other foreigners in the crowd had disappeared. Everyone around me was Vietnamese!

It was then that I noticed the *other* gate. Across the patio, on the other side of the pool, was a small gate, much narrower than the one we were waiting for. I had never even noticed it before. Even more amazing, no one was lined up behind it. And no soldiers were guarding it.

I did a quick reconnaissance and realized that to get there, we would have to leave our places in line, go back through the crowd, and run around the pool.

The plan was risky—perhaps crazy—but something prompted me to take a chance and try to convince my parents to follow me. "Let's go there," I whispered to my parents, nodding my head in the direction of the narrow gate.

God must have prepared their hearts in advance, because the entire family followed me without question. The crowd behind us was only too happy to see us give up our places, and before we knew it we had pushed our way back to the rear of the line. After urging a few other families to join us, we quickly ran around the pool and up to the narrow gate.

"Let's keep in order," I told everyone, taking charge like a drill sergeant. "We'll have more of a chance of getting through."

Beyond the gate, high up on a flat roof a few yards away, I spotted an official-looking white-haired man holding a walkie-talkie. I waved to him and smiled. "We're good!" I said, grinning broadly. "Please let us through, we're good!"

He bent down and said something into the walkie-talkie. A few seconds later, two soldiers guarding the other gate ran over to us and opened the latch. My family slipped through the narrow gate along with one other family, just as hundreds of people, seeing the soldiers run to help us, surged around the pool in our direction.

But they were too late. In the split second it took for us to get through, the soldiers slammed the gate shut behind us, locked it with a chain, and stood guard as a melee erupted.

We didn't know until later that although the family behind us had made it through as well, a third couple had shoved their children inside the gate without them, just as the soldiers barred the door. "Take care of our children," they begged the other family. "At least they will be safe."

Everything was happening so fast—we just kept running. The man with the walkie-talkie motioned us toward a fire escape, and we scrambled up the iron steps and onto the embassy roof.

There, in front of my eyes, was a flying machine, a monstrous, olive-drab steel realization of my prophetic vision. The hulking Huey helicopter stood with its rear door wide open, beckoning us to ascend.

As we piled into the chopper, a soldier barked, "Lie on the floor!"

We dropped to the floor and within minutes heard the clank of the metal door, the click of a latch, and the whir of rotating blades. Before long, we were airborne.

As the chopper pulled away from the embassy roof, I couldn't resist the temptation to look outside. Like a snake slithering up a wall, I stood up slowly and peered out of the little window.

Outside it was raining fire. Bright, burning bullet tracers, from rifles bent on bringing down our chopper, crisscrossed the night sky. The streaks were so close I could almost touch them. Off in the distance, I could hear the rumble of explosions. The Communists were finally moving into Saigon.

But I knew I was safe. The steady beat of the Huey's blades echoed with the sweet sound of redemption as we rose higher and higher.

"Farewell, country. *Tu biet*—farewell forever," I whispered under my breath. "Thank God I have *life*."

2

OPIUM DREAMS

It all began in a haze of opium.

My Grandfather Tieu desperately needed a pipe. He could feel the desire building all day as he went through the motions of his job at the government transit office in the city of Vinh, about three hundred miles south of Hanoi. By the Vietnamese standards of the early twentieth century, it was a plum assignment: he was first secretary of the Vinh Public Transportation Office. But deep inside, his whole being chafed under the oppressive yoke of the French bureaucracy, like a captive sparrow desperate to break free.

Memories of the night before, when the rickshaw driver had deposited him in front of the opium house, dominated his mind. From the moment he had alighted from the vehicle and pushed open the iron gate, he had been transported to a vaporous world where his dreams had become commingled with his destiny.

As always, Cho Lieu, the Chinese owner, had welcomed him at the door with a slight tilt of the head and a benign smile that beckoned him inside. Moving quickly and quietly, Cho Lieu had ushered him past dozens of figures who appeared like wraiths in the darkness. They were peasants, rickshaw drivers, and shopkeepers, men who would spend their last piaster for the pleasures of the pipe. On either side of him, they lay sprawled on mats or slouched against the walls, lost in phantasmagoric slumber. Here and there, Cho Lieu's attendants, young boys barely into their teens, slipped in and out, bearing long bamboo pipes with pills of opium primed for the next round of drafts.

The pungent perfume of the opium grew stronger as Tieu moved deeper into the den. There, partitioned by curtains in Cho Lieu's inner sanctum, Vinh's elite lay in pallets aligned like letter slots in a *bureau de poste*. Across the room, reclining on his customary bed, Tieu glimpsed Hiep, son of a wealthy rice merchant. Beyond the curtain next to him rested Bao, the reed-thin former owner of a rubber plantation, whose sunken cheeks and spindly limbs betrayed years of addiction.

These men shared a bond few could understand. Theirs was a brotherhood of brokenness, a fellowship of heartbreak sealed by the urgency of desire. One look into their rheumy eyes told the story as their vacant gazes laid bare their wasted lives.

Tieu climbed onto his pallet and reclined on his side, waiting. Within seconds a boy appeared, cradling in both hands the object of his redemption. Tieu's heart quickened at the sight of it: a nearly two-foot-long shaft of polished bamboo, punctuated toward the far end by a small bowl attached to the pipe by a narrow tube.

Tieu watched with longing as the boy speared the opium pill with a long needle, heated it over a small spirit lamp, and crushed it around the bottom of the bowl. With deftly orchestrated movements, the boy turned the pipe upside down and held the bowl over the flame until the opium bubbled up, releasing its sinuous vapors into the shaft. Quickly, he handed the pipe to Tieu.

With one practiced pull, Tieu inhaled the vapors and held them deep in his lungs. When he could contain them no more, he exhaled slowly, savoring each fume as his nostrils flared with pleasure. The effect was instantaneous, bathing him in an aura of exquisite comfort. It was as though a soft cloud enveloped him, cushioning his mind and body from every worldly blow.

A second pipe appeared, and a third, until finally Tieu drifted off to sleep. When he awoke an hour later, he felt supremely calm, yet invigorated. Purposeful, yet relaxed. What was it he had been worried about? The opium had the power to banish all cares. . . .

"Tieu! Come to my office, now!"

The staccato voice of *Monsieur le Directeur* echoed through the office, jolting Tieu awake. From the sound of his boss's voice, he was about to be berated for some foul-up in the local transportation system, a routine that had continued unabated ever since he had been appointed first secretary two years earlier. Is this what he had spent his life striving for?

Educated in French schools and armed with a coveted *diplôme*, Tieu had risen quickly in the vast bureaucracy that kept the magnificent system of rails working like clockwork. Under his sway, a small army of clerks, seated at desks in rows in front of him, filed reports, created timetables, and paid the bills in a never-ending flow of paperwork. Above him, *Monsieur le Directeur* ran the bureau with the precision of a commandant and a faint air of condescension that never let Tieu forget his position.

"Tieu," he would call out. "Why was the Number Four Train late getting into Hanoi? We can't have such shoddiness." Or "Where is the report on the repairs for the Thanh Hoa station? Why wasn't it finished earlier?"

Tieu's back prickled at the criticisms, but he didn't dare make a retort. Instead, as *Monsieur le Directeur* stomped off toward his office, Tieu followed meekly, with his head bowed low and a sheaf of reports under his arm. He could feel the eyes of his staff piercing his back as he hustled past their desks. When he returned to the floor, a hush swept over the room, and he knew his underlings had been talking about him.

The shame was unbearable. He was twenty-eight, a man of learning with a wife and three young daughters, and at the start of a promising career in the bureaucracy. But what was all of that worth, when day after day his superior emasculated, belittled, debased him in front of his staff?

Slowly he was suffocating. The ochre stucco walls of the transport office were nothing less than a prison and his life little more than a tedious repetition of tasks. Every day was the same: wake up at seven, eat a bowl of sticky rice with a few vegetables, head for work on his bike. By eight, he was bent over his desk, scrutinizing the latest report—trouble on the route from Hue to Saigon, or a request from the government of Siam to change the timetable for connections to Bangkok—predictable annoyances that never changed.

By 10:45 A.M., the day's heat settled upon the room, barely relieved by the faint breezes that wafted through the open windows. As sweat dripped off his brow and the drone of the mosquitoes echoed relentlessly in his ears, Tieu knew he was ready for a siesta.

Precisely at 11:00, *Monsieur le Directeur* emerged from his office, signaling the start of the midday break. The three-hour respite was intended to provide a break from the heat of the day and the tedium of work. But for Tieu, the break seemed only to prolong his agony.

It took Tieu less than ten minutes to arrive home, where a steaming bowl of *pho* awaited him. His ten-year-old daughter, Trung, had prepared his favorite soup just the way he liked it, with an extra touch of cinnamon and basil. But as the little girl chattered nonstop with the day's gossip from school, he ate his lunch listlessly. His muscles ached. Waves of nausea washed over him, and he tried in vain to hold down his lunch.

Overcome with fatigue, he collapsed on the hard wooden bed for an hour's nap. Then, with what seemed like monumental effort, he got up and bicycled back to work for the rest of the afternoon. By four, the office was humming, even as he was drifting further into the void.

He could think only of the pipe. He could taste it, smell it. The mental impression made the yearnings grow stronger. As he shuffled through the papers on his desk, he imagined how in a couple of hours he would be lying on a pallet, breathing in the magical elixir that would melt away his troubles. Nothing would matter then. Not *Monsieur le Directeur*. Not his staff. Not even his growing family, with needs that never seemed to stop.

"Mr. Tieu! Mr. Tieu!"

Looking up, he saw one of his clerks, Mr. Hung, waving some papers in front of him. Without even bothering to read the contents, he signed his name and affixed the Public Transportation Office's official stamp. Hung bowed and seemed to float away as Tieu returned to his reveries.

The pipe was the only thing that was keeping him sane. One pull at the long bamboo shaft would open up vistas of peace and tranquility that were as expansive as his father-in-law's rice fields: endlessly green and bountiful. With the pipe, he was free—unconstrained by convention, unshackled by familial duty, and untrammeled by officious superiors.

He reached into his pocket and pulled out his watch. Eight o'clock. Time to close up shop. Like clockwork, *Monsieur le Directeur* emerged from his office, tipped his hat, and said, *"Bon soir."*

One by one, the clerks filed past his desk and out the door. Only his clerk Ban was left, pulling fast the shutters on the windows and bolting them shut with a twist of a handle.

Finally Tieu was alone. He locked the massive wooden door, jumped on his bike, and with the instinct of a homing pigeon, headed straight for the opium house. Throngs of pedestrians and rickshaws filled the streets in the early evening, forcing him to weave in and out of the crowds. Occasionally an automobile bearing one of the French colonialists would take over the road, sweeping people out of its way as it muscled though the clogged streets.

The French. Tieu despised them and revered them at the same time. In the forty years since they had taken control of Indochina, they had transformed his country from a sleepy backwater into a burgeoning economic machine. Along the coast a paved highway, the Mandarin Road, stretched for more than fifteen hundred miles, linking together three parts of the once disparate land: the northern state of Tonkin; the central one-thousand-mile ribbon of coastal land known as Annam; and the fertile southern delta region of Cochin China.

What's more, on the backs of Tieu's countrymen, the French had laid track from Hai Phong to My Tho and then westward in a loop up toward Cambodia. As Tieu knew better than anyone, it was now possible for a passenger to hop on a train in Hanoi and go all the way to Bangkok.

Along with the roads and railroads, the French had brought with them every modern convenience: telephones, electricity, postal and telegraph systems, hospitals, schools. But they had also brought something more—a way of life, which, though alien, had become woven into his own aspirations and dreams. As a boy in Hanoi, Tieu had grown up under French rule, marching to Gallic rhythms that resounded in every area of his life. He had gone to their *lycées* . . . studied Charlemagne and Louis XIV . . . read Hugo and Voltaire . . . earned their *diplôme* . . . secured a place in their bureaucracy.

He had done everything right. And yet, where had it gotten him?

Tieu spat at the road and pedaled faster and faster as the rage boiled up inside of him. He deserved better, didn't he? For generations, the men in his family had been celebrated for their academic prowess, a legacy nurtured in his ancestral village, Hanh Thien, whose very name drew gasps of recognition and reverence. In the not-so-distant past, his forebears had been rulers of Tonkin, judges and governors, whose names were known throughout the northern region.

He had learned of these things, not from the history books, but from the tales his mother had spun for him as a child under the mosquito netting at bedtime. She told stories of Uncle Bao, the governor who had embraced French culture and built his province into a thriving commercial center; of Grandfather Long, the judge whose wisdom was legendary; and of his own father, who had been mayor of a province. These were men of influence who were masters of their own destinies. They were free. Powerful. Filled with zeal and purpose.

But that was long ago, too long ago to matter. The life they symbolized was gone forever. *Freedom, power, zeal* were meaningless words that could never apply to him, even in a whole lifetime of struggle. He was doomed to servitude and obsequiousness. Nothing was left for him but to endure the shame of his ancestors and hope that death would come quickly.

Now he was pedaling more slowly. He could feel his shoulders sinking as the energy drained out of him, forcing him to hunch over the handlebars like an old man. His feet had become deadweights, making every push on the pedal an excruciating ordeal.

If only he could hold on a little longer. The opium house was just around the corner. A few more rotations of the wheel and he would be there, pulling at the pipe, losing himself in its voluptuous vapors.

By sheer force of will, Tieu managed to turn onto Rue Clemenceau where two doors down the iron gate of the opium house beckoned. He was so focused on reaching his destination that at first he didn't notice anything strange. But as he got off his bike and headed for the gate, he came face-to-face with an odd little foreigner with a bag slung over his shoulder and a leaflet of some sort in his hand. The stranger wore a tie and a crumpled white cotton suit like *Monsieur le Directeur*. But something was different about him.

Tieu tried to avoid making eye contact, but as he walked past the man thrust a pamphlet into his hand and said in accented Vietnamese, "Peace, brother. Read what's inside for a lifetime of peace."

The man's boldness so startled Tieu that he looked up involuntarily. Their eyes locked, with the man looking directly at him as though he had known him for a lifetime. There was no condescension in the gaze. No hostility or even pity. Nothing but a burning intensity that seemed to Tieu to pierce his very soul.

For the first time in his life, Tieu was frightened. His hand tightened around the pamphlet and, without saying a word, he rushed past the foreigner into the safety of the opium house.

Unperturbed, the little man smiled contentedly and reached back in his bag for another pamphlet. He was so discreet that not even a passerby would have noticed his eyes closing for a brief instant and his lips moving in a silent benediction for the unnamed addict who was wasting himself to death.

Rich

Richmond Merrill Jackson may have been short in stature, but he possessed a huge sense of God's presence. For one thing, at an early age he developed the unswerving conviction that he would end up in Indochina as a missionary. His grandmother had prayed passionately for Southeast Asia from the time she was a teenager. She had offered her life to God and had begged her Congregational church to send her to the mission field, but for reasons known only to the dour Massachusetts elders, they rejected her.

So instead of joining the legions of young nineteenth-century women braving unseen dangers to spread the gospel around the globe, she married and had three daughters—all of whom she gladly dedicated to God's service.

Yet none of them heeded the call. They too married and settled down. But the next generation finally bore fruit. Three of the devout woman's grandsons entered the ministry, not the least of whom was R. M. Jackson.

Rich, as he was known, was born in 1894 in Georgetown, Massachusetts, where his paternal ancestor, Nicholas Jackson, had staked his claim more than 260 years before. Armed with a land grant from King James II, the twenty-three-year-old Nicholas had embarked from England in 1634 aboard a sailing ship bound for

Virginia. Once he hit shore, he walked with his meager possessions and his land title to the northeast corner of Massachusetts, a territory that became home to generations of Jacksons after him.

With this intrepid legacy, it wasn't altogether surprising that Rich had an adventurous streak. But as a child, he did nothing to show it. He was quiet and shy, growing up in the shadow of his cosseted older sister, Ardelle May, and extroverted younger brother, Herb. The story goes that his parents were so grief-stricken by the death of their first child, David, that when God gave them a daughter, they doted on her in a perpetual celebration. Rich, who came next, got lost in the shuffle, while Herb, who was five years younger, was a born raconteur and charmer who never lacked for attention.

When Rich was fourteen and Herb was nine, their mother died of consumption, leaving Rich with a hole in his heart that never quite repaired. Years later in Hanoi, when his own son, Bernard, turned nine, Rich delivered a stern lecture: "You be good to your mother. You only get one." When the boy turned fourteen, he got the same lecture.

In an odd way, death was never far from Rich's consciousness. His father owned a furniture store in Georgetown, and in those days the store sold coffins and doubled as a funeral parlor. From an early age, Rich and Herb had to help clean up the bodies of the deceased and put them in the coffins. They loaded the coffins on a four-wheel flatbed trailer and dragged it behind a black horse to the cemetery. Then they stayed for the funeral.

If the furniture business gave Rich a compelling sense of the transience of life and a commitment to hard work, it also provided him the wherewithal to follow his dreams. After high school he enrolled in Massachusetts Agricultural College in western Massachusetts, where he devoted himself to botany and animal husbandry.

But as graduation drew near, in the deep reaches of his heart Rich heard the echo of his grandmother's prayers, and he knew where he belonged. A summer visit to a camp meeting in an open-air amphitheater in Old Orchard Beach, Maine, sealed his commitment.

He had gone there with his favorite uncle and aunt, Wallace and Lydia Tenney, who had been lured by the prospect of hearing A. B.

Simpson, a fiery preacher with a passion for missions that had sparked a nationwide revival. Simpson's belief in Christ's imminent return was so powerful, and his heart for saving the lost so palpable, that his messages triggered an outpouring of young people eager to evangelize the hidden corners of the globe. The Sudan, Tibet, Annam, China—wherever the light of Christ had not yet reached was the territory Simpson staked out for his Christian and Missionary Alliance movement.

As Rich heard Simpson's appeal, his heart began to ache in an unfamiliar, highly disturbing way. His mind filled with images of those souls who had never known the power of God's love and forgiveness—souls like him, who were unworthy to receive such blessings. For a moment, his own guilt and sin seemed to overwhelm him. But as he heard Simpson's call, he understood that even though he himself was unworthy, God loved him so much that he had provided a means of escape from the certain death that awaited him: Jesus, the Lamb, who had died on the cross for him. And he knew that if God could love Rich Jackson, a sinner, he could love the whole world.

The organist had just started playing the opening bars of "Jesus Only" when Rich got up from the wooden bench and started moving forward. He didn't just walk; he ran, nearly tripping as he rushed down the grassy slope to the front of the amphitheater. When he reached the base of the speaker's platform, he fell to his knees, sobbing.

Rich felt a strong hand on his shoulder and heard the familiar, soft voice of Simpson, asking him what was on his heart. He looked up to see the famous preacher towering above him like a giant. The sheer physical presence of the man, with his huge head, white beard, and broad shoulders, was nearly overwhelming.

Yet there was another presence—a power emanating from deep inside—that commanded Rich's attention. He could feel it when Simpson knelt down beside him and began to intercede on his behalf. Something in the sweetness of Simpson's humility and in the intensity of his communion with God invited imitation.

As Simpson quietly pleaded for him before the Almighty; the amphitheater seemed to grow silent. The crowd of fifteen thousand, the dignitaries on the podium, and even Simpson's own ego seemed to melt away, replaced by a singular focus heavenward. It was as though nothing in all creation was more important in that moment than Rich's needs, his hopes, his fears. Simpson laid them all before God, certain that his prayers were heard.

When Rich left Old Orchard, he was on fire for the Lord. He withdrew from college and, with the backing of Uncle Wallace and Aunt Lydia, he switched to Nyack Missionary Training Institute, a school Simpson had established sixty miles north of New York City to prepare his global army. At Nyack, the fervor Rich had felt at Old Orchard only intensified as he studied Bible and evangelism and took classes on theology and missions from the aging Simpson himself.

After three years he was finally ready to serve in Indochina, and so, alone on a steamer ship, Rich arrived in Hai Phong Harbor in the fall of 1918 to join a team of English and North American missionaries who had established a beachhead in Tonkin. He walked down the gangplank, anxious yet filled with anticipation as the words of Simpson's prayer for him at Old Orchard echoed in his memory: "Oh, Lord, let Rich be your warrior. Bless him with a ministry so powerful he will convict even the most hardened sinner."

Tieu

Tieu had no intention of reading the tract the foreigner had given him. But too polite to say no, he had simply grabbed the small pamphlet and crumpled it up in his trouser pocket, expecting to throw it away at his first opportunity. Whatever peace the little man was talking about was of no consequence to him. His tranquility was closer at hand, in the vapors of the opium den that encircled him, tantalizing him with imminent possibilities.

Eagerly he wended his way back to his accustomed pallet, stretched out on the mat, and waited for his pipe.

The wait seemed interminable. Where was the boy? Where was his pipe? Everyone else seemed to be blissfully lost in sleep or smoke. When would his respite come?

Agitated, Tieu propped himself up on his elbow and scanned the room, hoping to catch sight of a rescuer. But the boy was nowhere in sight. Nor was Cho Lieu, the proprietor. Usually he was scurrying around like a high-class rat, poking his nose here and there to be sure his patrons were provided for. Now the only human forms Tieu could see were the flaccid bodies of his compatriots, lying like the dead in repose.

Tieu felt panic welling up in him. Beads of perspiration broke out on his brow as his muscles tightened and quivered with tension. The pipe would be there soon. He knew it would. He could hold out for a little longer, if he could just focus his mind on something, divert himself from the nagging pressure in his head.

He flopped back on the bed and stared wide-eyed at the ceiling. Out of the corner of his eye, he caught sight of a gecko darting across the wall, and desperate for a diversion, his eyes followed the little lizard as it ran back and forth as if on a quest. Without warning, it froze in its tracks and began to jerk its head up and down in syncopated rhythm—a rhythm meant for the eyes of its mate a few inches away. For a few minutes, Tieu lay mesmerized by the ritual, a dance primordially ordained to bring two living creatures together as one.

Then he found himself growing angry. What of *his* mate? What of *his* wife, Nhu, who lived several hundred miles away in her father's village with two of their three children? Their life together was no better than the geckos'—an occasional pairing of two bodies that was devoid of any emotion. Yet he was bound to her for life, and her life, it seemed, was wrapped up in having children: three girls, no less, whom he could ill afford.

The chance to work in Vinh had come as a welcome relief from her and the tedious cycle of family duties. Gladly he had packed his bags and left, leaving his wife and two youngest daughters in his father-in-law's care. He had even agreed to take his eldest daughter with him, if that meant his wife wouldn't bother him.

But even the relatively easy terms of the separation had not satisfied him. He had gradually drifted into a hellish existence that made him loathe himself even more. Many nights, he neglected his little daughter Trung, leaving her home alone while he attended to his habit. At other times, when the tug of parental responsibility became too great, he brought her along to the opium den.

"Stay here," he would insist, depositing her in the front room on a *chieu bac*, a low bed covered with a rice mat, where the gamblers whiled away the hours. As the men cursed over their card games, or drank rice wine served by fawning *co dau*, the entertainment ladies and prostitutes who sang sweet songs in their ears, little Trung would sit quietly, stoically resigned to her fate. At the end of the evening, Tieu would emerge from his stupor, collect Trung, and head for home, pretending that nothing was wrong.

But on this occasion, he felt more unnerved than normal. *Where was his pipe?* Didn't they know he was dying inside—that he couldn't wait another minute? Didn't they understand that it was the only thing he could depend on, the only thing that released him from Vinh, and his wife, and his daughters and *Monsieur le Directeur* and the haunting fears of a future filled with endless sameness?

As he turned over on the pallet, trying to get comfortable, he heard a crunch of paper in his pocket so loud it seemed to crackle like a string of fireworks at *Têt*, the Vietnamese New Year.

The little pamphlet. What could be so important in the handout that had caused the foreigner to press it upon him? *And the man's eyes.* Never had he seen such intense blue eyes. His heart had seemed to smolder within him at the very sight of them.

Tieu slipped his hand in his pocket, pulled out the tract, and held it up to catch the flickering light of the kerosene lamp hanging several pallets away. At first, he could barely make out the words.

Tin Jesus . . .

"Believe in Jesus . . ."

Ban se duoc tu do.

"And you will be free."

Tu do. The final words seemed to explode off the page. *Free!* He wanted true freedom more than opium—more than his very life. Was the foreigner still there? He had to be there. *Please be there.*

Like a tiger set on its prey, Tieu tore through the opium den, oblivious to everything but finding an escape. Cho Lieu, the smoke, the pipes, the addicts—all were a blur as he stumbled through the darkness and out the door into the early evening light.

Standing just a few meters away was the foreigner. Although his back was turned, there was no mistaking him: his white suit seemed to glow in the twilight, giving him an aura of otherworldliness. The foreigner was deep in conversation with a Vietnamese, who from the looks of the pamphlet bag slung over his shoulder was in the same line of work.

For an instant Tieu paused, pondering what to do next. But then the urgency that had propelled him out of the den took hold of him, and throwing aside all propriety, he ran up to the foreigner and cried, "Who is this Jesus? I want to be free!"

Before he heard any answer, his knees buckled under him and he slumped to the ground. The last thing he remembered was the warmth of the little man's breath in his ear and the words, "I will be with you, always."

Rich

Rich Jackson didn't know the first thing about opium addiction, but he did realize that the Vietnamese man at his feet needed help—fast. By now, a small crowd had gathered as Vietnamese on-lookers pressed in close, curious to see what he would do next.

Without wasting a second, Rich summoned a rickshaw, and with the help of his colporteur, the Vietnamese believer who helped him give out tracts, he hoisted the man onto the seat. Then he squeezed in beside him, but not before checking with the proprietor of the opium den to find out what he could about the addict's identity.

The information was sketchy: Nguyen Duy Tieu, first secretary of the Vinh transportation office. Lived somewhere near the rail-road station. Been patronizing the establishment for two years. The proprietor didn't seem to know anything about Tieu's family, al-though he did remember something about a daughter. He said a lit-tle girl had shown up late one night in the rain, barefoot and covered with a raincoat of reeds, to procure several pills of opium. She was a wisp of a thing—no more than about ten, he guessed. Still, she seemed to be very much in charge. Cho Lieu had given her the opium, he confessed, even though she didn't have enough money, because he felt sorry for her.

"That is all, *Monsieur*," he said. "That's all the information I have."

Rich Jackson doubted that the proprietor was telling all he knew, but he couldn't waste any more time. He ordered the rickshaw driver to the train station where, after a little discreet probing, he learned that Tieu lived just a few blocks away. With the rickshaw driver running as fast as he could, they arrived at Tieu's tiny house a few minutes later, with the colporteur right behind.

"*Chao em!*" the missionary called out as he knocked on the heavy wooden door. "I've got your father."

The door opened a crack, revealing a frightened girl clad in black pajamas.

"Please," said Jackson. "Your father is sick. We want to help."

The little girl opened the door and nodded her head toward the back room. The room was empty except for a low wooden bed covered with a thin mat of woven grass. Lying nearby was a polished bamboo water pipe, a cheaply crafted instrument that was sold in every market in Indochina as a poor man's ticket to paradise. Rich could see that the lip of the bowl was stained black with dross, the remnants of months or years of addiction. Next to the pipe, untouched, lay a bowl of rice with a few shreds of vegetables, which had dried up as the little girl who had prepared it had waited in vain for Tieu's return.

Jackson shuddered as he saw the vestiges of Tieu's wasted life. "I come to bring life abundantly," he sensed a voice echo in his mind.

He rushed back out to the rickshaw and with the help of the driver and the colporteur, he carried Tieu into his house and laid him on his bed. The man's body was like hot wax, rubbery and listless, incapable of movement on its own. Gazing into Tieu's eyes, Jackson could see his hunger, a wild, ravenous desire for something as yet unarticulated.

Jackson knew he was out of his element. The man clearly was on the verge of withdrawal, or worse. "Go get Pastor Diep!" he ordered the colporteur. "Quickly!"

As the American missionary waited for the arrival of the Vietnamese pastor, he sat on the edge of the bed, pulled out his Bible, and began to read aloud Psalm 46.

> God is our refuge and strength,
> a very present help in trouble.
> Therefore will not we fear,
>   though the earth be removed,
>   and though the mountains be carried into the midst of the sea;

Though the waters thereof roar and be troubled,
  though the mountains shake with the swelling thereof. (KJV)

Rich didn't know whether he was reading the passage for himself or for Tieu, who was tossing and turning on the bed, trembling uncontrollably. The man's gaunt body, slick with sweat, seemed to be shriveling up minute by minute. Rich watched in horror as fluid began gushing out of his nose and eyes, as if the very life force within him was flooding out. Rich continued to read:

There is a river the streams whereof shall
  make glad the city of God,
    the holy place of the tabernacles of the most High.
God is in the midst of her;
  she shall not be moved. . . . (KJV)

Rich closed the Bible, overcome by the words and the message. Could anything be any clearer? The river of anguish that was pouring out of Tieu was a flood of helplessness that, with God's help, might be harnessed into a torrent of hope.

But was Rich up to the task of ministering to this soul? He was just an ordinary, insignificant man, beset by fears of his own. Didn't he lock the doors behind him obsessively, to be safe from intruders? He was a missionary, to be sure. But his calling was to translate Bible texts. Was he also called to be the agent of deliverance for this pitiful opium sot? "God, help me!" Rich cried out. "Show me what to do."

Before Rich realized what was happening, he found himself kneeling over Tieu, massaging his legs, his arms, his body. Gently, he grabbed the man's right leg, squeezing the calf muscle and kneading it with his thumbs. Slowly he worked his way up the thigh, pressing and pulling until the tension gave way under his touch. From there, he moved to the left leg, working steadily, methodically, without even stopping to catch his breath.

Every now and then, Tieu would let out a small moan, but the sound, far from slowing Rich, spurred him on. It was as if in this one man's groaning, all of creation was calling out to him, laying bare all pain, fear, sin.

As his fingers slipped over Tieu's slick, sweaty skin, Rich became oblivious to the degradation before him. The man's clammy body, his odious smells, his nauseating secretions, all became like a sweet offering that Rich could give to his Lord.

Finally Rich cradled the man's head in his lap and slowly worked his fingers over his cheeks and brow. He gazed down at the man's face—hollow-cheeked, wide-eyed, filled with pain and loneliness— and somehow knew it was a face he had encountered before. Then he understood. He would recognize this face anywhere: the face of his Lord Jesus, agonizing on the cross.

An hour later, Tieu fell asleep, and Rich sank, exhausted, into a chair. The missionary was too numb to pray. Too drained even to open his Bible. All he could do was stare straight ahead and trust that unseen hands would care for the man sleeping fitfully before him.

Rich didn't hear the girl come in. The clink of a tray on the tile floor roused him, and he looked up to see the little girl kneeling beside him, arranging a humble treat of tea and bean cake. Deftly, she poured tea into a little porcelain cup and then presented it to him with two hands, as though he were royalty.

"*Cam on em,*" he said thankfully, referring to her affectionately in the Vietnamese manner as "little niece."

She nodded her head and quickly averted her eyes. Then as quietly as she had come, she left.

Rich thought nothing had ever tasted so good. One sip of the tea, and the hint of jasmine revived his spirit as his mind filled with images of fresh white blossoms. And with the sweet surge of the tiny rectangle of bean cake, he felt a burst of energy that bolstered him just enough for the next round of challenges.

A few minutes later, Pastor Diep arrived as a reinforcement, giving Rich yet another reason to hope. But had Rich known what a hell on earth he was about to enter, perhaps he would have shied away from the fight that loomed before him.

*T*ieu

Tieu awoke terrified. It seemed that some creature was deep inside him, trying to claw its way out. He could feel his body lurching, heaving, straining—fighting to keep hold of the terrible addictive force that had insinuated itself into every corner of his being.

He couldn't stop yawning, but these weren't normal yawns. They were huge, gaping chasms that wrenched his mouth apart and left his jaws and ears aching. It was as though some demon were prying his mouth open as a means of escape.

Next came the deluge, a tidal wave of secretions that poured out of every orifice, leaving him drenched in his own tears and mucus. One minute he would be choking on the mucus, certain he was drowning. The next minute he lay shivering so hard that the hairs on his arms stood on end.

Just when Tieu thought he could bear the cold no more, the demonic presence began to rip him apart from the inside out, convulsing his stomach and intestines in spasms so excruciating he nearly passed out from the pain. Not once, not twice, but for hours on end, he found himself doubled over, simultaneously spewing out streams of vomit and excrement as his body erupted with volcanic force.

Through his tortured screams, he could hear the steady drone of human voices in some distant place, pleading, begging, crying. Once, in a heroic effort to relieve the pain, he rolled to the side of his bed and staggered to a half-standing position. Before he collapsed back onto the mattress, he imagined he could see the figures of two men kneeling by his bedside, keeping a steady vigil.

Rich

How long, O God, how long?

It had been nearly two days since Rich and Pastor Diep had knelt almost without ceasing on Tieu's bedroom floor, yet the addict's ordeal showed no sign of abating. Sweat continued to pour out of him, and he refused all food and drink.

Although the paroxysms of vomiting had stopped, Tieu was shivering so much they had covered him with whatever they could to keep him warm—blankets, straw, rags—until there was nothing left in the house. His entire body kept twitching, and every now and then his legs would start kicking reflexively as though he were trying to rid himself forever of Satan's grip.

The stench was unbearable. Rich and Pastor Diep had tried to bathe Tieu and clean up what they could, but they had more immediate concerns: their own flagging energy and a driving certainty that prayer was the only way out for this captive soul. So for the next few days, they ignored the physical hardships and spelled each other at Tieu's bedside, praying in shifts to cover the man in a blanket of grace.

Rich knelt on the tile floor, weeping for God to listen. He knew the depth of God's mercy. He had received it himself, day after day, as he had struggled to live faithfully.

He knew too the awesome power of God's deliverance. He had seen it firsthand in Hanoi in the transformation of a sorcerer who had been his first convert. He remembered how he had come upon the man plying his magic in the square in front of Saint Joseph's Cathedral. As a crowd watched with their mouths agape, the Vietnamese sorcerer had driven a sword through his face from cheek to cheek, without drawing so much as a drop of blood.

For days Rich had dropped by to watch the spectacle, until one day he called out to the man and asked if he wanted to know the one true God. The sorcerer was so startled by the question that he immediately stopped what he was doing and asked for help. There, in front of the crowds, Rich had prayed with him for deliverance.

Moments later, the sorcerer tried to put the sword through his cheek as usual, but this time, at the very prick of the point, blood gushed out. The man had shouted with joy to have his body back, freed from the terrible demon that had held him captive.

Rich knew that the God he served was greater than any demon. Greater than the powers, the principalities, and the hosts of wickedness that were keeping Tieu's body in bondage. God would heal this addict. Rich had no doubt of that. And so he kept praying.

By the seventh day of the prayer vigil, Tieu finally lay quietly, seemingly at rest. Gone were the twitching muscles, the drenching sweats, the anguished moans. Instead, he was almost motionless; only his chest moved up and down slowly, in sure, steady breaths.

When Tieu awoke, soon afterward clear-eyed for the first time in a week, he turned his head toward Rich and said, "I am free."

3

WHISPERS OF LOVE

Grandfather Tieu may finally have been free of his opium, but he had an even bigger hurdle to cross: his wife—and my grandmother—Nhu. She had started reaping the benefits of his changed life almost immediately, as more income began flowing her way each month. But she scoffed at rumors of conversion and refused even to believe such transformation was possible.

She remained mired in denial after Pastor Diep showed up at her father's door in Kien Giang to tell her the news. "Mrs. Tieu," said Pastor Diep. "Your husband is a Christian now. He's a new man."

But Nhu didn't want to listen. Instead of inviting the pastor in for tea, she kept him standing in the courtyard for nearly an hour. Finally she came out with a broom and started sweeping the tiles, hoping that like the dust, he would be swept away and never come back.

Pastor Diep bowed graciously and slipped out.

When Grandfather Tieu arrived in Kien Giang unannounced, Grandmother started crying in hysteria at the sight of his beaming face.

"It's a disgrace!" she shouted. "You are an embarrassment to your ancestors. I have to be loyal to my father and my grandfather."

Then she turned on her heels and ran inside the family worship house, where she burned a stick of incense to chase away the evil spirit that had come upon her family. As the smoke curled toward the ceiling, she looked at the daguerreotypes of her grandfather and grandmother perched on the altar and wondered if they too were cringing in shame at what she had become.

They had been sturdy folk who had worked all their lives, adding field after field to their holdings. Her father had followed their example, turning barren land into lush rice fields and bringing untold hectares of rice paddies under his sway.

She remembered how at her own wedding, hundreds of peasants from throughout Nam Dinh province had appeared at the village just for a peek at the bride and groom. She could almost hear the titters of approval for Tieu, the handsome young man from Hanh Thien village who had brought to the marriage an educational pedigree unmatched in the region.

At the time, it had seemed like a worthy arrangement: he was the scion of a family who had prized education for generations; she was the child of a prosperous farmer whose daughters were among the most sought-after brides in Tonkin. As a dutiful daughter, she had understood the trade-offs: for her and her family, the luster of status from his elite education at the *Lycée Protectorat Truong Buoi*; for him, the promise of wealth from her land-rich parents. But from the outset of the marriage, it was clear that Tieu had looked at her with disdain.

"Peasant!" His eyes seemed to shout the word like a curse every time she opened her mouth to offer an opinion. She knew she could never hope to understand what was in the books he pored over every night. She had barely gone past the third grade. But was that any reason for him to ignore her? All she had ever wanted was to be a good wife, to bear him children, to make him proud. Instead, as each daughter had come, he had drifted further and further away from her, until finally he had left more or less permanently for Vinh and his cursed opium. He seemed to want no part of her, except for the occasional physical release when he visited.

With Tieu unable to support her in Vinh, she had been forced home to Kien Giang, where, living under her father's roof, she had to endure the pitying stares of the villagers. Lately, whenever she went to the market, she could see them eyeing her swelling stomach—a token of Tieu's last visit—and hear them clucking in dismay at her misfortune.

And now this. A supposed change of heart. "A Christian," the pastor had said. After such an affront, could the gods indeed ever again bring blessings to her family?

As the joss stick crumbled into ashes, she rang a little gong and bowed at the altar, hoping desperately that the pastor had been mistaken. The baby inside her jumped in her womb, apparently disturbed by the sound of the gong. Nhu gently patted her stomach, and sighed.

❋❋❋❋❋

The baby, a fourth daughter named Nghia, was born just after the family was reunited in Vinh. But the change of scene and her new child failed to bring Nhu happiness.

Why did Tieu bring me to this wretched place? Nhu wondered as she tried to wipe away the inch-high growth of mold that had collected on her husband's leather shoes.

Vinh. The humidity hung so heavy on the city it was impossible to breathe. Every day was more of the same: devastating heat and dampness so unyielding nothing ever seemed to get dry. Early in the morning, she would go to the market with a list a yard long, and a half hour later she would return, dripping with sweat and exhausted from the effort, with only a few of the items she needed.

Whatever had possessed her to leave her father's house and agree to join her husband? He had gotten a raise, Tieu had said. Found a little house perfect for their growing family. "The opium is in the past," he had told her. "Please come to Vinh. I beg you."

Maybe it was the pregnancy that had made her soften. Or perhaps it was the fact that the new life Tieu had promised was everything she had dreamed of during the two years they had lived apart. Whatever the reason, she had relented and moved to Vinh, where a few months later she gave birth to Nghia.

At first, at least on the surface, everything had seemed as Tieu had promised. The nice house. The happy little family with four healthy daughters. His increasing stature at the transportation office. But underneath, Nhu was certain it was a sham. *The gods are laughing at me. At any moment, I will be punished. My baby will die. The opium will be back. My ancestors will be angry.*

As the threats multiplied in her mind, Nhu's fears flooded into oceans of tears. Finally one day her chest grew so tight with anxiety that she thought she would be squeezed to death. Forgetting the children, she raced out the door to the nearest temple, where in giant stone urns she burned fistfuls of fake red paper money to appease the gods.

She stared bewitched at the orange flames leaping toward the sky and for a brief moment, she could feel the tension lessen. But the minute she returned home, the old doubts resurfaced.

This is all Tieu's doing, she told herself, convinced that disaster was imminent. She blamed her husband for everything. The humidity . . . the burnt rice . . . the front gate that wouldn't close properly.

As if these difficulties weren't enough, Tieu returned home from work a half hour late that night, and she lashed out in a suspicious rage. "It's the opium, isn't it?" she cried, pounding her fists on his chest. "That's where you were!"

Without saying a word, he grabbed her hands and held them tight until she finally relaxed and let down her guard. Then, gently, he wrapped his arms around her, holding her close as she sobbed into his chest. "Things will be better in Hanoi," he said, hoping to lift her spirits. "We're moving there next week. I've been promoted to manager of the transportation office. And there is no opium anymore. You must believe that."

But Nhu was barely listening. Why should she believe that a move to Hanoi would improve her miserable life? Why not stay in the unpleasant place she knew, rather than take a chance on making things even worse? But even though she continued to grumble, she had no choice but to comply. That was what dutiful wives did—especially when their husbands got a better job.

When they finally completed the move to the big city, she had to admit, if grudgingly, that their new situation was quite bearable. They had actually improved their standard of living. The house was bigger; there was a better variety of food. She and the children even began to make a few friends.

Then tragedy struck.

Tieu

Tieu was terrified. The wild, incessant screams of his baby daughter shocked him and Nhu bolt upright out of their early morning slumber. Nghia's little eyes were so completely caked with dried pus that she couldn't even open them. He immediately rushed the child to Hanoi's Central Eye Institute, where the diagnosis left him speechless.

"Syphilis," the doctor said. "Very serious case. She may die. If she lives, she could go blind."

My baby die? Go blind? The very words sent shudders down his spine. Everything had been going so well. A new baby. The promotion to Hanoi. A comfortable home for his wife and children. And now this. He couldn't understand how the disaster had struck.

There seemed no way for such a disease to have entered his home. He had been faithful to his wife. And he was certain she had been faithful to him. *But still, it must somehow be my fault. The opium. It must have been the opium.* He couldn't imagine how that might have happened, but a lingering sense of guilt made him wonder. Tieu always remained suspicious of the long-term consequences of his drug habit. That seemed the only answer. *Yes, it's all my fault. Please, God, help her—despite my sins.*

He was hardly consoled when the doctors told him that they thought the source of the disease had been Nghia's wet nurse, who they believed had also infected other children. Racked by grief, Tieu could only imagine the future for his little daughter, who in the end might never again see the sunlight, or the faces of her sisters or parents.

Desperate for help, and sensing that little Nghia's situation was now beyond the capacities of the medical community, Tieu started running in a panic toward the Protestant mission compound, which was a short distance away from the hospital. His ultimate objective was the compound's printing operation, which was the bailiwick of William Cadman, the missionary who had become his *Giao Si*—his mentor and teacher in Hanoi.

Tieu knew that what he needed most urgently was prayer, the kind of prayer that had raised him from his opium pallet and would transport his daughter out of her illness to live and thrive another day. Bible stories he had been studying swirled about in his mind. Hadn't Jesus raised Jairus's daughter from the dead? Hadn't the centurion's servant been healed? All those miracles had required was a word from Christ. As soon as Tieu reached *Giao Si* Cadman, he would claim just such a word for his daughter.

He had just turned the corner near Saint Joseph's Cathedral, a few blocks from the Protestant mission, when by chance he bumped into the missionary. "*Giao Si* Cadman!" exclaimed Tieu.

"My daughter is very sick. She may die, the doctors say. It's syphilis. From her wet nurse. I need you to pray."

"Let's go to the hospital immediately," said the missionary.

"We can't," said Tieu. "My wife is there and she is not a believer. But if you just say the word, my daughter will be healed."

If the British man seemed a little taken aback by Tieu's bold certainty, he didn't show it. Nor apparently did he stop to question why God would spare this child—and not his own dear daughter, Agnes, who had been choked to death at the age of six by a worm growing inside her body. Without hesitating a second, he ushered Tieu to a nook at the side of the cathedral. There, hidden in the shadows, Cadman began to beg for Nghia's life.

"O Lord, pour out your healing power on this little child!" Cadman cried. "Like the blind man at Siloam, and the lepers on the road to Jerusalem, let her be healed!"

Tieu left with a smile on his face, certain that a miracle had taken place. It wasn't until several days later that he ran into *Giao Si* Cadman again, this time near the train station.

"How is she, my man?" asked the missionary. "You never came by to tell me."

"Why, I thought you would know," Tieu said, disconcerted by the question. "*Of course* she was healed! By the time I got to the hospital, her eyes were open and she was laughing."

As it happened, there was more to *Giao Si* Cadman's fervent prayer of healing than either of them knew—because the deathly ill child Nghia grew into the intrepid young woman who later became my mother.

Nhu

Despite baby Nghia's healing, my Grandmother Nhu clung to her joss sticks and daily offerings of bright pink dragon fruits, determined to maintain the family honor. But one day, just as she started to burn incense at the small red altar she had set up by the entrance to the family's house, she stopped herself. Looking at the little wooden altar with its gold trim, empty blue-and-white teacups, and urn filled with burned ash, she wondered what it all meant. Why did she have five joss sticks in her hand instead of six? Why would it matter to her ancestors whether she burned an odd number or even? Why would *Ong Troi*, the honorable heaven, care about incense or dragon fruit or tea?

All the rituals and fears that had consumed her for years suddenly seemed empty and shallow, leading to nothing but confusion. She couldn't even remember why she had come to the altar for prayer. Instead, images of her husband flooded her mind. She saw him coming through the door of their little house, his white shirt damp with sweat from the bike ride home, and his broad face radiant with excitement. She saw him sweep a wayward lock of dark hair from his forehead and then throw back his head in laughter as the girls came rushing out to greet him. She saw the twinkle in his eye, a roguish gleam that always signaled a surprise that he had brought especially for her.

"For you, my dearest," he would say, bowing like some courtier. Then, with a gallant flourish, he would pull out a gift from behind his back. Fresh frogs one week. Her favorite chocolates the next. A silk scarf from Paris, in blue, her most becoming color. Always something irresistible, wrapped to perfection. There were live crabs tied in elegant knots of straw, bundles of cakes wrapped in colorful foil, or armfuls of bright yellow chrysanthemums so magnificent they didn't need any wrapping.

One day he came up behind her, put his arms around her waist, and kissed her on the neck, sending tingles up her spine. At first she steeled herself to his overtures, shooing him away with excuses. "I must get back to the kitchen," she insisted.

But the next day he once more crept up on her catlike. He kissed her once, then twice. Day by day, she found herself looking forward to his lavish attentions, until finally she melted at his touch.

And how he loved the girls. Every Saturday, without fail, he piled them into a rickshaw and took them to Ho Hoan Kiem, the Lake of the Returned Sword, leaving her at home to catch up on her errands. Around the lake, they would while away the afternoon, sitting on its banks under a frangipani tree or playing badminton on the footpaths. By five o'clock, they rushed in the door, chattering excitedly.

"Daddy showed us how to make fishing poles," sister An would exclaim.

"We walked all the way up Hang Dao to Cho Dong Xuan to buy lichees," said sister Trung.

On Sundays, he took the children with him to the little church in the mission compound on the other side of Hang Da, the Leather Market. Week after week, Nhu defiantly dug in her heels and refused to go, but invariably, the children came home all smiles, singing songs about Jesus and bubbling over with Bible stories.

"Momma, did you know about Jonah?" asked Tinh. "He was swallowed up by a big fish and lived in its belly for three days, until God told the fish to spit him out."

The more she heard, the more she wondered. And deep in her heart, she felt a stirring.

But what stirred Nhu most was the image now imprinted in her mind of her husband praying. Early one morning, she peeked from behind the covers to catch Tieu kneeling by the bedside, lost in whispered conversation. Another time, near midnight, she stole by the bedroom door to sneak a glimpse of him at his nightly vigil. In the darkness, she could barely make out the faint contours of his body as he knelt ramrod straight, with his arms outstretched and his face turned heavenward in humble supplication.

Whatever his prayers were, they must have been answered, because he never once strayed back to the opium. When his cravings came, she would see his eyes grow wide as rice bowls and his limbs hang limp as noodles. He would then head directly into the bedroom, lie down, and begin to pray.

Even the children knew the warning signs. Wanting to help him banish the threatening demons, they would rush to his bed, jump on his back, and start pounding the muscles until the yearnings passed. It seemed to work.

"Me, I'm home!" Tieu's voice cut through her musings. He always called her Me or "Mother." Quickly, she got up from the altar, stuffed the joss sticks in her pocket, and ran to greet him. Shyly, she smiled and bowed, but he scooped her up in his arms and exclaimed, "Garlic—you're making my favorite thit kho!"

Could any woman be happier? Despite herself, she couldn't suppress a giggle. To be loved by this man—respected for herself alone—was something she had once dreamed of. Yet now her dreams seemed to be coming true. Every day, she was not only loved but also treasured with such affection that at times, she thought her heart might actually burst with joy.

"Behold, you are beautiful, my love," he whispered to her in the night. "You are all fair, my love. There is no flaw in you."

She knew from things Tieu had read to her and the children that some of those words came from his Bible. Yet somehow they seemed to her to have more power than if they had been original with him. In his eyes, she really did seem beautiful. Beloved. Blessed. Who could deserve such a gift?

Finally, Nhu decided that she had no choice but to respond to him. The very next Sunday, she decided to take a significant risk. She rolled her long hair like a halo in a tube of black velvet cloth, put on her very best *ao dai*, and accompanied her family to church. As she picked her way through the muddy streets, she wondered what she was getting herself into. Would she become a laughing-stock, as she had been in her father's village? Would she be asked to do things she was ill-equipped for? Would she feel stupid? Overwhelmed? Lost?

She didn't have any direct knowledge of this God, this Jesus. All she knew was that she wanted what her husband had. She wanted to feel the power that had pulled him away from opium, to know the love that never stopped pouring out of him, and to experience the joy that always surrounded him.

They were getting closer now. Tieu led the way, taking a short-cut through the market, which was bustling with stalls. All around Nhu, gap-toothed merchants were hawking their wares: fresh chicken feet, Chinese noodles, live ducks, prawns, bean curd. It was all there, spilling over baskets and buckets brought in early that morning straight from the countryside.

But today they didn't stop. They walked purposefully past the stalls, past the shoppers caught up in their daily haggling, until they reached the open doorway that led to Rue Bourret. There, just out-side the door stood the mission compound, its gate flung open in a bold gesture of welcome. As her children bounded past her into the courtyard, Nhu hesitated a moment, afraid to take the next step. She felt Tieu's strong body next to hers and heard his voice whisper tenderly. "Let's go in, *Me*."

Too scared to look up, she kept her eyes focused on the ground and followed him into the church. Her heart was pounding as they walked down the center aisle and slipped into a pew. Out of the corner of her eye, she could see people smiling and nodding in approval. But the biggest smile was Tieu's.

How could he be so bold? His eyes danced with that twinkle that always meant something good was in store. What present did he have for her now? Surely he wouldn't do anything rash.

At the very thought of Tieu's impetuousness, Nhu began to blush. Then she smiled. Soon she became so relaxed that she lifted up her head and looked around. By the time the missionary lady, Mrs. Cadman, hit the chords of the opening hymn on her portable keyboard, Nhu was open to receiving whatever God had for her.

From that moment on, it seemed that the entire service was meant for her. When the preacher, a Vietnamese evangelist from Tourane, gave his message, she drank up the words like a thirsty sponge.

"Every good endowment and every perfect gift is from above, coming down from the Father of lights," the preacher said, quoting from the Book of James.

My husband . . . my daughters. Perfect gifts. It seemed they had been given to her from "the Father of lights," as the Bible said. *The Father brought my husband back to me. He healed my little daughter Nghia.*

"God's greatest gift is Jesus," the preacher declared. "He will never turn away from you, never leave you helpless and alone."

Could this be true? Please let it be true. . . . I want it to be true. . . . It is true.

Such a wave of peace surged over Nhu that she stayed fixed to her seat, even as Mrs. Cadman began banging out the closing hymn. One by one, Tieu and the people around her stood up and opened their hymnals, and still she didn't budge.

Nhu felt a strange sense of dislocation. She could see her husband and the preacher and the missionary lady, but she was somehow separate from them. It was as though she were floating, hovering over them, up close, yet at a distance at the same time. Oddly enough, she didn't feel even a hint of fear. At another time or place, she would have been petrified, certain that the gods were toying with her. But there in the little church, she felt enveloped in tranquility, cushioned at last in the pure love of the God who was Lord of all.

The congregation was singing now, their voices joined in a rousing hymn that brought her down to earth. The melody was unknown to her, but the words had a familiar ring, as though they had been written just for her.

"I will say 'yes' to Jesus, oft it was 'no' before," she heard the people sing. "As He knocked at my heart's proud entrance, and I firmly barred the door."

As her mind began to absorb the meaning, Nhu rose to her feet and stood next to Tieu, who pointed to a page in the hymnal. She started to sing along with him: "But I've made a complete surrender, and given Him right of way. And henceforth it is always 'yes,' whatever He may say."

Nhu noticed a tear rolling down Tieu's cheek, but she never mentioned it. After she released her life that day, she never looked back. As for the ancestral altar, it remained in a corner of the little house, untouched, as a reminder of the life she had left behind forever.

4

A NEW CREATION

The house crackled with excitement. To the outside world, there was nothing special about that August day in 1928, but inside the little house on Rue Duvillier, the air was brimming with expectation.

In less than an hour, Le Van Thi would be commissioned as the first Vietnamese pastor of the Hanoi Protestant Church, an event that Tieu had been praying for ever since he had moved to Hanoi and become a church elder. The commissioning was the culmination of years of spadework by the foreign missionaries, people like his mentor *Giao Si* Cadman, the printer from England, and his tall, angular wife, Grace, who had planted the seeds for the church more than a decade earlier. Now, because the French were cracking down on overt evangelism by the missionaries, it was more important than ever that the mantle of spiritual leadership pass to Vietnamese hands, and no one was more overjoyed than Tieu.

This is the beginning—the spark that will light a fire in Hanoi. And I am part of it. Thanks be to God.

He smiled as he watched his wife shouting orders and fussing over the girls in an effort to get them to church on time.

"Ca, don't wear that old rag," Nhu told Trung, the eldest, who had stood by him faithfully through those disastrous opium years in Vinh.

"Be careful how you comb your hair, An and Tinh," she ordered daughters number two and three. "Nghia, what are you doing with that doll?"

Nghia. Every time Tieu looked at his youngest, who was now four years old, he marveled at God's goodness. She had walked in the shadow of death, and yet here she was, running around the room with the energy of a little boy. With her crisp black tunic, white pants, and short haircut, she even looked like one. Only the doll, which she refused to part with, betrayed her.

"Let's go, children!" he heard Nhu say. "We can't be late."

With that, his wife hustled him out the door along with the rest of the family and into waiting rickshaws for the three-block trip to church. When he started to protest about the extravagance, Nhu stopped him short. "This is a special day," she explained. "We can't even think of walking."

They pulled up at the mission compound just as a photographer was lining up people outside the church for a shot of the entire thirty-member congregation.

Tieu got out of the rickshaw and stood off to the side for a moment, proudly surveying the scene. All the church stalwarts were there: Mr. Truong Van Hoang; Mr. Nguyen Duc Thuc, a noted sculptor who was head of the *Academie des Beaux Arts*; Mr. Trinh Van Nhi, treasurer of the Far East Bank; and of course, Pastor Thi, flanked by two missionaries, *Giao Si* Cadman and *Giao Si* Van Hine. Seated together in white were the missionaries' wives, Grace Cadman and Nellie Suzanne Van Hine, a Swiss. The "Frenchie," everyone called her.

Tieu noticed that the only people with a hint of a smile for the camera were the foreign missionaries. Everyone else—women, children, and his fellow elders—stared solemnly ahead, their faces heavy with the magnitude of the occasion.

"Nghia, sit down!" he called to his youngest daughter, who was jumping up and down next to her sister in the very front row. Still clutching her bald baby doll, she squatted low and looked wide-eyed as the photographer popped a flashbulb into the boxlike apparatus.

Tieu slipped into his place, second row from the back, assumed his most austere demeanor, and looked directly into the camera. Seconds later, the photographer squeezed the shutter, capturing the group for posterity.

From that auspicious day the church started to grow rapidly, and Tieu was at the center of it. He may not have been the richest member of the congregation, nor the most prestigious, but he became known far and wide as the most Christlike. Still, the public image didn't always tell the full story of the inner man.

Even though outwardly Tieu appeared to be a model of righteousness, inwardly he struggled daily with his own desires, not the least of which was the temptation to return to opium. It was the thorn in his flesh, an ever-present specter that hovered over him, threatening to destroy the new life he had built and keeping him on his knees day and night.

There was also the lure of prosperity. At work, he watched through the door one day as his boss, Mr. Linh, the *chef de bureau* of the Public Transportation Office, met with one of the contractors who supplied coal for the trains. Tieu knew that this particular man was notorious for gouging the railroad and everyone else in Hanoi, and he expected a showdown.

Instead, Mr. Linh slapped the man on the back and laughed with him uproariously at some joke. A few minutes later, as the contractor bent over Mr. Linh's desk to sign some papers, the man casually slid an envelope across the desk. Still smiling, Mr. Linh picked up the envelope and pocketed it.

With their business concluded, the men bowed simultaneously, a routine formality that ended every business deal in Indochina. But Tieu recognized immediately that something was amiss. Usually in such transactions it was the contractor who would bow the lowest, signifying his gratitude for the favor that had just been bestowed upon him. But this time, it was Mr. Linh who seemed to be doing obeisance. He bowed so deeply and so long that Tieu was almost embarrassed for him.

Tieu had just started to turn his head away when Mr. Linh caught his eye. The boss glared at him for a second, and then, without skipping a beat, he smiled broadly and ushered the contractor directly over to Tieu.

"I want you to meet Mr. Tieu," Linh said to the contractor. "He is one of my most valued employees. He will take care of you in any way he can." Mr. Linh gave Tieu a knowing wink and then maneuvered the contractor toward the door.

Later that afternoon, Tieu found an envelope lying on his desk. No message was inside to indicate the sender, no inscription on the front with telltale handwriting. The envelope was empty except for a crisp, neatly folded bank note.

Twenty *dong*. A week's salary. That's when Tieu sensed the voice, almost as though it were whispering in his ear: "Take the bribe. It's okay. It's the way business is done. Look at Mr. Linh."

Tieu knew that like Mr. Linh, everyone around him was on the take. Without the extra cash, no bureaucrat could ever hope to get ahead on the meager wages the French paid. Mr. Linh had done so well it was rumored that he was buying up land around *Le Grand Lac*.

"You need a bigger house," the voice persisted to Tieu. "You need a new rickshaw. Take the money. It's there for the asking."

Caught on the edge between duty and desire, Tieu eyed the envelope. Then, unable to bring himself to take the money yet uncertain where to return it, he tossed it in the wastebasket and walked out the door.

"You're a fool," the voice said, but he kept on walking, trying hard to ignore it.

As if opium and wealth weren't temptations enough, there was also his pride, a nagging, self-important murmur that threatened to taint the overwhelming love he felt for his wife, Nhu. "She doesn't know anything about the realities of the world," the voice said. "She can't carry on an intelligent discussion. What good is she?"

But Tieu steadfastly refused to succumb. The minute the voices started echoing in his mind, he steeled himself through a sheer act of will to turn to the one resource that could keep him on the path of truth: prayer.

Remembering the example of Jesus in Gethsemane or on the Mount of Olives, he retired to a place apart. Alone in the morning and at night, Tieu knelt at his bedside, thanking, praising, pleading, until he was drained of all desire except the will of the one who had saved him.

After supper every night, he gathered Nhu and the children together for a time of Scripture reading and prayer. One time he pulled out the Bible for a lesson on Zacchaeus. As the children listened intently, he expounded on the little man who climbed the sycamore tree to see Jesus and later entertained him at home for dinner. "Who can tell me why Jesus went to his house?" he asked.

A chorus of voices shouted out, "I can," as the children vied with each other to go to the head of Tieu's class. He called on each one in turn, giving all the children a chance to show off their knowledge. When he was confident that they had understood the lesson, he closed his Bible to signal that it was time to pray.

Tieu folded his hands on the table and bowed his head. For the next twenty minutes, as he poured out his thanks and requests, he entered a realm of exquisite transcendence, aware only of the one to whom he spoke and totally oblivious to anything going on around him.

Nhu

Nhu couldn't suppress a smile. Through her half-opened eyes, she saw Tinh, daughter number two, slip under the table along with little Nghia, while Tieu droned on with his prayers. Nhu didn't have the heart to stop them. Let them play their silly games. Someday, when they were older, they would understand what it meant to have a father like Tieu, who cared for them so deeply that he would try to teach them and pray with them night after night.

Her own father wouldn't have dreamt of spending time with her or her sisters. Like most Vietnamese fathers, he had been a distant, formidable figure who had never taken the time or interest to be part of her life. He had housed her and clothed her and fed her, but that's where his sense of duty had stopped.

Tieu had been that kind of father—once. But since he had left Vinh and the opium habit, his attitude had changed radically. Nhu had to admit that his intentions toward the children were incredibly endearing, even if his approach was sometimes a little stiff. He had never quite figured out how to adapt to the children's limited attention span.

The scene that evening was typical. The children stayed engaged for most of the Bible story, but by the time the prayers came around, they were already squirming. Tieu was so absorbed in his prayers that he didn't seem to notice the girls sliding under the table or hear their muffled giggles.

But as the moments started to tick by, Nhu began to worry. *I hope they get back to their seats before he finishes,* she thought. *If he catches them, they'll get spanked.* With a wave of her hand under the table, she alerted Nghia and Tinh, who slithered back into their seats and bowed their heads just as Tieu's voice mounted in a crescendo toward the *Amen.*

When the prayers had ended, Tieu looked over at her and beamed. "We have been blessed," he said.

And so they had, in ways she never would have expected. *Look at this house,* Nhu thought. *Who would have imagined it would ever be ours?*

She remembered the day *Giao Si* Cadman had shown up at the tiny two-room house they were renting and had given them an astonishing offer: he would dip into his own pocket to buy them a house, if they would agree to pay him back over time.

"How much can you afford to pay each month?" *Giao Si* Cadman had asked Tieu. "After you pay for food and necessities, how much is left over?"

"Twenty *dong,*" Tieu had told him.

"Then pay me twenty *dong* a month, and the house is yours," *Giao Si* Cadman had replied.

A few days later, they had moved into their little house on Rue Duvillier, which quickly became a thoroughfare for children, relatives, and various young Bible students whom Tieu was mentoring. The house was much larger than their previous one, with three bedrooms, a dining room, a living room, a courtyard with a big water container to collect rainwater, and an outhouse all the way in back behind the kitchen area. But more important, the place was cozy and welcoming, with bright pink bougainvillea cascading over the walkway as a herald of joy to all who entered by the narrow wooden gate.

There always seemed to be room for one more, especially little Esther Van Hine, daughter of the missionaries, Jake and Nellie Van Hine, who had moved north to Lang Son. Mrs. Van Hine was sick much of the time, and often the family would come to Hanoi for her medical treatment. They would no sooner arrive than *Giao Si* Van Hine would stop by the house on Rue Duvillier and drop off Esther to play with Nghia and the other children.

The house was only a small part of the Lord's bounty. As Nhu was coming to understand more clearly every day, it was Tieu's single-minded focus on spreading the love of Jesus that was the biggest blessing of all.

Once when a Canadian named Robert Jaffray came to the Hanoi Church to preach, he asked at one point, "Who will pray for the mission work in Indonesia?"

Tieu had stood right up and said resolutely, "I will." Then, to Nhu's shock and amazement, in the next breath he ignored any semblance of propriety and started pouring out his deepest feelings to the entire congregation.

"The Lord knows I want to be a full-time Christian worker," he said. "But I have a big family. I pray that God will one day accept one of my children to be a full-time servant."

Nhu watched her husband move constantly among friends, family, and strangers, serving in his own way as a missionary at home. Every Wednesday night, she saw Tieu head out the door to the church, where he was part of a little band of three who met in the library to intercede for the lost. The prayer group grew to seven, then to ten, then to fifteen people, as the small room became the fireplace of the Hanoi church in the midst of its spiritual winter.

"Pastor Thi was inspired tonight," he would tell her, brimming with excitement on his return. "Two more people joined our group, and we could feel the Spirit among us."

Before long, the prayer group had grown so large that it had to move to the church, where it ignited a spiritual fire inside many church members and encouraged them to bear witness for the Lord wholeheartedly. The result was that dozens of people became believers in God.

A few years later, when the French lifted the ban on proselytizing by foreign missionaries, the work of the church—which the prayers of Tieu and Pastor Thi had sustained—exploded.

Year by year, as the church prospered, Nhu treasured these things and pondered them in her heart. And her love for her husband grew even more.

Tieu

If only I could be more like Giao Si *Cadman,* Tieu thought.

Some people, particularly his colleagues at the mission, considered Bill Cadman brusque and demanding, quick to erupt in anger if a job hadn't been completed perfectly. But to Tieu, the stocky missionary was everything a man of God should be. He worked tirelessly, dressed simply, ate and drank sparingly, drove an old car, and even slept on church benches when necessary. And always, he considered others better than himself. "If I had been born Vietnamese, then God's work for me would be more successful," he often told Tieu.

Taking a cue from Cadman, Tieu tried his best to live abstemiously. He denied his own needs and put others first, especially his family, which soon grew to five children, then six, then seven, then eight, with the birth of his only son, Trach, or "Tam" as he was known. Overjoyed at this bounty, Tieu gladly gave up his rickshaw and rode a bike to work every day, ordering the rickshaw driver, Quoc, to take the children back and forth to school and his wife on her errands. "Be sure to take care of whatever they need," he told Quoc.

On the job, Tieu tried to "work as to the Lord," as he paraphrased the New Testament verse, always keeping alert for ways to improve the quality of the department and using his position to help whomever he could: church members, distant relatives, friends. When he learned that his sister was nearly destitute, and that two of her sons were out of jobs, he immediately put them to work at the Public Transportation Office. His nephew, Nam, became conductor on the Hanoi-Hue run, while Diem became a gas station attendant for the department's fleet of vehicles.

It didn't take long before the Public Transportation Office was peopled with dozens of employees who owed their jobs to Tieu. But he never expected or asked anything in return, except a good day's work and unswerving personal integrity.

Over the years, Grandfather's work ethic and honesty caught the eye of his French bosses, who promoted him to ever-increasing positions of responsibility. By 1938, he was *chef de bureau chargé du personnel* of the Railway Division of the Public Transportation Office, which meant he was in charge of hiring for the entire railroad, from Lang Son to My Tho. The new position ranked just below that held by Mr. Linh, who was *chef de bureau* for the entire railroad.

On the day of his promotion, Tieu was so excited by his new

status that he allowed himself his first luxury in more than fifteen years at the railroad: a shiny gold pocket watch, imported from Switzerland. It was unusually large, with fine Roman numerals raised in gold and long, graceful hands that swept across its face in rhythmic precision. On its cover, Tieu had taken the bold step of having his initials engraved in a florid cursive script.

Later that afternoon, Nhu showed up at his office at the central railroad station with Bay and Tam, numbers seven and eight, the two youngest children. He grabbed their hands and, as they stood mesmerized, showed them around the cavernous marbled waiting room whose ceilings were three stories high. They didn't seem to notice that everyone, from the cone-hatted peasants on the platform to the ticket sellers in the booths, were nodding to Tieu. The word had already gone out: "Mr. Tieu is *chef de bureau chargé du personnel.*"

Proudly, he led Tam and Bay outside to the platform to await the arrival of the Number Five Train from Hai Phong. As he saw the smoke rising from the oncoming train, he pulled his watch out of his pocket, flicked open the cover, and with the gold chain dangling from his trousers, started counting down the seconds to the train's arrival. "Five, four, three, two, one."

The engine let out a great belch of steam as the engine came to a halt.

"It's right on time," he said to the children, as though he were personally responsible for its efficiency. With that, he snapped closed the cover on the watch and slipped it back in his pocket.

If the pocket watch was a symbol of how far Tieu had come, his rickshaw became a reminder of how far he still had to go. Over the years, the family rickshaw, which Tieu had so selflessly given up for the use of his wife and children, became tattered and worn. In particular, the black accordion-folded hood, which had once been slick and shiny, was now covered with an ill-matched assortment of patches whose glaring colors only accentuated the decrepit state of the vehicle.

One day during *Tết*, Mr. Duong, a representative from a village that produced seat covers for all the trains in the system, happened by the station just as Tieu's family was leaving in the rickshaw. It so happened that the village was now prospering because of the seat-cover contract, which Tieu had arranged several years earlier. At the time, Mr. Duong had begged Tieu for a chance to show what his village could do. "We'll produce seat covers for five *dong* less than the going rate, and we'll guarantee a better product," Mr. Duong had told him.

Tieu had looked at their work, compared it with the current contractor's seat covers, and sent Mr. Duong to Mr. Linh with the recommendation that Duong be awarded a contract.

For years afterwards, Mr. Duong had offered to compensate Tieu personally for arranging the deal, but always Tieu refused. "Your good work is all I ask for," he would say with a wave of his hand.

But this year at *Têt*—the traditional time of gift giving—Mr. Duong took one look at the rickshaw and made Tieu an irresistible offer. "Mr. Tieu," he said, "I see your rickshaw cover is in need of repair. Please let us fix it for you. This is what we do best. It is the least we can do to show our appreciation."

Tieu hesitated a moment. *It's Têt, after all,* he thought. *And the rickshaw is an eyesore. What could be the harm in having it fixed?*

"That would be nice," said Tieu. "I would be very grateful."

An hour later, Mr. Duong appeared at Rue Duvillier and took away the rickshaw. "For repairs," he explained to Nhu.

Two weeks later, Tieu arrived home from work to find the entire family standing outside the gate of the house, circling a brand-new rickshaw. It was the latest model, with chrome wheels, a leather seat, and a black accordion bonnet made of sturdy fabric just like the seats on the railroad trains.

Tieu took one look at it and winced.

"A man just rang the bell and left it here," said Nhu, sensing his discomfort. "He said you knew about it—and that it was a gift for *Têt*."

"We can't keep it," he said. "It's too generous."

"But Daddy," protested Nghia, "the old one is falling apart. This is so beautiful."

"It's for *Têt*," shouted Number Six. She jumped onto the seat and struck a pose, as if she were an elegant lady on a holiday. "Take me to Pho Hang Khay, Quoc," she said, pretending to order the rickshaw driver to the priciest shopping street in town.

The children burst into joyous giggles and came running over to Tieu, begging for a reprieve. "Please, Father, please!" they said almost in unison.

He looked from one child to the next. At the sight of their happy faces, bubbling over with excitement, he found his resolve slipping away. "Just this time," he said with a sigh. "Only because it's for *Têt*."

But still, he didn't feel right about accepting the gift. He knew he hadn't accepted Duong's generosity in return for recommending him for the contract. But even though he was aware that some would dismiss his concern on the ground that he was making too-subtle distinctions, there did seem to be at least the appearance of a conflict of interest.

That night, as Tieu knelt at his bed for prayers, he begged God's forgiveness. He knew that he had fallen short and that he would fail again and again. His only hope was to humble himself before his Savior, and trust as he had many times before that in his own weaknesses, God's power would be revealed.

"I praise thee, for thou art fearful and wonderful," Tieu prayed from Psalm 139. "Thou knowest me right well; my frame was not hidden from thee."

He got up from his devotions certain that his sins were washed away. But from that day on, every time he looked at the rickshaw he felt a twinge of sadness. And he steadfastly refused to set foot in it ever again.

Sometimes Tieu wondered if his transformation into a spiritual "new creation" should involve a paring down of earthly rewards. Did God expect him to give up more of his worldly possessions, such as the new rickshaw? Did true faith require renunciation of all wealth and status?

As if in a counterintuitive answer to such a question, Tieu was hard at work in his second-floor office at the Hanoi train station when several low-ranking officials stopped by his desk.

"Congratulations!" they said.

"Thank you," he responded, not knowing what they were referring to. It wasn't until a French railroad official asked him to sign the contracts for some new railroad cars that he realized what the fuss was all about.

Mr. Linh's job. I've been promoted to chef de bureau of the entire railroad!

As it turned out, the French had finally gotten wind of Mr. Linh's bribery schemes and had unceremoniously given him the sack. To replace him, they had turned to the one man whose record was without blemish: Tieu.

But inexplicably, when he rushed home to tell the family the news, he was greeted by seeming indifference. "I've been promoted," he announced breathlessly, as he threw his briefcase on the dining table at Rue Duvillier.

"That's nice," said Nghia, without even looking up from her *lycée* textbook.

"You always do so well, dear," said Nhu. "How about something to eat?"

Tieu was quiet for a moment. Then he nearly shouted: "You don't understand! It's not just *any* promotion. I've got Mr. Linh's job!"

Finally his words began to register. "Mr. Linh?" his wife responded. "You're now at the *top*?"

"And that means more *money*?" Nghia asked.

Grandfather Tieu had now become the highest-ranking Vietnamese in the nation's railroad system, and it seemed to him that his struggles might be over. From Hanoi to Saigon, no one could be hired, and no contract concluded, without the signature of the former opium addict who had been reborn.

But beyond the Chinese border loomed an even bigger challenge, one that would threaten my grandfather's hard-won security and change his life—and the lives of my entire family—forever.

5

RUMORS OF WAR

The Japanese soldier jabbed a pistol in Jake Van Hine's ribs and shouted something unintelligible. But the missionary was too outraged to be frightened.

"I'm an American," Jake said indignantly. "A missionary. I must go back home to get my belongings. You have no right to stop me."

The soldier just spat on the ground and kept the pistol aimed squarely at Jake Van Hine's chest.

The missionaries had never expected events to deteriorate so rapidly in Lang Son, the city north of Hanoi where the Van Hines had been stationed. Certainly, they had known that a Japanese attack was imminent. By 1940 rumors of a Japanese invasion from China had created havoc in the missionary community, which stretched at three-hour intervals by train from Lang Son in the north on the Chinese border, to My Tho in the south. With the threats mounting daily, each family—whether the Richmond Jacksons in Vinh; the Cadmans in Hanoi; or the Van Hines in Lang Son—had to decide for itself whether to leave or to stay.

Due for a second furlough after more than a decade in the field, Jake and Nellie Van Hine had opted to leave. They had sent word to their ten-year-old daughter, Esther, who was at boarding school in Da Lat, to rendezvous with them in Hanoi. There, they planned to say good-bye to friends like Mr. Tieu, Nhu and Nghia, and then return briefly to Lang Son to collect their belongings before shipping out.

Jake and Nellie packed all their worldly belongings in steamer trunks and had just gone to Hanoi for a day to pick up Esther at the train station when the news hit that the Japanese had swarmed into Lang Son.

"We've got to get out of Indochina—now!" Jake said to his wife and daughter. He put Nellie and Esther on the next train to Hai Phong, with instructions to book passage on a ship to Hong Kong. Then he hopped in a friend's truck and raced back to Lang Son to retrieve the steamer trunks.

By the time Jake arrived in Lang Son the next day, the Japanese had the city completely under their thumb. Soldiers had stopped his truck on the outskirts of town, forced him out at gunpoint, and refused to let him go back to his house for his belongings.

"Everything we own is there," protested Jake. "You must let me go back."

But the pointed pistol in his chest was the only retort. Soon an officer appeared, and after a few heated words, he agreed to bring the Van Hines' property to Jake later that night. Hours later, a truck did indeed appear, along with the same officer, who waved a sheaf of papers in Jake's face.

"Sign this document saying that you received everything," he demanded.

Again, Jake protested. "I can't sign anything until I see the contents of the truck," he insisted.

"Just sign," ordered the officer.

Reluctantly, Jake scribbled his name and watched as the Japanese soldiers transferred his precious trunks to his truck. When they were finished, the officer motioned for him to leave. It wasn't until Jake got back to the mission compound the next day and reunited with Nellie and Esther that he dared open the trunks. Fearful of what he might find, Jake called Nellie into the bedroom, shooed Esther out of the room, and shut the door.

❖❖❖❖❖

Esther stood just outside the door, straining to hear any tidbit of conversation. As minutes passed, she heard only the squeak of metal hinges as her parents opened the trunks, one by one. Then, there was no sound at all. No high-pitched exclamations from her Swiss mother. No deep throaty baritone sigh of relief from her father. Not a whisper.

Unable to restrain herself any longer, Esther burst through the door, only to find her parents ashen-faced, sitting like statues behind the open trunks. Quickly, she ran to check the contents. There, stuffed inside each trunk, was a pile of trash. Tin cans, pieces of wood, soiled rags, any detritus the Japanese could find had been dumped in the trunks to replace their belongings.

Gone were the family heirlooms: sterling silver, china, Belgian linens, all treasures that her mother had brought from her home in Europe. Gone, too, were their clothes, her toys, her father's books, her mother's tennis racquets, and the special Bible story scrolls they had used for teaching. Every vestige of their lives had disappeared, stolen from under their noses. It was as though their personalities and histories had been erased. Eliminated.

Esther didn't understand. *Why would anyone do such a thing? How could they be so cruel?*

She looked from her father to her mother for an answer, but they were far away, lost in their own separate grief. Then, on the floor next to her mother's hand, she caught sight of something familiar.

Books! A picture! Something of our own.

Esther's heart leaped with excitement as she knelt down beside her mother and pored over the precious remnants the Japanese had left behind. Here was her grandfather's French Bible, inscribed by his hand in the flyleaf. There was her baby album, bound in weathered leather. The pictures were all there: one of her and her beloved *amah*; another of her with her blonde hair done up in Shirley Temple corkscrews; still another of their house in Lang Son, down the road from the French doctor and across the street from the provincial *Résident*, the government official who headed the province.

As she flipped through the album, which was filled with so many happy memories, Esther began to relax a little, more certain now that things would work out. *God will take care of us. He always does.*

She closed the baby album and reached for the large photo lying on the floor. Even without looking at it directly, she knew it instantly as her favorite picture of her father, the one with him resplendent in his white tropical suit and pith helmet. She had seen it countless times before, sitting framed in the parlor.

But his photo didn't have a frame. The edges were torn, and something seemed to have damaged the picture. Esther picked up the photo and let out a gasp. There was her father, smiling broadly under the pith helmet. But slashed across his white suit in the form of a cross, two bold knife strokes had nearly ripped the picture apart, as some mad swordsman had sent a terrifying message. It was as though a samurai sword had sliced straight across her father's heart.

■■■■■

Two days after the invasion of Lang Son, the Japanese moved in on Hai Phong, bombing the harbor and attacking a French garrison. For the next few weeks, Esther slept with her shoes at the end of her bed in Hanoi, ready at a moment's notice to run out to the trenches that had been dug in the mission compound as a makeshift air raid shelter. Although her mother had managed to secure tickets for the family on a Norwegian oil tanker that was scheduled to depart from Hai Phong the following month, their entire escape was now jeopardized by the tense political situation. Morning after morning, Japanese bombers appeared in the sky in a show of force aimed at cowing the French colonial government into submission. The message was clear enough: open the doors of Indochina to a Japanese military presence, or be destroyed.

Esther was too young to understand the subtleties of the political maneuvering between the French and Japanese. All she knew was that at five in the morning, when the wail of the sirens pierced the air, her job was to jump out of bed, throw on her clothes, grab her doll and head for the trenches. Quivering in the dirt, Esther and her parents would wait for hours until the sirens stopped, which meant the planes were headed back to China.

Eventually, the French caved in and gave the Japanese military access to Indochina, but the easing of tension didn't make the Van Hines' situation any more certain. On the day of their scheduled departure from Hai Phong, they arrived at the docks to find the captain reluctant to take them on board.

"It's too risky," he said. "I can't take responsibility for foreigners."

Esther and her mother took this response as a final rejection and started wondering what would happen to them now. But Jake didn't give up so easily. He argued and cajoled until, finally won over by the fervent entreaties, the captain relented. He gave them a berth in the cramped crew quarters in the bow of the ship, and they immediately leapt on board.

But from the moment they left the harbor, they faced trouble. The sea was the first enemy, billowing up in violent swells that rocked the tanker and sent giant waves crashing over the decks. Jake became incapacitated by seasickness, and at mealtimes, Esther and her mother had to rely on a burly missionary friend to help them fight their way across the slippery deck through sheets of rain and crashing waves to get to the mess area. He held them tight so that they wouldn't be swept overboard and led the way to the dining facilities.

Other terrors appeared from the skies. On Esther's first morning at sea, she awoke to hear an ominous, deep buzz in the distance. Frightened but curious, she jumped out of bed and ran up to the deck to see what was happening. Many of the crew had gotten there ahead of her. Their fearful eyes and wild gestures told the story: the Japanese were coming out of the clouds.

Esther's eyes scanned the horizon. Far in the distance, a tiny black dot seemed to be growing larger and larger as the buzz turned into a steady roar. "Come quickly!" she shouted below deck to her mother. "The Japanese are coming!"

Her mother rushed to her side, and as the silhouette of the plane came into view, Mrs. Van Hine spontaneously burst into prayer in French, as though she thought the Almighty might better hear her in her native tongue. "*Mon Dieu, protège nous,*" Esther's mother prayed. "*Fais que l'ennemi disparaisse, que nos vies soient protégées.*"

Ester picked up snatchers of her mother's prayer: "Protect us . . . make the enemy disappear."

The plane drew closer, so near that Esther could see the bombs under its belly and feel the vibrations of the engine penetrating her bones. Instinctively she grabbed her mother and held her tight, too frightened to watch, yet too mesmerized by fear to turn away.

"*Seigneur Dieu, je t'implore . . . je te supplie.*"

Little by little, the steady rhythm of her mother's prayers almost seemed to drown out the drone of the oncoming Zero, and Esther felt a strange sense of security. Seconds later, the plane dropped lower in the sky and started heading straight toward them. This time, Esther could even make out the features on the pilot's face.

Esther and her mother ran for cover just as the plane swooped over the deck and then banked and turned for a second run. Again, the Zero swooped low, buzzing the deck and sending waves of panic through the onlookers.

Then, as quickly as it came, the plane left, only to return the next day, and then the next, to continue its barrage of intimidation.

"Here he comes again!" Esther shouted. As the plane coursed by, she recognized the pilot's face. "It's the same pilot we saw yesterday," she exclaimed.

Through it all, Esther's mother kept praying.

The captain, terrified, chose another means to assuage his fears: a bottle of whiskey that never left his hand. "I don't understand why they don't bomb us," he said one night at dinner.

"Because we prayed for God's protection," said Esther's mother.

"Then please keep praying!" the man replied, taking another swig out of his bottle.

Though buoyed by her mother's faith, Esther still couldn't quite shake her fears. *What will become of the Vietnamese? What of my friends? Mother's friends in the French government? Will God protect them too?* These were questions she dared not ask out loud, but they weighed heavy on her heart.

By the time the tanker steamed into Hong Kong Harbor, the ship was out of water, out of food, and one week late. "I can't believe we're seeing Hong Kong," the captain said to Esther's mother as he leaned over the rails watching Victoria Peak gleam in the sunshine. "You were my good luck."

But as young as she was, Esther knew it was more than luck. Her family had faced down the Japanese in Lang Son, evaded Zeros, and survived treacherous waters and storms. They might have left Indochina *tay khong*—empty-handed—with barely a shred of the past to their names. But at least they had their lives.

As for those they had left behind—Mr. and Mrs. Cadman, Mr. and Mrs. Tieu and Nghia, and her friends at the mission school in Da Lat—Esther could only look at the cloudless sky above her . . . and wonder.

The arrival of the Japanese in Indochina during the fall of 1940 had little immediate impact on Grandfather Tieu and his family. Under an agreement signed by the German-controlled Vichy French government and the Japanese, the French colonial government retained control over Indochina, operating the schools, the railroads, and the police, while the Japanese gained a military presence and a ready source of supply.

Except for the appearance of increasing numbers of Japanese on the streets, life went on as usual. Tieu went to work every day as head of the Public Transportation Office; Grandmother Nhu kept cooking and shopping; and my mother, Nghia, finished her studies toward her *diplôme* at the *Lycée Hoai Duc*. With the three eldest daughters, Trung, An, and Tinh, already married, Nghia and her four youngest siblings were the only children still at home. Absorbed in the daily details of work, school, and church, the family temporarily felt cushioned from the political maelstrom that was building around them.

Under the surface, Vietnam was beginning to boil. With one stroke of the pen, the French had lost their claim to any status and authority among the Vietnamese people, and throughout the country a variety of anti-French and anti-Japanese nationalist groups began to assert themselves. Not the least of these was the *Viet Minh*, or "Vietnam Independence League," a group organized in early 1941 by the leader of the Indochinese Communist Party, who took the name Ho Chi Minh. Ho encouraged his comrades to downplay their Marxist agenda and create a coalition across all social and economic strata to fight for Vietnamese independence.

Before long, the universities began to seethe with political activism, the *Viet Minh* staged isolated guerilla attacks on Japanese outposts, and cells of revolutionaries enlisted adherents throughout the cities and the countryside. In retaliation, the French security police, the *Sûreté*, aided by the Japanese, launched a relentless dragnet. They pulled suspects from their homes for interrogation and threw insurgents into jail. Before long, Hoa Lo prison, the nineteenth-century fortress built by the French in what later became downtown Hanoi, was jammed with more than one thousand alleged conspirators.

Throughout this turmoil, Grandfather Tieu stayed outside the orbit of politics. He had a job to do and a family to feed, and for a while that was all that mattered to him. Slowly, however, any semblance of ordinary life began to erode.

Many of the Europeans and Americans whom Tieu knew, including most of the missionaries, grabbed the chance to evacuate on a Swedish ship in July 1942. A few stalwarts, including Grandfather's mentor, *Giao Si* William Cadman, and his wife, stayed behind in Hanoi. *Giao Si* Richmond Jackson, showing the same grit that had helped him free Tieu from opium nearly two decades before, opted to remain in Vietnam. But the Japanese forced him to move from Vinh to Da Lat with his wife and youngest son, Victor. There he coordinated the work of various local churches.

In 1943, the Japanese rounded up the missionaries and interned them with other foreigners in a prison camp in My Tho.

As the war dragged on and the fortunes of the Japanese began to wane in the Pacific, the invaders focused on tightening their economic and military grip on the Vietnamese populace. Food began to grow scarce, and fears of Allied bombing sent thousands of city dwellers—including my Grandmother Nhu and her youngest children—to the relative safety of the countryside.

Tieu and Nghia continued to seek shelter in Hanoi at their little house on Rue Duvillier, with the aid of the family's faithful rickshaw driver, Quoc.

Of course, no place in war-torn Vietnam was truly safe. Just outside Hanoi, Allied bombers were targeting industrial centers and Japanese military bases. In the city, the songs of the noodle vendors grew silent, and were replaced by the wail of sirens and random pop of explosions. But Tieu, Nghia, and Quoc remained firmly resolved to face the dangers together, however severe those dangers might be.

6

BROTHER QUOC

The little child sat by the gate, not saying a word.

What does he want? thought Tieu. The young boy didn't act like the usual beggars, who yelled and screamed in a desperate plea for leftovers. He simply appeared after lunch each day and squatted on his haunches, watching the house with wide, soulful eyes.

Tieu went behind the house to the kitchen and scooped out a bowl of rice from the pot, as he did routinely every day. Then he walked to the front of the house, down the narrow path, and quietly passed the bowl through the gate. "The Lord bless you," he said to the boy.

The child grabbed the bowl and started shoveling rice into his mouth with his fingers faster than he could swallow it.

Why does he come here? These days so many beggars were on the streets it was hard to know whom to feed. The Vichy French didn't care. They were so firmly under the thumb of the Japanese that they did whatever they were told. The Japanese certainly didn't care. They had even forced the farmers to grow jute instead of rice to produce burlap bags for the war effort. The fact that millions of peasants were starving meant nothing to them.

Tieu cringed as he thought of the invaders, whose alleged cruelty was whispered on the lips of everyone in Hanoi. According to one story making the rounds, a Japanese colonel had killed his Vietnamese servant over nothing more than a bucket of wheat. The servant's job had been to feed wheat grass and grain to the officer's horse. But one day, the servant's children were so hungry that the poor man had substituted regular grass for the feed and had given the wheat to his family instead. The horse ate the ordinary grass, choked on a thistle, and died. When the colonel found out what had happened, he was so enraged that he had the entrails removed from the horse and forced his servant to crawl inside the carcass. Then he sewed up the carcass and left the servant to die.

As the war raged on, such stories multiplied, and tragedy continually unfolded before Tieu's eyes. All around him people were dying, and all he could hope to do was try to help them one by one, just as he had responded to the little boy at the gate.

Fortunately, Tieu's job at the railroad kept him solvent. What's more, every few weeks, his wife came back to Hanoi with a bag of rice, salted fish, *nuoc mam* sauce, and vegetables that she had stored up in her father's village during more prosperous times. At each visit, Nhu carefully counted out a few *dong* and gave the money to the family's rickshaw driver, Quoc, so that he could buy fresh eggs at the market for Tieu and Nghia.

"Brother Quoc," as Tieu called him, was the only one keeping the household afloat in Nhu's absence. Tieu could never call him *thang*, or "trash," as most people did their servants. He had worked for them so long that he was almost a part of the family. Before the war, he had carted the children back and forth to school. Now his job was to manage the household in Nhu's absence, running errands, doing the shopping, washing clothes, cooking the food, and taking Tieu back and forth to work.

Quoc's personal life remained a mystery. From what Tieu could tell, Quoc lived a solitary life, content to do his job and nothing more. One day, however, instead of waiting for Quoc to pick him up for lunch, Tieu arrived home earlier than usual. He opened the front gate only to discover Quoc holding the little beggar boy in his arms. Stunned, Tieu asked, "What is the meaning of this, brother Quoc?"

Quoc tightened up and immediately set the boy down. "I didn't give him anything from the house. I give you my word. I gave him my own food." With that, he turned to the boy and tried to shoo him away. "Go home now," Quoc said. "You can't stay."

"Wait," said Tieu, who in a flash of understanding realized that the child was Quoc's own son. Why hadn't he figured it out before? The boy waiting patiently by the gate . . . Quoc's secretiveness . . . his increasingly sickly appearance. Over the past few months, Tieu had sensed that Quoc was getting thinner and thinner, but he had been so absorbed in his work that he hadn't really paid attention. Now it all made sense. How could he have been so obtuse? Quoc was sacrificing his own health for the sake of his family.

"Just let him eat," Tieu said tenderly. "And please, you go get something to eat as well."

Brother Quoc seemed so relieved by Tieu's kindness that the words started spilling out of his mouth in a torrent. "I was afraid to tell you," he said. "I was scared that if you knew I had a family, your wife wouldn't trust me to take care of you and elder sister Nghia. But every penny Mrs. Tieu gave me, I spent for you."

There was something oddly familiar about Quoc's story that tugged at Tieu's heart. Then he recalled the verse: "Well done, good and faithful servant; you have been faithful over a little, I will set you over much; enter into the joy of your master."

"You are a good man," Tieu told him. "With the money my wife gave you, you were always able to get what we needed. You never tried to cheat us."

From then on, Tieu sent rice home with Quoc every day. And he never saw the little boy at the gate again. But as sensitive as Tieu was to those around him, he was mostly oblivious to his own needs—particularly when it came to his health. His appetite wasn't what it used to be. And every now and then, he felt so weak he had to close the door to his office and lie on the floor until his energy returned.

It must be the aftereffects of the opium, he thought, a sense of resignation creeping over him. *It's catching up with me.*

Tieu's increasing preoccupation with the war and his responsibilities at the railroad caused him to overlook not only himself, but also other challenges close at hand. One of the most important and potentially far-reaching for him was the transformation in his daughter, Nghia, a change that had actually begun just before the Japanese invaded. Under his very nose, Tieu's precious little girl, who had once almost died of syphilis, was growing up.

7

RED RIVER RHAPSODIES

As the clouds of war were first gathering over Indochina, Nghia, then a teenager on the cusp of womanhood, found her attentions drawn to dreamier pursuits. Overnight, it seemed, the boys she knew had turned into young men, and she felt the first stirrings of emotions so rapturous they brought a blush to her cheeks.

Even the loss created by the abrupt departure of her friend, Esther Van Hine, and the imminent wartime dangers on her doorstep couldn't fully penetrate the gauzy world of romance that Nghia was creating in her imagination. In that emerging inner world, where love was becoming paramount, the young girl's hopes and dreams sought fulfillment in deep relationships that endured beyond hardships, beyond war, and perhaps even beyond life itself.

Yet for Nghia that kind of love wasn't merely a fantasy. It was a blissful reality she saw played out as she had watched her father shower affection on her mother with shameless abandon. "He loves his wife as Christ loves the church," Nghia heard people in their congregation whisper.

Nghia knew it was true. She could still picture the gleeful look on her father's face the day he surprised her mother in the kitchen, not long after his big promotion to *chef de bureau*.

It was just before *Têt*, and Nhu was hard at work, feverishly pounding pork into a fine paste with *nuoc mam* sauce and garlic to make *gio*, a delicious sausage. The entire household was in the kitchen—the housemaids, Quoc the rickshaw driver, Nghia, and all her sisters—chopping, cutting, and cooking in a scramble to get the food prepared before the holiday. As everyone knew, superstition dictated that if anyone dared cook or clean on the first three days of the New Year, he would spend the rest of the year laboring without rest. Christian or not, none of them was about to put tradition to the test.

Nhu had just dumped potato starch into the ground-meat mixture and was kneading it with her hands when Tieu came up behind her and put his arms around her. "Me, I have something for you," he said.

"Don't bother me," Nhu responded, trying to wriggle away from him. "I have to get this done by midnight. Besides, it's your favorite dish. It even has chopped pigskin in it."

But not even the lure of pigskin could dissuade Tieu. In front of *everyone*, servants and children alike, he pulled Nhu's hand out of the pile of raw meat and slipped a beautiful gold bracelet on her greasy wrist. Then he walked around in front of her and grinned like a little boy.

Nhu seemed so embarrassed that she picked up a bowl and hid her face behind it, even as she held up her hand for all to see her prize.

For a few minutes, Nghia stood motionless, entranced by the scene she had watched unfold: her father's love-struck eyes, her mother's shy delight, and the golden bangle, gleaming in the harsh glare of the kitchen light. She couldn't resist the temptation to run over and take a closer look.

The bracelet was extraordinary. It was yellow gold, about two centimeters wide, engraved with sinuous dancing dragons holding a blazing fireball between their mouths. She recognized the design as a classic symbol of wealth and prosperity—a sign, perhaps, of the glorious future Tieu was promising his adored wife.

But to the teenaged Nghia, the dragon bracelet came to symbolize something much more profound: a rare kind of love that was passionate, unself-conscious, and utterly committed. For months after *Tết*, the romance of the bracelet enveloped her as she replayed that scene in the kitchen over and over in her mind. She imagined the day when she would know that kind of love, when she would meet a man like her father, who loved so completely that nothing else in the world mattered.

Then, one day, it happened.

She was sitting in the living room doing her homework, when her older cousin Dan, a poor relation from the countryside whom her father was raising as a son, arrived with a new schoolmate. Cousin Dan was forever bringing friends home for dinner or a card game and usually she paid no attention. Most of them were egotistical louts, consumed with posturing and raucous chatter.

But when Minh walked in the room, he and Nghia locked eyes and never let go. Something about him was different from all the other young men she knew. He had an elegance about him, a strong, masculine grace that projected an air of supreme confidence, yet unusual sensitivity. He might have been a young professor. Or perhaps a poet. Snatches of conversation she overheard made it clear that he was intelligent. Something of an intellectual, perhaps.

At the first sight of him, Nghia felt her face redden and her legs grow weak. She even thought she might faint as she watched him move across the room in her direction.

"*Chao em,*" he said when he reached her side. Hello, little sister.

From his lips, the ordinary greeting sounded like nothing less than a prayer, a touch, a kiss. She answered back. "*Chao anh.*" Big brother. Friend. But she also wondered, *Lover too?*

It seemed that he might be all that and more. "O God," she prayed, "is he the one you've chosen for me? Is this what love is?"

From that day on, the two became inseparable, yet they orchestrated their friendship so discreetly that not even her family grew wise to their affection. Every day after school, Dan and Minh would arrive, overflowing with vitality. When Nghia would hear the front gate slam shut and the sound of their feet running up the narrow stone path, every nerve ending from her fingertips to her toes would tingle with anticipation.

Dan and Minh would burst through the door and throw down their books, just as Nghia emerged from the kitchen with a plateful of noodles. The three of them would sit around the table, eating and laughing and talking, until it was time for homework. Then, invariably, Minh would offer to tutor her, and Nghia would sit at the table with him, poring over the day's assignments.

Day by day, his tutoring became the perfect cover, one that gave them precious moments in each other's company and seemed to endear the young man to her father. Minh seemed so like her father, always filled with conversation about books, or politics, or music. But it was his tenderness that had especially touched her, a sweetness that showed itself in his concern for her every need.

"Are you thirsty, *em?*" he always asked. "How about some fresh coconut juice? I know where to find just what you like." Or, "Can I bring you a book tomorrow from the library?"

The months and weeks passed and still, their secret remained hidden even from Nghia's friends. When the school bell rang at the end of the day, she would walk out the south gate of *Lycée Hoai Duc* and head down the broad avenue with her schoolmates toward her house.

Seeming to ignore Nghia and her girlfriends, Minh would appear on his bike from a side street and ride nearby at a pace to match that of the young women. He didn't talk or even give her a glance until her friends had parted from her. Only then did he get off his bike and walk her the rest of the way home. Sometimes, though, they would meander down other streets, especially those that led to the *Song Hong,* the Red River, where lovers often strolled and lingered. Many times, dusk arrived before they said their good-byes.

❖❖❖❖❖

As the months passed, their passion grew, fueled by love notes hidden in the covers of the books his sister delivered back and forth, or by stolen glances over tea and bean cakes. Although they were continually surrounded by family and friends, they found secret moments together even in the midst of the throng, and their hearts grew heavy with longing.

Not once in the time she had known Minh had they kissed or even touched. Somehow, they didn't need to. Their desire for each other was bathed in a love so pure and constant that they could wait forever, if necessary, for the time when they would finally be together.

Our time will come—I know it will. After the war. I will be waiting.

But it seemed that Minh had no intention of waiting for the end of the war. He broke the good news to Nghia at their favorite weekend rendezvous, a bench overlooking Ho Hoan Kiem. By then, Nghia had blossomed into a young woman of nineteen, while Minh had established himself as a rising intellectual with plans to study law.

As the morning mist rose from the lake, he looked deep into her eyes and said the words she had longed to hear ever since they had met. "We will be married," Minh told her. "My parents have agreed to it, and soon we will be one."

Nghia was delirious with happiness, and her imagination immediately took flight. She could see the future clearly: They would read books together every night . . . talk until they fell asleep in each other's arms . . . have a brood of children—boys just as intellectual as Minh, and girls just as inquisitive as she. They would take walks on Saturdays . . . they would eat *pho* till they burst. He would be a lawyer; she would be a teacher. What a life they would have together!

A few weeks later, in the early evening, she looked out of the window of her house to see an elegant rickshaw pull up in front of the gate. A stately, middle-aged woman in a formal *ao dai* and velvet headpiece alighted and made her way up the path.

Nghia had never seen the woman before, but she knew instantly why she had come. *A go-between! Sent by Minh's parents. Our dream is finally coming true.*

With her heart pounding, she joined her mother and sisters to greet the woman at the door. Then, according to custom, she disappeared to a back room and waited. Fortunately, Nhu was in Hanoi from the country for a few days, so this visit by the go-between could be counted as official.

Though almost too impatient to observe the formalities, Nghia understood that she would have to stay out of sight and rely on her married sister Trung, who had dropped by on a visit, to help serve the woman tea. But she also expected Trung to report back to her regularly with any tidbits of news.

Twenty minutes later, Trung appeared with a smile on her face. "Minh's family is eager for the match," she said. "Mother just sat there listening and nodding. She told the woman it's up to Father to make a decision."

Later that night, after Tieu returned from work, Nghia listened in eager anticipation through the doorway for the words that would bind her to Minh forever.

"He's a wonderful young man with a bright future," she heard her father say to her mother.

Yes, yes, she thought. *A bright future, indeed. If anyone understands the value of Minh's education, it's Father. He'll have a law degree. From Hanoi Law University!*

"He is everything I would want in a son-in-law," Tieu added, pausing just long enough for Nghia's heart to stop. "But Nghia cannot marry him."

8

DIVIDED ALLEGIANCE

Nghia was stunned. It was as though a spear had been thrust in her heart. The minute she heard the words "cannot marry," she ran to her room and threw herself on the bed in tears. She was too distraught to ask for—or listen to—any reasons for her father's decision.

Why is Father against Minh? Money certainly wasn't a factor. Minh's parents were Mandarins, so wealthy they made hers look like peasants. Besides, her father had seen him practically every day for years at the family's house with cousin Dan. *What could possibly be wrong?*

As she lay sobbing, Tieu slipped into her room and sat by the bed. Gently, he put his hand on her head. "I'm sorry, Nghia," he said. "You know I want only the best for you. But Minh is not what God wants for you. His family is Buddhist. We are Protestants. They are Mandarins, who have known a life far beyond ours. The gulf between our families is too great. In the end, you would be disappointed. Trust me. I know what's best."

She didn't understand—might never understand. But because she loved and respected her father above all others, she reluctantly acquiesced in his judgment. Each of her older sisters had married the man he had chosen for her. He had even turned down promising seminary students to make what he thought was the perfect match for them.

Still, she wondered, *does he really know what's best?* Then her father dealt her an even more crushing blow: "One more thing,

Nghia," said Tieu as he stroked her head. "You must never see him again."

▦▦▦▦▦

For more than a year and a half, Nghia obeyed her father's wishes. But as the war dragged on late into 1944, and as life in the perennial war zone of Hanoi grew more and more severe, her heart cried out for the sight of Minh. Her anguish grew so great that finally, against every dictum in her strict upbringing, Nghia abandoned all sense of filial duty and followed her passion. Even though she knew it would pain her father deeply, she started seeing Minh again.

They got into the habit of meeting secretly several times a month at Voi Thuc Temple in O Cau Giay, the "Paper Bridge" neighborhood far from her home. It was wrong, and Nghia knew it. Just the whisper of her disobedience would scandalize her father. But Nghia couldn't help herself. She rationalized that seeing Minh was her only possible source of happiness, her only hope of joy in the midst of the chaos and suffering that surrounded them. She became convinced that they must capture the moment, steal whatever pleasure they could in these uncertain times. At any second their lives might end. Yet she sensed that their love would go on forever.

But in the end, the rationalizations failed to banish the doubts and guilt that gnawed away inside her. These misgivings finally reached a climax on a particular sunny weekday just before Christmas in 1944, when the lovers had scheduled one of their trysts.

Nghia had awakened that morning in turmoil. In less than an hour, she would be meeting Minh at Voi Thuc Temple, yet she felt strangely disconnected from him. Usually, she would be tingling with excitement at the prospect of seeing her lover. But today, she wasn't so sure about anything. About Minh. About her life. About their future. Where was the relationship going? Should she keep seeing him? Should she put an end to it now? She was almost sick with indecision.

Without any clear answers, Nghia threw on her clothes and slipped out of the house. As she walked down the path and out the gate at Rue Duvillier, she prayed that by this time of the morning, the death carts would have carried away the bodies that had died on the streets the night before. Her heart was too heavy from her own problems to deal with anyone else's tragedy.

As she picked her way along the street, she had to avert her eyes to avoid looking directly at the bodies of the peasants that lay grouped together, in the same configurations where they had died during the night. The horror of it was too overwhelming for her to contemplate. Husbands, wives, children lay all around her, entire families forced by famine and flood from the countryside to Hanoi, where they had hoped to find relief. Instead, during the chill of the previous night, they had died where they had slept, trying unsuccessfully to huddle together for warmth.

To Nghia, the corpses were silent witnesses to the ravages of a war that had snatched away her youth and to the heartbreak that seemed poised to shatter her dreams. Only a single thought kept her moving forward: Minh. She had agreed not to marry him, but she could never agree not to love him. He was her first love. Her truest friend.

Nghia knew her relationship with Minh was pure, as pristine and noble as any could be. But it was frustrating that he still remained just beyond her reach—so close, so dear, yet so untouchable. How could she continue to torture herself week after week, seeing him young and vital and alive, yet fearing that their love could never be consummated? The agony was becoming unbearable.

Finally, as she walked toward their meeting place, she made up her mind. She would see him this one last time . . . she would tell him she couldn't see him anymore . . . explain that it would be better for both of them if they just drifted apart . . . better if they each found someone else to share their lives. "It will spare both of us more pain," she would tell him.

With her decision in place, Nghia walked quickly along the street toward the temple. But the closer she got, the shakier her resolve became. She started to rationalize: Maybe it wasn't necessary to initiate a permanent breakup. Perhaps she should wait until next week, or next month. By the time she crossed the street and turned into a little side street toward the temple grounds, she had forgotten her decision and everything she had planned to say. She could feel the familiar rush of adrenaline, the surge of excitement as she drew nearer to her love.

Any minute now, she would be sitting next to Minh on the little stone bench, listening to him expound on the outlook for the end of the war, or the poetry of Rimbaud, or the prospects of the *Viet Minh*. It didn't matter what they talked about. All she really wanted was to drink in the sight of him. His tousled black hair . . . his deep-set eyes . . . his wispy beard that reminded her of some *Rive Gauche* artist she had seen in a picture in a French magazine. Nghia was about to turn into the temple when she heard footsteps behind her. She spun around to find herself face-to-face with him.

"Minh!" At the sight of him, her knees seemed to melt the way they had the very first day she had met him. Shyly, she gave a little nod of greeting. Side by side, they walked into the temple grounds, their hands just a whisper apart. Somehow she knew she could not obey her father. She had no choice but to see her beloved again and again.

❖❖❖❖❖

The next Sunday, Nghia sat in her usual pew at church, third from the front, staring pensively at the Bible on her lap. But she was oblivious to the festive Christmas decorations or what was happening in the worship service. Instead, she continued to grapple with her conscience over her clandestine relationship with Minh. Occasionally she shot a glance to her right toward her father, Tieu, who was sitting next to her. His head was bowed and his hands folded in prayer as he waited for the pastor to deliver the sermon. The sight of her simple, pious, somewhat frail father only aggravated Nghia's sense of guilt.

But Nghia's inner turmoil would never have been apparent to any casual observer. Outwardly, she was the picture of understated elegance, with porcelain skin as delicate as eggshells, and large luminous eyes that peeked out as innocently as a doe's from under her lashes. She wore her straight black hair swept back from her face and pulled together in a loose bun that barely brushed her neck, giving her a hint of propriety. A navy-blue silk *ao dai* with tiny white polka dots, worn over a loose pair of white silk pants, graced her tiny frame and lent her an air of glamour that only seemed to accentuate her piety.

Fragments of Bible verses and prayers drifted through her mind. "My peace I give to you." If she could only allow herself to settle her mind, to release her guilt and her struggles with Minh, per-haps she might find some of that peace.

"Abide in me." Nghia knew that this sanctuary was the one place where she could abide, a place where hope and expectation had always been a constant. For as long as she could remember, the Hanoi Protestant Church had been at the center of her exis-tence. As a child, when she hadn't been in school, she was at Thursday afternoon Bible meeting, or Sunday school, or the mis-sionary convention, hearing preachers from as far away as North America, and singing robust hymns that resonated with a sense of possibility.

She needed those assurances now; she longed to hear the promises that would lift her spirits and resolve the inner conflicts of her heart. Her eyes drifted to the Bible in her lap, which was open to Psalm 119: "Open my eyes, that I may behold wondrous things out of thy law. . . . My soul cleaves to the dust; revive me according to thy word!"

My soul cleaves to the dust. . . . Wasn't that exactly what she was feeling? Like King David in the wilderness, running from his enemies, she was weary and parched. She was emotionally dry. Drained of all energy and feeling. It wasn't just the war, though that was reason enough for her utter exhaustion. Certainly, the threats, fears, and un-certainties had worn her down and helped extinguish the fire within her. But the dominant reason for her spiritual drought was Minh. The war that raged inside her could be traced directly back to her decep-tion and disobedience to her father.

Are we really doing anything wrong? she argued to herself. *Is there something wrong with loving someone so completely?* Nghia looked over at her father and sighed. *It's all so complicated.* After all, it was because of Tieu that she had fallen in love with Minh. Her lover was nothing less than a younger version of her romantic, faithful father.

How could Nghia forget the delight in Tieu's eyes when he gave the dragon bracelet to her mother? How could she overlook the affectionate hugs and words Tieu bestowed on Nhu? How could she ignore his selflessness toward his wife—and also his children—when he had elected to ride his bike to work day after day so that the family could use the old rickshaw they had once relied upon?

From the time Nghia was small, Tieu had shown her by his every action what a man could be: not hard and arrogant like many men she knew, but tender, and sensitive, and humble. Over dinner just a few months before, he had even apologized to her for the recurrent bouts of sickness that had plagued her as a child. "It was all my fault," Tieu had told her. "Because of the opium, my sperm was not strong, and so after you were born, you suffered."

But if she had suffered as a child, she had long since forgotten it. Now her only suffering was because she ached to be with Minh, and yet she felt guilty even for wanting this relationship because her father had rejected him. *So complicated.*

Nghia couldn't be angry with her father. She really couldn't fault him for the way things had turned out with Minh because she had known all along that he had just been trying to protect her spiritually. More than anything, he wanted her to be faithful—not just to an earthly husband, but to God. He had taught her that true joy and happiness had to begin with God, and that the marital relationship had to be built upon that foundation.

But it's so hard when you're in love. . . . Slowly Nghia began to understand that there might be a way out of her dilemma. She knew that Tieu's unbending faith in God was the source of all his strength, even his ability to love Nhu as devotedly as he did. His faith was the reason that she herself had come to know the true meaning of love. Nghia needed that kind of faith now to revive her own flagging spirit. She needed to ensure that nothing—not her love for Minh, nor war, nor famine, nor even death—would separate her from the greatest love of all, the love of Christ. Her eyes drifted again to Psalm 119: "Keep steady my steps according to thy promise, and let no iniquity get dominion over me."

Steady steps, one by one: that was the answer. She didn't have to have everything figured out at once about Minh, or even about her own personal faith in Christ. She simply had to trust that step by step, God would guide her decisions, and that he would guard her very life.

As she heard the congregation around her beginning to stir during a soaring Christmas carol, Nghia could feel herself growing stronger. Looking around at the other worshipers, she thought of the steady steps that had brought each one of them to church year after year and Sunday after Sunday and of the struggles that each had endured.

Shopkeepers and tradesmen sang with gusto, even though they periodically had lost everything to the invading Japanese or to the bombing. Her father's good friend, Mr. Hoang, was sitting nearby with his two wives—a difficult cultural situation that had been settled to the satisfaction of the elders. His son had even become a pastor. For each of these people, the transition to a life with Christ had been demanding. But if anything, their spirits seemed more alive than ever before.

Yet none in the congregation was more faithful than her father. Nghia marveled at his devotion. Every few weeks, just after work on Fridays, Tieu would hop on his bike, as he had done this very weekend, and ride four hours through the countryside to see his wife, Nhu. Along the way, he had to dodge bombs and pass through military checkpoints under the watchful eyes of French and Japanese soldiers. Then, two days later on Sunday, he rode back without fail to Hanoi in the wee hours of the morning so that he would arrive in time to join Nghia for church. The pace was excruciating, and it was beginning to show on his face.

Without thinking, Nghia reached over and touched his sleeve. Tieu looked up from his prayers and smiled. "The Lord is good, Nghia," he whispered. "He has been faithful."

His eyes look so heavy, Nghia thought. *When we get home from church, I'll tell him to sleep.*

Nghia was so absorbed in concern for her father that she failed to notice the rugged-looking stranger sitting several benches behind her, watching her every move. She didn't know that the man's name was Phuong—or that he was on the run.

9

GUERRILLA GAMES

The shackles on Phuong's ankles were so tight the pain was excruciating. A heavy chain that linked the leg irons had so little give he had to shuffle every time he walked. "Hurry up, you scum!" the Japanese guard yelled to him. "Get into the truck. Move it!"

Phuong edged his way out the door of *Maison Centrale*, the main gate of Hoa Lo prison, and lined up behind three other prisoners who were waiting to board the truck. The four of them were being transferred to another facility on the outskirts of Hanoi, where, it was said, the guards were even more vicious. It had been bad enough in Hoa Lo, where the guards' idea of fun was to put him in an empty oil barrel and bang on the sides until his nerves were so rattled he wanted to die. But the place where he was now going was worse.

"Nobody comes back alive," his fellow prisoners had whispered.

I've got to break out, he thought, searching the street for a possible means of escape. *There's got to be a way.*

He looked to the left and right. *No luck.* The Japanese were everywhere. Guards on the right and left of the gate. Guards by the truck. If he bolted, he'd be shot straightaway. *I'll bide my time . . . wait for my chance.*

"Get moving!" shouted the guard, clapping Phuong on the back with a bamboo rod.

Phuong was about to pull himself into the truck when, out of the corner of his eye, he caught sight of a movement at the far end of the street. A lime seller was squatting by the road with two flat baskets filled with fruits piled up in geometric pyramids. He was haggling with someone, and as they talked, the two men kept looking toward the truck.

It's Binh and Khang! Phuong thought. Just knowing that the two *Viet Minh* operatives were keeping watch at the prison's edge gave him a surge of confidence. *I can do it! There's got to be a way.*

He climbed up into the open bed of the truck and sat on the floor with the other three prisoners, waiting for his chance. He eyed the two guards. They were sitting at the back of the truck with their rifles resting on their knees, watching him.

But the minute the tailgate clanked shut, their attention seemed to wander. They began whispering to each other and laughing. Then one pulled out a cigarette, and as he lit up and started puffing, Phuong could see the man's shoulders relax.

They're manageable, he thought. *They think they're just out for a ride!*

The truck pulled away from Hoa Lo and was ready to turn the corner onto Boulevard Carreau when one of the prisoners started to vomit.

"Stop the truck!" a guard yelled. The driver slammed on the brakes, and one of the guards rushed over to the prisoner and held his head over the rail.

Phuong didn't waste a second. He shoved the other guard toward the cab of the truck, hurled himself over the rear end, and rolled to the side of the street. Then, before the guards could regroup, he jumped up, and doing a fast two-step in his leg irons, he shuffled quickly past Binh and Khang. It was almost dark, and he hoped the lengthening shadows and darkening alcoves would help shield him from the eyes of his pursuers.

Glancing over his shoulder, he saw that the truck driver had jumped out and was starting to run after him, but his friends Binh and Khang managed to block the way, sending the two baskets of limes rolling all over the street.

"What did you do to my limes?" Binh yelled, pointing his finger and gesturing wildly at the soldier. "You've ruined my business. No one will want to buy damaged fruit."

The soldier just shook his head and walked back to the truck empty-handed. For the time being, at least, Phuong was free.

The forlorn moon soon spread out a pale blue blanket over homes and shops that were deep asleep as Phuong hobbled swiftly along the narrow cobblestone streets. Only a few more blocks and he would reach Hang Da Market, where the maze of shop stalls could serve as his hiding place.

I'll be safe soon, he thought. He was exhausted. Suddenly, he heard footsteps and foreign voices.

I will not be caught again! I'd rather die. With teeth clenched, Phuong grabbed the chain by his ankles and slithered noiselessly into an alley like a vole in the darkness. A few minutes later, he reached the empty market, where he slipped under a wooden platform in one of the stalls and hunkered down for the night.

Sleep eluded him. His mind still churning, he thought back over his narrow escape and the direction his life had taken.

◼◼◼◼◼

At thirty-one, Vu Duc Phuong was a wanted man, a Communist, a revolutionary. There was no turning back.

How different my life might have been, he mused. He hadn't been raised to be a radical. He was a rice farmer, a landowner, heir to his family's fortune in Hoanh Nha village, where two wealthy families had been joined in marriage. His father came from Mandarin stock. Didn't he have the old picture to prove it? Back home in Hoanh Nha, the photo of a dignified man in a hat and silk Mandarin robe sat on the altar in his ancestral worship hall, next to the incense his mother never allowed to burn low.

As for his mother, her parents came from a long line of landowners. "Co bay thang canh" was the way the villagers described his mother's holdings: "Geese would fly with straight wings into the horizon, and even that wasn't where her land ended," the villagers said. The property was so vast that people from several villages away came to seek work in his mother's fields. A shrewd businesswoman, she seldom paid their wages in cash. Instead, she provided an incentive for hard work by guaranteeing them a percentage of what they harvested.

It would have been easy for Phuong to share in that life. He could have stayed back in Hoanh Nha to help his mother manage the property. With his father dead, his two brothers fighting for the revolution, and three unmarried sisters at home, perhaps it had been his duty to stay. But his need for adventure was too great, and the call of revolution was too strong.

"I'm sorry, *Me*," he had told his mother. "I wish I could be a dutiful son. But I can't stay here and watch the French tear our country to pieces like wolves and chickens."

His mother had supported his decision and, from time to time, she had sheltered him and his *Viet Minh* comrades in tunnels dug behind the house when they were on the run. But after the French finally raided the estate—tipped off, Phuong was sure, by one of the servants—he had decided to stay away indefinitely.

Phuong knew how much the separation must pain his mother. He hadn't been back to Hoanh Nha in a couple of years, and his six months in Hoa Lo after the *Sûreté* fingered him must have been excruciating for her. She probably didn't even know if he was dead or alive.

He knew his mother well enough to understand that even though she might be helping to support the revolution, underneath it all, she wanted nothing more than to have him living close at hand with a family of his own. Her biggest fear, she confessed, was that he and his brothers would be killed in the war. "No sons, no grandsons to worship me after I die," she had often said, echoing the old Vietnamese adage.

Phuong shuddered at the thought of his mother alone for eternity. "I promise, *Me*," he vowed to his mother as he drifted off to sleep, "I promise that someday, you'll have the grandest worship house you can imagine."

※※※※

Underneath the platform in Hang Da Market, Phuong lay quietly waiting for the shops to come to life. It had rained during the night, and the ground was still damp, smelling of garbage and fermented vegetables. He was cold and very tired, but he fought the unyielding desire to keep sleeping. The last thing he wanted was for a merchant to arrive and find a stranger in shackles under his stall.

I must find Ha, he thought, as he slid out from under the platform. *His bicycle repair shop is around here somewhere. I'll get him to cut the leg irons. After that, I'll try to find Uncle Qui.*

Phuong knew he couldn't stay anywhere for long. If he was lucky, he could hide out at his uncle's apartment for a day or two at the most, and then, like a rat, he'd have to scurry off again. The *Sûreté* had a wide net, and the only way to slip through it was to keep on the move.

As the faint light of dawn began to creep into the market, Phuong did a quick reconnaissance. From what he remembered, Ha's bicycle shop was just a few rows away. Quickly, he passed through the maze of stalls until he reached his comrade's place.

"Ha! Are you in there?" Phuong rapped gently at the shutters that covered the stall at night to ward off thieves. "Ha! Answer me!" Phuong was on the verge of walking away when he heard heavy breathing on the other side of the shutters. "Wake up, Ha! It's me, Phuong!"

He heard the sound of quick movement inside the stall, and then, like magic, one shutter board opened up low to the ground. The smell of rubber and glue nearly knocked him over.

"*Nhanh len, nhanh len,*" Ha said. "Quick, quick."

Phuong crawled through the opening, and Ha slipped the shutter back on the stall.

"I got news that you had escaped," Ha said. "I stayed at the shop, hoping that you might show up."

"Could you help me with my shackles? 'Chief *Ha Can Do*!'— that's your slogan, isn't it?"

The two friends clasped hands, not daring to make a noise. But in the darkness of the shop, their eyes shone with laughter.

Phuong had met Ha two years earlier in the *Viet Minh* training camp, where they had struggled with little food, less medicine, and more rain than he ever hoped to see again. It was Ha's sense of humor that had made the experience bearable, and together they had forged a bond, not only with the Communist cause, but also with each other, despite the differences in their backgrounds.

Phuong had gone to school only through the seventh grade, while Ha had an impeccable pedigree: a *baccalauréat* from *Truong Buoi*, the elite boys' high school in Hanoi, and the start on a promising career at the *Banque d'Indochine*. But when Ha left the bank after a year to join the *Viet Minh*, his father, a prosperous silk merchant, disowned him. In the camp, Phuong had become his family, and the two had grown even closer since their training was completed.

The two of them had been at home in Hoanh Nha for the sixth anniversary of Phuong's father's death when the French had raided Phuong's family estate. The only way they had eluded the Sûreté was by jumping in his mother's pond and staying underwater for hours, using hollow reeds to get air. Afterward, Phuong's mother gave Ha the money to start the bicycle repair business, which had since become a crucial meeting ground for their comrades in the middle of Hang Da Market.

As they talked in the shop, Phuong could hear the clanging of shutters and the noise of conversation as one by one, the merchants opened their stalls. "I've got to leave," he said. "I'm trying to get to my uncle Qui's apartment."

"Isn't he the one I met at your father's death anniversary?" asked Ha, as he started sawing the shackles off Phuong's ankles. "I see him around the market every now and then. He's a Christian, isn't he? It's Sunday today, and he'll probably be at church. It's just around the corner. The services last all morning.

"You can change into my clothes and then blend in with the Sunday shoppers. Tonight there's a full moon, and the crowds today will be huge."

Phuong nodded. The full moon always brought people out to buy food, incense, and flowers that they could bring to family grave sites or temples to ask favors of their ancestors.

"The place should be jumping in a few minutes," said Ha.

Phuong pulled on Ha's trousers. "You're fat," he chided his friend, drawing in the waist with some twine. "I haven't eaten for a couple of days. They like to starve you at Hoa Lo." Now he could really feel his hunger. "I could kill for a bowl of *pho*."

"Some *pho* can be arranged," said Ha, as he wrapped Phuong's prison clothes and the pieces of iron shackle in some oil-stained paper. "We can eat at the market, but we can't sit together. Four stalls to the left and then follow the aroma of *pho*, and you should see the best soup place in Hanoi."

Ha smiled at his fugitive friend and clapped some money in his hand. Then he peered through the shutters, and when the crowd thinned, he removed one of the shutters and let Phuong crawl through. "Good luck, my brother."

By the time Ha arrived at the soup place a few minutes later, Phuong was already sitting with a steaming bowl of *pho* in front of him. Ha took a seat in the far corner of the stall and then shouted out his order: *"Mot thit chin gan,"* he said. "One well-cooked meat with tendon in soup."

Across the stall, Phuong slurped down the noodles, pretending not to notice Ha. But as he lifted the bowl to his mouth, he looked over the rim at his comrade, and their eyes met. Phuong could feel his body grow warm all over. Hot soup. A good friend. Life was almost bearable. And the breakfast energized Phuong for his next round of challenges.

Don't rest on your laurels. The game is far from over. He got up from the stool and made his way through the maze of the market, heading for his uncle's church. Hang Da Market was in full swing now, with the voices of shoppers ordering and bargaining in lively counterpoint to the merchants who called out invitations to their stalls.

"Look at these chickens!" one merchant said.

"Deliciously fat!" exclaimed another, holding out a pudgy bird. Next to her, an old man cleaned a duck amidst a mess of feathers while across the aisle, a middle-aged woman arranged round plates of blood jelly in perfect order.

As Phuong wended his way through the cavernous market, he drank in the sights and smells that had been denied him for so long in Hoa Lo. He passed the food stalls, where cleavers moved up and down in harmony as if performing in some butchers' orchestra: *Kop, kop, kop!* Meat of all kinds hung on hooks on the wall, waiting to be taken down and fondled by housewives demanding to know if it was tender or firm. A large female customer sniffed a pig head and complained of the price.

Phuong couldn't help but smile. As he turned a corner to the long row of vegetable stalls, the aroma of basil, ginger, nutmeg, star anise, fresh pepper, cilantro, and mint danced around him, seducing his senses. He craved the chaos of smells, colors, movements, noises—rich, everyday pleasures that he had almost forgotten in the dank gray cells of Hoa Lo. Suddenly he was keenly aware of how glorious it was to be alive.

Next came the flower row, which assaulted him with colors so dazzling they almost blinded him with their beauty. He looked from one blossom to the next until finally, at the end of the row, he found himself emerging from the market.

Across the street, just where Ha had directed him, stood a simple white building with a cross on its roof. *"Nha Tho Tin Lanh Ha Noi,"* said the sign hanging over the front door. "Hanoi Protestant Church." The metal gate was wide open, as if beckoning him to enter.

Phuong crossed the street and walked through the gate into a small courtyard ringed with trees. The place was so serene that not even a birdsong broke the silence. Quickly he walked up a few steps to the little church and stopped at the entrance. An elderly man with a gentle face came out to greet him. *"Chao ong,"* the man said warmly.

"Chao cu," Phuong responded. "I'm looking for my uncle, Thay Qui. Is he here?"

"He's in Sunday school," the man said, pointing to a long building across the courtyard. "He'll be here for the service shortly."

"May I just sit in the church and wait for him?" Phuong asked.

"Oh, yes, this is God's house," the old man said, ushering him into the empty sanctuary. "Anyone is welcome to stay."

Phuong quietly took a seat in the last pew, which was hidden in the shadows, untouched by the light that streamed through the windows.

Whether it was because of the shadows, or the stillness, or the strange peace that he had never sensed before, Phuong closed his eyes and succumbed to a calm, blissful sleep.

◼◼◼◼◼

The sun rose high above the church and cast a beam directly onto Phuong's face, causing him to stir out of his slumber.

"Blessed are the poor in spirit, for theirs is the kingdom of heaven. Blessed are those who mourn, for they shall be comforted."

In that strange interlude between sleep and consciousness, Phuong could hear a man's voice, reading. The words were crystal clear, but somehow they seemed almost surreal, far away, as though they were in some distant dream world. As the sun streamed down on him, he felt so warm that he didn't want to move for fear he might lose this sense of utter tranquility. *Such peace!* The last time he had felt like this was as a child, sitting in his mother's lap, enveloped in her comfort and love.

"Blessed are those who hunger and thirst for righteousness, for they shall be satisfied."

Hunger . . . thirst . . . poor in spirit. The words were calling to him.

Dear heaven, he thought. *Are you talking to me? Yes, I am poor in spirit. I am frightened . . . hunted . . . alone. I am hungry for righteousness. But can I know what's right? I am lost. How do I find the way?*

"Take my yoke upon you, and learn from me," the reader continued in a sure, steady voice. "For I am gentle and lowly in heart, and you will find rest for your souls. For my yoke is easy, and my burden is light."

"Amen!" A chorus of voices startled Phuong awake. He looked around and realized he was no longer alone. All the pews were occupied, including his. Up in front, someone was saying something, but Phuong wasn't listening. His mind was still grasped by the tender words he had heard in his sleep, words that were now resounding somewhere deep inside. *You will find rest . . . my yoke is easy.*

Distracted, Phuong let his eyes wander around the congregation to look for his Uncle Qui. He checked the row in front of him, and then the next. Suddenly, up ahead of him, in the third row from the front, an image stopped him short. It was just a gentle nape of a neck. But that elegant curve of pale skin told him everything he wanted to know about the young woman. Her hair was loosely gathered together in a bun, and her head was bowed slightly—in prayer, he supposed.

He had known many attractive women, comrades from the training camps, who were as intense as they were beautiful. But none like this one, none with such exquisite femininity that caused his heart to skip a beat.

For the second time that day, Phuong felt life might be bearable. Even more than bearable.

10

PASSAGES

Nghia couldn't say when she first noticed that her father was failing. For the past couple of years, he had seemed tired a lot, but she wrote that off to his grueling schedule. Ever since her mother had gone to the country with the four youngest children, he had often shuttled back and forth from Hanoi on his bike just to see them. The constant travel would have been enough to drain the energy of anyone, even a much younger, healthier person. But then just after *Tết* in 1945, Tieu came down with a cold that he just couldn't seem to shake.

"You need to see a doctor," Nghia would tell him, switching roles from daughter to mother.

"It's nothing," he insisted. "Just a cold. Don't worry."

But she did worry. On her way to school each day, where she was finishing her teacher training, she fretted about his health. Some days she was so distracted she couldn't concentrate on her studies.

For the next couple of months, Tieu would come home after work and fall asleep right after dinner. He might pick up a book and head for the living room, but within minutes his eyes would close, his head would fall on his chest, and the book would slip to the floor, unread.

Also, his breathing was heavy. *Too heavy*, Nghia thought.

Spring came, and then summer, but still Tieu showed no improvement. In an odd way, his health seemed to mirror the fortunes of Indochina, which appeared to be declining day by day. In March, a year after the Allied liberation of Paris, the Japanese had engineered a coup against the French in Indochina, interning soldiers and high-level French bureaucrats. Those French civilians who remained free were living under a cloud of fear.

As for the Vietnamese, the Japanese dangled a hope for autonomy by encouraging Emperor Bao Dai to set up an independent government made up of Vietnamese nationalists. But the government turned out to be devoid of any real power, and the people's hope of security for the future faded still further.

As the Allies closed in on Japan, the lives of ordinary Vietnamese were swept up in a surge of uncertainty as the forces of revolution began exploding around them. In the early months of 1945, the *Viet Minh* guerrillas, led by General Vo Nguyen Giap, had wrested control of the countryside north of Hanoi. By early summer they stood poised to enter the city whenever the opportunity seemed ripe.

For Nghia, these events were merely a backdrop to the more personal drama unfolding in the house on Rue Duvillier. One day in early August, Tieu came home from work and started coughing. The next day he complained about feeling chilled. "Just a little feverish," he told her. By the next morning, he was so weak he couldn't get out of bed.

Nghia was beside herself. *I've got to get him to the hospital.* "Brother Quoc, come quickly!" Together, Nghia and the rickshaw driver lifted Tieu into the vehicle, and she jumped onto the seat beside him.

"Don Thuy Hospital!" she said, directing Quoc to the best hospital in Hanoi. Nghia knew that only the French and high-level Vietnamese public servants could receive treatment there, and she was determined that her father would be one of them.

Once at the hospital, Nghia sprang into action, calling in French for orderlies to come with a stretcher, and oozing charm as she negotiated with the staff to secure Tieu's admission. "*Il est très malade,*" she said. "*Il est chef de bureau des Transports Publics.* He's of the highest rank . . . I know that only you can save him! *Vite! Vite!* We need help!"

A stretcher appeared, and Tieu was whisked away to an examination room.

In the reception area, Nghia waited anxiously, surrounded by men and women both French and Vietnamese, who were buzzing with the latest war news. But the words barely penetrated her consciousness.

"*Les américains . . . une bombe atomique.*"

"The war will soon be over . . . Japan will surrender . . . good news!"

Nghia was too numb to care. The only news she wanted to hear was that her father would be all right. After an hour, she heard her name called and looked up to see a nurse coming her way.

"We need to keep your father here for tests," she said. "It's his lungs. We'll know in a few days."

Nghia nodded, her mind racing as she thought of the possibilities. *It can't be tuberculosis. Please, God, no.* Her mind clouded with ominous images: Bac, her father's sister, who had died of TB only two years earlier . . . her mother, Nhu, out in the countryside with the four youngest children . . . little brother Tam was only eight . . . younger sister Bay was eleven. How would they cope? How would *she* cope?

The tests took several days. Blood tests. Sputum tests. She came to the hospital as often as she could manage—at lunchtime and after school to feed him *pho*, or *banh cuon*, or whatever could give him strength.

By the time the tests were finished, the outside world had turned upside down—a fact that Nghia was finding very hard to ignore. The Japanese had surrendered to the Allies, and Hanoi was gripped by a sense of unease that only heightened Nghia's anxiety. Would the countryside rise up? Would the nationalists take over? Would there be more bloodshed? More war? More tragedy?

She headed for the hospital laboratory, mindful at that moment only of her father and the personal tragedy she feared was coming. "*Monsieur Tieu?*" she said to the orderly, inquiring about the lab results in her perfect French. "The tests were run two days ago."

The man shuffled through some files and pulled out a thin white envelope. He handed it to her wordlessly.

"*Merci,*" she said, clutching the envelope tightly. Out in the corridor, with no one in sight, she ripped open the envelope and scanned the results.

Sputum. *Positive.*

Blood test. *Positive.*

Advanced case, the doctor had scribbled.

At that moment she knew Tieu would never leave the hospital. He would never see his beloved house on Rue Duvillier, never go again to his marbled office or to his ancestral village.

Nghia willed herself to walk toward Tieu's room, the click of her heels echoing in the hallway like a death knell. She would have to control herself. She *must* control herself.

But even as she tried to hold back the surge of feeling that had welled up inside her, her throat choked up and tears cascaded down her cheeks, dripping in spreading stains of sorrow on the bodice of her blue-and-white polka-dot *ao dai.*

Several nurses and orderlies came rushing by, and quickly Nghia turned her head away. She couldn't let them see her crying— couldn't let them know her weakness. She had to be strong for herself, for her mother, and above all, for her father.

Down the hall from Tieu's room, she saw a little alcove, and she slipped inside to regain her composure. *I've got to think this through,* she thought. *What do I tell him? When do I tell him? What should I do?*

The answer came like a gentle breeze, whispering in her mind in a verse from Hebrews: "I will never fail you nor forsake you."

All of a sudden, she knew what she would do—what she *had* to do. She would care for her father until the day he died. Whether it took a week, a month, or a year, she would be there for him, sleeping at his side, sharing snippets of conversation, and tending to his every need. It was a small gift she could give him in gratitude for the lifetime of love he had given her.

Nghia sighed, a deep sigh of conviction and resignation. She dabbed her eyes with a linen handkerchief and rehearsed what she would say. She couldn't bear to tell him the truth. Not yet. Let him have some peace for a little while longer.

She tiptoed into the room and pulled up a chair. He was sleeping like a baby. But his face—why hadn't she ever noticed it before? The lines were etched deep in his cheeks. His skin was sallow, nearly drained of life. He was only fifty, and yet he looked somehow ancient, as though he had lived for a century.

"God, please spare him from pain," she prayed silently.

As if he had heard the cries of her heart, Tieu opened his eyes and gazed at her lovingly.

The twinkle is still there, she thought, *but I can't bear to see him like this.*

"Nghia," he said weakly, "have you learned the results of the tests?"

"Don't think about that now," she said, trying to deflect his question. "There's so much to tell you. The Japanese have surrendered. No one seems to know what it means for us. But there are rumors of an insurrection." Then she paused. "But whatever happens, I'm here with you," she continued. "I'll always be here."

Nghia's older sisters came the next evening, when they heard that Tieu had been taken ill. As each one arrived, Nghia broke the news, swearing them to secrecy. One by one, they approached his bedside, but their eyes said it all: *Tuberculosis . . . a death sentence . . . perhaps for each one of us.*

Tieu didn't say a word. After they left, he turned to Nghia and asked again: "Did you pick up the results yet? What did the tests say?"

Still, she couldn't tell him. Finally, a few days later, when Tieu started wondering why the family hadn't returned to see him, she knew she could hold out no more. "It's TB," she said. "Everyone's scared to come. They're afraid for their children. Mother and the little ones are still in the country. But I will be here as long as you need me."

Tieu shut his eyes tight and turned his head away from her toward the wall. But she had already seen his tears. *Why did I have to be the one to tell him? Why is life so hard?*

That night, despite the health risk to herself, my mother, Nghia, moved into the room with her father, sleeping in the empty bed next to his. She spent her days reading to him, or running to the market at lunch to buy noodle soup and rice, things her mother had made for him at home.

Her only solace in these dark days was Minh, who met her as often as he could during breaks from his activities with a university group affiliated with the *Viet Minh*. Always he was filled with talk that kept her blissfully distracted. He would share with her the latest rumors of the war, and wax eloquent about the cause for independence. "The *Viet Minh* are ready to strike," he said optimistically. "Soon Vietnam will be free."

Events came to pass just as Minh had predicted. One day in mid-August, Nghia had just come out of the market when hundreds of brown-shirted young people surged past her, led by a standard-bearer waving a red flag emblazoned with a yellow star. With her way temporarily blocked, Nghia stood mesmerized as column after column marched by. First came the women, clad in black pajamas with rifles slung over their arm. Next came the men, erect in their khaki uniforms.

"Who are they?" she asked the shopkeeper.

"They call themselves the People's Liberation Army," he said. "Didn't you hear? Yesterday morning at the Municipal Opera House, there was an uprising. The *Viet Minh* stormed the theater and deposed the nationalists. Now their army has just taken over the viceroy's residence. They're led by a general named Giap. Vo Nguyen Giap."

◈◈◈◈◈

Just as rapidly as Vietnam was coming under the control of Ho Chi Minh and the *Viet Minh*, Tieu's life was slipping away. He was so weak he could barely talk. But his pride was intact, so much so that he refused to soil the bed. In the middle of the night, using every ounce of his energy, he would try to get out of bed to relieve himself.

Nghia would hear the rustle of the bedclothes and jump up to help him. As he sat on the edge of the bed, she stood in front of him, letting him grip her arms to pull himself up. Then, as he leaned his hand on her shoulder for support, she led him to the toilet.

In the waning days of August, Tieu could no longer get out of bed. But his mind remained lucid, and with his last ounce of energy, he scribbled a note on a scrap of paper.

There's money in the bank: 9,500 *dong*. Two thousand is God's money. Bring it to the church, two hundred a month, until it is gone. Three thousand is for Nghia to take care of her disease. She is sure to contract it. The rest goes to my beloved wife.

A few days later, as Tieu neared death, Nghia tried to rally him one last time. "Vietnam is free," she said, knowing how he had dreamt of the day when the people would be rid of the French and the Japanese and control their own destiny. "It was announced on the radio today. Ho Chi Minh is president of the Democratic Republic of Vietnam."

For a brief moment, Tieu's eyes lit up and he mustered a weak smile.

"Rest now," she said. "Close your eyes and get some rest."

The next day Nghia sent for the family and they gathered around his bedside for the last time. By then, her mother had returned from the country with the children, Ai, Sau, Bay and Tam. Nghia's three older sisters were there too, along with cousin Dan, whom Tieu had raised as a son. Rounding out the mournful group was one of Tieu's oldest friends from church, Hoang, who had once been addicted to opium himself. Tieu had led him out of darkness, and then Hoang and his two wives had become believers.

"I'm going home to Jesus," Tieu told Hoang.

Hoang gripped his hand and smiled. "Yes, my friend. It will be glorious."

Tieu called for each of his children and one by one, they came to his bedside. He lifted a feeble hand to each head, and like some biblical patriarch, he gave each one a final blessing.

"Bay," he said to daughter number seven. "A perfect number in the Bible. God has something special for you."

"Nghia. You are my rock. Take care of them for me."

With that he turned to his beloved wife, Nhu, and with his eyes smiling, he took his last breath.

❖❖❖❖❖

The funeral was Nghia's magnum opus, an event so grand people in Hanoi still talk about it with reverence, along with the funeral of Dr. Hung, a famous physician who had died a few weeks earlier. "No funerals were more elegant than Mr. Tieu's and Dr. Hung's," people agreed.

Nghia arranged for everything. First she sent her siblings to the tailor to get special white outfits made for the funeral. Then she got on her bike in the pouring rain to announce Tieu's death to their friends at the church. Finally, she wrote an obituary for the newspaper.

But the most dramatic touch of all was the carriage: a white, four-wheeled, fairy-tale chariot driven by two liveried servants and pulled by four black horses. Feather plumes topped the roof corners in a flourish fit for a king.

How twenty-one-year-old Nghia orchestrated such a gala send-off for my grandfather in those topsy-turvy days of Ho's ascent to power, no one will ever know for sure. But as Hanoi reeled and reveled under the new political order, the funeral went forward exactly as she had planned: after a short service at the hospital, Tieu's nephews placed the coffin in the carriage, and then the entire funeral party followed behind on foot for the three-kilometer trek to the cemetery.

But this was no ordinary procession. Along the way, the crowd of mourners grew larger and larger, as people who had arrived late for the service fell in behind the carriage. Before the cortege reached the cemetery, there was one final stop: the house at Rue Duvillier. At my grandfather's request, the coffin paused in front of his house so that he could make a final good-bye.

The carriage had no sooner stopped in front of the house when six young men Nghia had never seen before rushed toward the vehicle. They were wearing crisp white suits with black armbands on their left sleeves. "Please let us walk alongside the carriage," one of them begged. "Mr. Tieu supported us while we were in seminary. We want to do something for him."

So for the last leg of the journey, the six young seminarians walked as an honor guard next to the carriage. When they reached the cemetery, they carried the shiny wooden coffin to the burial site and placed it in the tomb. And then they wept.

But Nghia's eyes were dry. Even as the Vietnamese pastor was saying the benediction, her mind was spinning, overwhelmed by the responsibility that had been thrust upon her. How could she take care of her mother? Would her father's pension be enough? What of the house? Would they be able to keep it?

The questions would have been daunting in ordinary times. But as Nghia would soon discover, the times would never again be ordinary. As Tieu's body was being laid to rest at the cemetery far across town, in a large open square near the French viceroy's palace, preparations were being made for a massive celebration.

A few days later, Ho Chi Minh ascended a platform before thousands of well-wishers who had streamed into the city to support him. The announcement he would make would forever change his countrymen—and test Nghia's mettle far beyond anything she had yet endured.

11

A WARRIOR'S DREAM

Phuong elbowed his way toward the front of the jubilant crowd to get a closer look. Any minute now, his hero, Ho Chi Minh, would be stepping in front of the microphone to speak, and he didn't want to miss a word.

He had never seen such a crowd: young women with rifles slung over their shoulders, middle-aged men in mufti, peasants in pointed cone hats, old men with swords, children. Tens of thousands like him had flooded into Hanoi from the provinces and found their way to the broad grassy square, where on September 2, 1945, they waited expectantly in the hot afternoon sun.

Up ahead of Phuong the podium rose like a giant confection, frosted in white and decorated with garlands of red bunting and a huge red flag with a yellow star. Straining his eyes, he could see that high on top, the dignitaries were already starting to assemble, and so he muscled forward a few more steps for a better view of the man who was turning his dreams into reality.

Ho Chi Minh. President of the Democratic Republic of Vietnam. Under his breath, Phuong repeated the words like a mantra.

"Uncle Ho," as their leader was known, was the reason he had given up everything—school, a comfortable living off his parents' vast rice fields, and the hopes of a normal family life—to gamble his fortunes on the Communist cause, the people's cause. Now Phuong's gamble seemed to be paying off.

In the confusion after the surrender of the Japanese, Uncle Ho had seized the moment to wrest control of the government and bring the north under his sway. Two weeks later, the *Viet Minh* had gained the upper hand in Saigon in a coalition controlling the south. Ho's aim was to stake his claim for an independent Vietnam before the Allies carved up Indochina permanently. By striking swiftly, he hoped to preempt the return of the French, undercut his internal opposition, and gain the support of both the Vietnamese people and the international community.

Although the future of Vietnam was still in the balance on that September day, for Ho's followers, these were heady times, and Phuong was swept up in the fervor.

At age thirty-two, Phuong sensed that the moment was Vietnam's and felt vindicated by his choices. He had spent his youth in the *Viet Bac*—the mountains north of Hanoi—learning Communist doctrine, training for combat, living on meager rations with his comrades, and enlisting the support of peasants in village after village.

But he had also done something more: over the years, he had used his financial savvy to create a lucrative lumber business, which was providing a major income stream for the *Viet Minh*. That money, and his mother's financial support for the *Viet Minh*, had helped fuel the revolution, and now he was witnessing the fruits. Uncle Ho had promised that all Vietnamese—landowners, peasants, workers, merchants—would share in the victory. Phuong claimed that victory with pride. *This is the day*, he thought. *Our future begins today.*

Off to his left, he could hear children's voices chanting an exultant song of revolution. He craned his neck over the heads of the people next to him to get a look. That's when he caught a glimpse of her. She was standing about twenty meters away in the row in front of him, with her head turned away. The minute he saw the nape of her neck with the soft bun gathered at the top, he knew it had to be the same young woman he dreamed of—the one he had spied in church just after his escape from Hoa Lo prison.

It's Mr. Tieu's daughter! Phuong softened at the thought that she was so near. From the moment he had seen her in church, she had consumed him. He couldn't explain why he was so smitten. Maybe it was because of his months in prison, where the shackles, the putrid smells, and the ugly yellow teeth of his tormentors had made him forget that such beauty was possible. Or maybe it was his years of hardship in the north in the *Viet Bac*, where the Communist cause had become his obsession, taking the place of lover, mother, spouse.

Whatever the reason, that day in church he had fallen in love instantly with Mr. Tieu's daughter and wanted to be with her forever. He had no sooner left the church than he pleaded with his Uncle Qui to to intercede for him. "I want to marry this girl," he had said. "Please ask her father if he will agree to the arrangement."

At the time, Uncle Qui had seemed genuinely pleased at the prospect, but he was also a bit circumspect. "Does that mean you've made a decision to accept Christ?" he had asked Phuong. "That's the only way her father will permit her to marry you."

Phuong had agreed on the spot. "I'll become a Christian. Whatever it takes, I'll do it for her."

The next day, Uncle Qui had sent a go-between to Rue Duvillier to ask Tieu for Nghia's hand. The answer came back just as fast: No.

"He may *say* he's a Christian," Tieu had said. "But his faith has not stood the test of time. What's more, he has no education. And he's eleven years older than Nghia—much too old. My daughter cannot marry him."

Upon hearing the news, Phuong had been despondent. But despite Tieu's rejection, over the next few months he had kept alive the hope that somehow, someday Nghia would be his bride. Now she was right in front of him, waiting along with the crowd to hear Uncle Ho. Was this a sign from heaven? A divine blessing on this day of rejoicing for all of Vietnam?

He fixed his eyes on the young woman, hoping desperately that she would turn her head in his direction. All he wanted was a fleeting look, a fresh reminder of her delicate face, her dainty nose, and her sensuous lips, that he could hold in his mind like a cameo.

Suddenly, Phuong felt the mood of the crowd shift. He was just about to give a quick look at the podium to see what was happening when he saw the young woman's head start to turn. Phuong's heart was beating so hard he could hear the pounding in his ears. *Her face. Let me see her face.*

Ever so slowly, the young woman's head turned toward the podium, but as soon as Phuong saw her profile, he realized his mistake. It wasn't Nghia at all. It was someone much more pedestrian, with coarse cheeks and a nose so flat she might have been a tenant farmer in Hoanh Nha, his mother's village.

How could he have been so weak? It had all been a dream, a tantalizing trick played by the gods to remind him of his frailties. He had allowed his own desires to seduce him. What would his comrades think of him? He was *Viet Minh*—a warrior, a patriot—but not some love-besotted fool.

As he responded to the call of the fighter within him, Phuong felt his body stiffen. This was not the time for womanish fantasies; it was a time for heroes to be born, for men to lead, and for a nation to be established.

Phuong could hear the static of the microphone and the voice of someone calling the crowd to attention. The next thing he knew, General Giap had presented Ho Chi Minh, and the new president was standing at the mike in a crumpled khaki suit speaking glorious words that linked the Vietnamese to free people everywhere.

"All men are created equal," Ho told the crowd. "They are endowed by their Creator with certain unalienable rights; among these are life, liberty, and the pursuit of happiness."

Phuong felt a rush of adrenaline as Ho explained that the words were from the American Declaration of Independence. He got even more excited when he heard Ho reiterate that Vietnam had become a "free and independent country." And when he heard Ho exhort the people to "mobilize all their physical and mental strength" and "sacrifice" for the sake of freedom, he was ready to run out of the square and lay down his life that very day if it would help further the cause of Vietnamese independence.

The struggle will soon be over, Phuong thought. *Vietnam will be ours.*

◻◻◻◻◻

Whatever dreams of imminent glory Phuong may have had for his country that day in Ba Dinh Square soon faded as little by little, the shaky foundation of Ho's self-proclaimed Democratic Republic of Vietnam began to crumble.

On the international front, no foreign power had yet recognized Vietnam's new independent status. What's more, the country was still at the mercy of the Allies, whose short-term plans called for the occupation of Indochina by the Chinese and British to disarm the Japanese.

Within days of the gathering at Ba Dinh Square, the Chinese army rolled into Hanoi, and the British moved into Annam and Cochin China according to the prearranged terms of the Potsdam Agreement. Within weeks, the French were back in control in the south after having successfully pressed their case with the British to reclaim their old colony. By October, the French flag was flying over government buildings in Saigon, martial law had been imposed in the south, and French troops were routing the *Viet Minh* from the cities and sending them fleeing to the villages.

With his *Viet Minh* now embroiled in guerrilla skirmishes against the French in the south, Ho Chi Minh struggled to maintain his grip on the north. Internally, he worked to shore up his political base by publicly embracing a broadbased nationalist image. Covertly, his supporters were liquidating his opposition through a widespread campaign of violence.

On the diplomatic front, Ho sought to rid the north of the Chinese, whom he distrusted, and to prevent the return of the French. To that end, over the next few months, Ho negotiated with the Chinese, and then with the French to reach a solution that would insure Vietnam's independence. By March 1946, Ho had to settle for the best deal he could wrangle: the Chinese would leave; a small contingent of French troops would return to the north; and France would recognize his government as a "free state"—but not yet as an independent republic.

On March 16, at Ho's invitation, the French troops entered Hanoi in what would be the beginning of the end for Ho's immediate hopes for full independence for the north and south. After several more months of fruitless negotiations in Paris, the French and Ho reached a stalemate. The climate was incendiary, and by November, fighting broke out between the *Viet Minh* and the French in Hai Phong, culminating in a French massacre of thousands of Vietnamese civilians. A month later, on December 19, 1946, the *Viet Minh* army struck the French in Hanoi, and General Giap declared war. The next day, Ho Chi Minh issued a call for a general insurrection.

As these cataclysmic events were unfolding, my mother, Nghia, already burdened by personal tragedy, came face-to-face with seemingly insuperable obstacles. From the moment my grandfather took ill, she had assumed an uncomfortable leadership role in her family. Now, in the wake of his death and the country's tumultuous political and economic upheaval, she was forced to push herself beyond the limits of her youthful experience simply to survive. Like Joshua facing unknown perils in Canaan after the death of Moses, she sensed she would need to draw on every ounce of her faith to heed God's battle cry: "Be strong and of good courage; be not frightened, neither be dismayed; for the LORD your God is with you wherever you go."

12

MONKEY BRIDGES

"Bay *oi!* Sau *oi!* Ai *oi!*" Nghia yelled to the back room, calling for her younger sisters. "Come here this minute!"

"Tam!" she said to her little brother, frowning at the squirming lizard in his grasp. "Put down that gecko right now and go get your Bible!"

Nghia was so furious that her eyes smarted with tears. It had been weeks since her father's death, and yet not once in that time had the children shown any inclination to read the Scriptures or even to pray. In fact, every time she had brought the subject up, they had actively opposed her.

"I don't want to," one whined.

"It's so boring!" said another.

What infuriated Nghia the most wasn't their disobedience, but their outright rejection of the values that had been at the core of her father's life.

"Father wanted us to follow Christ!" Nghia reminded them when they finally lined up in front of her. "You are disgracing his memory. You don't want to pray. You don't want to have devotions. This is wrong, and it's going to stop. From now on, we're having devotions every night, and whoever isn't here is going to get spanked."

The words had barely come out of her mouth when Nghia burst into sobs. "I can't do this," she prayed, appealing to God for a reprieve. "I gave everything I had to take care of my father. Why are you asking me to do this too?"

She hated being the taskmaster—hated stepping out of the benign role of elder sister to become disciplinarian, teacher, and father. But as the weeks had passed, it had become clear that no one else could shoulder the burden. Her mother, dear as she was, was incapable of making decisions and imposing order on their lives. Nhu could feed them and clothe them and love them, but beyond that, she was helpless.

Tieu had been the axis around which the family had turned, the driving authority and force behind their education, their prosperity, and their spiritual growth. With him gone, and with their livelihood snatched from under them, they were left rudderless in a sea of uncertainty. If they were to survive as a family, Nghia knew it would be up to her, and no one else.

"But I'm too weak," she complained to God. "Too vulnerable. What about Minh? What about my future? I'm only twenty-one . . . and a woman. What good am I?"

Nghia already knew the answers. All she had to do was open her Bible and the pages would come alive with story after story of God's power made perfect in the weaknesses of men and women like her: Sarah and her barren womb. Moses with his speech impediment. Jonah and his pride. Elijah and his fear. There was no hiding behind excuses with God; no running from his purposes. If she really believed the lessons she was insisting her sisters and brother learn, she had only one choice: to commit her way to God with the simple faith of a child, knowing that in his time, he would act.

"Here I am!" she said with a sigh, echoing Samuel's cry. "Here I am."

It took only a few days after Nghia's outburst at the children for them to fall into line. She made good on her threats, and soon her sisters and brother were gathered at the table, dutifully listening to Bible stories and saying their prayers.

But getting tough with her siblings on spiritual matters was only the beginning of Nghia's challenges. Money was growing tight, and even though she had managed to finish teacher's college in the months before her father's death, no jobs were available. Her father's pension provided a mere one-tenth his former salary, barely enough to feed the six family members still at home.

Little by little, in a desperate quest to sustain the family, Nghia started trading whatever she could on the black market: pieces of fabric, medicines, rice, yarn—a hodgepodge of items that her mother had collected over the years. She was so consumed by the need to survive that she rarely saw Minh, who by now was deeply embroiled in political activities with his university group of the *Viet Minh.*

Yet whether they were apart or together, she never doubted the certainty of his love. Like his very name *Minh,* which meant "light," his love shined like a bright beacon in her heart, illuminating her inner spirit even as the world outside her was growing darker.

By the summer of 1946, with her family's resources nearly exhausted, Nghia despaired of a solution and prayed for a sign. The very next day, her cousin Nam, whom her father had once employed at the railroad as a conductor, appeared at her door with a daring proposition. He asked her to join him in a trading business between Hanoi and Hue. "It will be dangerous," he said. "But the profits will be greater than anything you have ever imagined."

❖❖❖❖❖

The train rumbled south toward Hue in the pitch-black darkness, shaking and heaving as it skidded over the ruptured tracks. Nghia lay her head back on the wooden seat and tried to sleep. She had never felt so exhausted. Piled next to her were the wares she would sell at the market along the Perfume River in Annam's ancient capital: watches, medicines, fabric—imported items that were hard to come by in the outlying cities. *Better rest while I can,* she thought. *Any moment we might have to stop and get out.*

For months now, she and her cousin had worked the railroad route so often that they had become quite expert at the operation. Every few weeks, they would hop on a train in Hanoi laden with small goods, and return a week later with sugar, salt, sticky rice, betel nuts, and cone-shaped poetry hats with special poems woven into the straw, a specialty of Hue that was always in hot demand in Hanoi.

But there was a hitch. Because Allied bombing during the war had disrupted the train rails and bridges, at least two or three times a day the train would come to a complete halt on the edge of a deep ravine. When that happened, everyone in the train poured out to transfer to the rickety railroad cars and engine waiting on the other side. If they were lucky, they would find a "monkey bridge," made by the Japanese out of ropes, to enable them to cross the yawning canyon. Sometimes, though, even the monkey bridge was out. In that case, hauling all of their belongings, Nghia and Nam would have to climb down the steep incline and up the other side to the waiting train.

It was arduous work. But the return trip from Hue could be even more grueling, as Nghia had to carry fifty-pound bags of sugar on her four-foot, nine-inch frame. Over time, though, Nghia and Nam had gotten savvy and had hired local townspeople along the way to be their beasts of burden. Whenever the train came to the end of the line, Nghia would call out the window to her "staff," and they would rush on board to do the heavy lifting.

The system had worked like a charm until the war started with the French. Since that time, the daylight hours had become too risky, with French bombs dropping helter-skelter on suspected *Viet Minh* targets all over the countryside. To avoid the danger, Nghia and Nam decided to travel only at night, but in some ways, that made the journey even more perilous. Thieves were afoot, and every transfer from one train to another held the risk of physical injury or worse.

✠✠✠✠✠

The train screeched to a halt, jolting Nghia awake.

"Everybody out!" the conductor yelled.

"Hurry, *Chi* Nghia!" Nam said. "The other train is leaving soon."

Nghia leaned out the window and searched the darkness for her helpers. "Duong, Tung, Vong, come quickly!" she shouted.

Three men, whose faces were so weathered they appeared permanently creased, jumped on board and started loading up her wares. Then they all walked silently and swiftly to the monkey bridge, where Nghia began barking out orders. "Duong, you go ahead to the other side with Nam and the first part of the merchandise. Tung, you and Vong follow them across the bridge with the other bundles. I'll bring up the rear. But hurry! We've got to hurry. We can't miss that train!"

Nam and Nghia had decided to organize the transfer of goods

from one side of the ravine to the other so that one of them was either at the front or end of the line. They had worked with these men before and trusted them, more or less. But they weren't about to take any chances on anyone absconding with their valuable goods, which represented food on the table for the family back in Hanoi.

The bridge swung perilously as the many passengers rushed across in a near-frenzy. If they missed the train on the other side, there wouldn't be another one for a day or two, and they would lose precious time and money. Even worse, they would be stuck out in the middle of nowhere, offering a ready target for the *Viet Minh* by night, or the French bombers at the break of dawn.

Except for the flickering torches that illuminated the first few rungs of the bridge, the way across was shrouded in darkness.

"My packages!" a woman screamed. "Help! Someone, help!"

In the darkness, Nghia could see no more than a meter in front of her, but she guessed that the woman had been carrying too much. Several parcels must have slipped off her back and tumbled into the ravine. *Poor thing,* Nghia thought. *She'll never get them back. A week's wages at least—gone.*

Gingerly, Nghia stepped onto the first rung of the bridge and gripped the ropes. She let her body sway with the movement, as freely as a primate swinging on a jungle vine. She knew that if she fought the rhythm, she wouldn't make it across. As she moved steadily, step by step, the ropes slipped through her hands, burning her skin. But that didn't matter. The goal was what mattered. At that moment, the only thing she cared about was getting her goods to market.

"Ayee!"

The bloodcurdling shriek stopped Nghia short. She heard a thud and then a commotion beneath her, as dozens of peasants rushed down the ravine.

"He's bleeding!" someone shouted. "Get him to the village."

It happened night after night. Someone would lose his grip or miss a rung and fall through the ropes to the bottom of the ravine. Two weeks earlier a man had hit his head on sharp rocks below and had died. But Nghia couldn't allow herself to think about such possibilities, or even to hesitate as she moved across. *Just get to the train. Just keep moving forward.*

About ten minutes later, Nghia reached the other side. Nam and their helpers were already loading the train—or what was left of a train. At this junction, there was only an engine and one car, but she knew they were lucky to have anything. Parts were so scarce that some nights a mechanic had to remove sections of an engine from one train and transfer it to the other before the journey could continue.

Nghia hopped on board and tried to wedge herself inside the car, but there wasn't even a centimeter of space left for merchandise or people. She waved to Nam, who was sitting on top of their packages. Then she climbed up the metal ladder to the roof of the train and stretched out on top.

The night was clear and cool, and as she gazed up at the stars, she imagined that Minh was lying by her side, whispering the melodic lines of a love poem he had written just for her.

Suddenly, a shooting star arched across the sky. Nghia smiled as she watched its trail of light. Surely Minh had read her thoughts and was sending her a greeting.

As the train began to move, Nghia could feel the car rattling underneath her. The car was moving faster now—faster and faster, until the wind whipped her eyes half-shut, and the stars went by in a blur. She stretched out her arms to grab hold of some wooden stays and pressed her body tight against the roof to keep from sliding off. And almost without thinking, she began to pray from Psalm 121: "He will not let your foot be moved, he who keeps you will not slumber. Behold, he who keeps Israel will neither slumber nor sleep."

13

AU REVOIR, MON AMOUR

The French are coming! The French are coming!"

A young man, his shirt splattered with blood, burst into the church, disrupting the worship service with a frantic appeal. "*Giao Si* Cadman, come quickly! People are lying dead on the street, and the soldiers are headed this way."

The missionary dropped his Bible and rushed down the aisle, followed by a handful of the sixty parishioners inside. He had never expected to be caught in the middle of a war zone again, certainly not so soon. He had returned to Hanoi simply to continue the work of the gospel printing press and to finish his translation of a Bible dictionary.

It wasn't that he was afraid. After his release from the Japanese prison camp in My Tho, he had made the risky choice to remain in the south. Although he had survived, the war had taken a terrible toll on those dearest to him. His wife, Grace, had been so weakened by their internment that she had died in Saigon several months after the surrender of the Japanese. His friend, Tieu, had succumbed to TB.

With all these losses, Cadman was determined to do all he could to prevent anyone from taking away friends or loved ones again—especially not his flock of faithful Christians, whom he loved like sisters and brothers. Through the open windows, Cadman could hear the *rat-tat-tat* of rifle fire punctuating the air. *They're already on Rue Bourret*, he thought.

By the time he swung open the door of the church, a platoon of

French soldiers was already pouring through the gate of the mission compound and rushing straight toward him.

Raising his hand in defiance, Cadman positioned himself in front of the church door and glowered. "If you're going to shoot them, you'll have to shoot me first!" he shouted.

The French lieutenant hesitated a moment. He looked at Cadman and then glanced over the missionary's shoulder into the church at the frightened faces of gray-haired men, old grannies, young women with babies, and teenagers.

"Hold your fire," he said to his men. "I'm sorry, *Monsieur*," he said to Cadman. "We're looking for insurgents."

With that, the soldiers left. Moments later, rifle fire resounded from inside the nearby market. Hanoi was in chaos. For weeks since Ho Chi Minh had issued a call for insurrection, the French army had been sweeping through the city, street by street, destroying *Viet Minh* strongholds and routing out the rebels. Ho and his comrades had reportedly retreated to the *Viet Bac*, but before he left, he had issued a call to duty that inspired thousands of citizens to abandon the city for the countryside: *"Tieu Kho Khang Chien!"*

The cry reverberated through the streets. "We must be willing to live hard; to live in poverty! Leave your homes! Leave your jobs! Go to the villages and leave the city to the French!"

Responding to the call for an urban strike, at least half of Cadman's church members had uprooted themselves and left for their ancestral villages, along with nearly one hundred thousand other residents of Hanoi. The missionary knew that those church members who remained, including his friend, Mrs. Tieu, were torn between patriotism and the desire to hang onto what was left of their lives and property.

"I can't leave my house," Nhu had told him. "I can't leave Rue Duvillier. It meant too much to my husband. But we are running out of money, and I am afraid to stay."

As a stopgap, *Giao Si* Cadman had begged her and her children to move into the mission house, where he could take care of them. "Please stay, Mrs. Tieu," he had urged her. "You'll be safe here. I'll see that you are protected."

But a few weeks later, Nhu came to him with the news: "We're leaving for my brother's village. My son-in-law says it's our patriotic duty. We have no choice but to follow Ho Chi Minh."

❖❖❖❖❖

Nghia couldn't bear the thought of leaving Hanoi without Minh. They had always known it was a possibility. But once her mother made the decision to flee, she and Minh were forced to make some decisions of their own. Would they go together? Or would they separate for the duration of the war, however long that might be?

Both of them knew there was only one answer. No matter how radical it appeared, or how many tongues would wag, they would go together. They would live side by side as "brother" and "sister" in Hanh Thien, her uncle's village, until the day that they could be one forever.

"I want to spend my life with you," Minh confessed to Nghia. "I'll wait as long as it takes."

A week later, Nghia put her mother and the four youngest children on a ship bound for Nam Dinh. From there, they would catch a boat down the Red River and navigate the canals to the little village of Hanh Thien, just a few kilometers from the Tonkin Gulf. Nghia and Minh planned to catch up with them a few days later, after they finished some last-minute business in Hanoi.

The next morning, Minh dropped off a duffel bag with all his belongings at Rue Duvillier, and with his eyes gleaming he said to Nghia, "Meet me this afternoon at four o'clock at our special place, at the *Van Mieu*. Let's seal our plans and say farewell to Hanoi at this sacred location."

Nghia had agreed instantly, but for the rest of the day she was so distracted she could hardly keep her mind focused on packing. What was Minh thinking? Going anyplace in Hanoi these days was dangerous. With the French still ferreting out the *Viet Minh*, any street could become a battleground. And the *Van Mieu*—the Temple of Literature—the nearly thousand-year-old seat of learning just south of the beleaguered citadel seemed like an invitation to trouble.

The more Nghia thought about the prospect of meeting Minh, the more nervous and uncertain she became. She had to admit that the idea of sealing their commitment to each other today was deliciously daring, especially at the Temple of Literature. The aura of romance surrounding the site had come to mean so much to the both of them because, after all, the *Van Mieu* had sometimes shielded their secret assignations. No spot in Hanoi could be more idyllic in Nghia's imagination.

Also, while the Temple of Literature was a link to the past she had shared with Minh, it was also a promise for their future. For centuries, the landmark had withstood wars and emperors and invaders. Yet still it remained as a monument for her people to all that was noble and beautiful and good. The very notion of stepping once again through the main gate, the *Van Mieu Mon*, into the placid grounds where for hundreds of years scholars had studied the Confucian precepts, made her almost dizzy with desire for that perfect relationship she had sought for so many years. *The temple is like our love*, she thought. *Noble. Beautiful. Good.*

Despite her longings, Nghia also sensed a nagging uncertainty. Her family responsibilities had escalated since her father's death. Many people depended on her now. She had gone one way, and Minh another. Could they really somehow merge their respective duties and commitments into one life? The warnings from her father, Tieu, still echoed at the back of her mind.

Nghia looked at the clock on the wall. Three o'clock. She had to hurry to get there on time. She threw on her blue-and-white polka-dot *ao dai* and her cone hat and raced out the door. Then she jumped on her bike and searched the street. *No soldiers. I'm safe for now.*

The streets seemed unusually empty, almost as if the way had been cleared for her to pass by. Nghia quickly pedaled west and then turned south toward the temple. Block by block, the French colonial buildings, with their ochre walls and green shutters, went by in a blur.

Soon she was standing in front of the *Van Mieu*. She smiled as she read the Chinese characters inscribed above the entrance: "*Ha Ma*"—"Get off your horse." She parked her bike, stepped through the dragon-sculpted main gate, and walked slowly down the ancient stone path through the first courtyard.

Where's Minh? Off to her right, she could see a student lighting a joss stick. On the left, a young woman was lost in a book. She stepped into the second courtyard and looked toward the poets' gate, the *Khue Van Cac*, where the most learned scholars of Tonkin had once stood reciting their poems. The gate was an airy pavilion, with four stone pillars supporting a soaring, double-tiered, red-tiled roof whose upturned corners reached toward the sky as if in a gesture of praise.

As she drew closer to the gate, she saw Minh standing in the shadows. He was leaning nonchalantly against a stone pillar, watching wordlessly as she moved toward him. Their eyes met, and in that moment it was as if the war had disappeared. Whatever their lives were outside the temple gate—whatever tensions and fears and unanswered questions threatened to tarnish their hopes and dreams—simply drifted away, like a bubble floating toward the sky. For a moment, they were like the poets, the Pleiades, caught up in a heavenly constellation of illusion.

Slowly she walked up the steps until they were face-to-face.

"*Chao em,*" he said, calling her "little sister" as he often did, just as though she were still fifteen.

"*Chao anh,*" she replied.

Then, before she could say another word, he reached his hand around her waist and pulled her toward him. She didn't resist. Couldn't resist. She felt her body give way and merge with his until suddenly she felt his breath hot on her cheek and his lips pressing into hers.

Abruptly she pushed him away. *What have I done? How could I have been so indiscreet?* But even as she turned her head away, her heart was aflutter.

Too embarrassed to speak, they stood quietly. Finally, Minh broke the silence. "Nghia, I don't know how to tell you this, but I can't go with you to Hanh Thien right away. My organization has assigned me to a secret mission. I can't even tell you what it is, or where I'll be. But trust me, I'll join you soon. Very soon. Can we meet tomorrow, one last time?"

Nghia nodded, but a hollow feeling swept through her—a feeling of inevitability about their relationship that she realized she had somehow been expecting. Something had changed between them. She knew that they wouldn't meet again. At least not the next day. And perhaps not for a long, long time.

Quickly she turned away and walked down the steps and along

the path through one courtyard and then the next. But before she reached the *Van Mieu Mon*, she stopped and glanced back. Minh was still there, leaning against the same stone pillar, staring at her.

Au revoir, mon amour, she thought. *Au revoir*.

14

CHANGE OF HEART

Hanh Thien was more deadening than Nghia could have ever imagined. From the moment she arrived in her uncle's village, there was only one thing on her mind: survival.

If daily life in Hanoi had been hard, in Hanh Thien it was impossible. The village was a farming hamlet deep in Nam Dinh province, with small mud houses surrounded by walls joined together like a labyrinth. Although the village was only about forty kilometers from the city of Nam Dinh, it took two days by foot and by boat along narrow canals to reach it. But little was left in the city to make even that trip worthwhile. The *Viet Minh* had swept through ahead of the French, burning houses and government buildings, and leaving nothing but a shell of a city behind them.

In Hanh Thien, thanks to Nghia's uncle, her family had a roof over their heads, but little more. She and her mother, Nhu, were crammed with her three sisters and brother in one tiny room in a thatched-roof hut, where they slept on mats on the floor and cooked out back on a makeshift stove.

To make ends meet, they resorted to barter. Nghia's mother had managed to bring a few items to the village: a sewing machine, silk flowers, soap, medicine, pictures, empty tins, and satin fabric. To the simple villagers, such items seemed like treasures, and so each day Nghia traded what she could: a bar of soap for a chicken, or some medicine for rice. But as the weeks turned into months, they sold off everything one by one until nothing was left except for a few precious keepsakes.

One day, in the middle of summer, when the heat covered the

village like a blanket, suffocating anything that breathed, Nghia's mother turned to her and said numbly, "Everything is gone. We have to sell your father's pocket watch."

As soon as the words left her mouth, Grandmother Nhu went to a corner of the room and returned with a red-silk pouch, one she had made especially for the watch soon after Grandfather Tieu had bought it. As she handed it to Nghia, she averted her eyes. "I can't bear to look at it," she said. "I was saving it for your brother, Tam."

Nghia opened the pouch, which was shirred together at the top with a golden cord. Then she reached in and pulled out the watch. *Eighteen-karat gold,* she thought. *Father had been so proud.*

She lifted the ornate cover and gazed at the face. The hands were still moving perfectly. Just what she would expect. She pictured her father standing on the train platform, pulling the watch from his pocket, flicking open the cover, and counting down until the train arrived. A tear dropped from her cheek onto the crystal watch face. She gently wiped it on her sleeve. Then she snapped the cover closed and slipped the watch back into the silken pouch.

For my mother, the time for tears was over. Like my grandfather's watch, her life as she knew it was gone, snapped shut, never to show its dazzling face again. She could no longer afford her golden dreams—dreams of Minh, or of the sweet, sheltered life of her childhood.

Nghia sold the watch the very next day for some rice, vegetables, and fish sauce. Then she put on her cone hat, threw off her wooden clogs, and walked barefoot down the dusty paths of Hanh Thien toward the road, which would take her toward the canals and distant villages. There she hoped to trade the fresh food for whatever trinkets she could find to please the fancy of the villagers in Hanh Thien. Then she would parlay the trinkets into extra food and basic supplies for their survival.

As for the dangers that might lie ahead, she couldn't dwell on them. Would she run afoul of the French, who were coursing through the countryside, recapturing village after village? Would suspicious *Viet Minh* attack her? Whether she lived or died was out of her hands. All she could do was keep moving forward.

Every now and then, Nghia stopped along the road and squatted to rest her weary body. Occasionally, when she was lucky enough to see a traveler coming her way, she reached out her hand, and like the peasants she had once seen in Hanoi, outside the gates of her house on Rue Duvillier, she called out in a plaintive song: "Lichees. Vegetables. Fresh from the countryside."

Times remained hard, and even Nghia's efforts as a roadside vendor couldn't provide enough food for the family. So they moved from Hanh Thien to another nearby village. Then they moved back to Hanh Thien but had to flee when the French raided the village. Finally, they ended up in Hoanh Nha, where the family knew there were relatives and friends who might help if their situation grew so desperate that they might face starvation. Anything to survive.

Phuong

Phuong couldn't believe his good fortune. He had just left a meeting with the village elders and was walking along the pond near his Uncle Qui's compound when he spotted Mr. Tieu's daughter turning into his uncle's gate.

This time, I'm right—it's really Nghia! he said to himself, remembering his mistake three years earlier at Ba Dinh Square. *But what's she doing here in Hoanh Nha?* He quickened his pace and turned into the gate after her. Not a soul was in sight, and so he headed for the house on the far side of the paved courtyard, expecting to find Nghia sipping tea in Uncle Qui's front parlor.

Uncle will introduce us, Phuong thought. *He'll invite me in for tea, and I'm sure I'll make an impression.*

Phuong had every reason to feel confident. As the Communist chief of Hoanh Nha, he had status and position far beyond his thirty-five years. What's more, he had earned his place, not simply because of his parents, who owned huge tracts of land in the village, but because of his years in the mountains with the *Viet Minh.*

Up north amidst the *Montagnards,* the tribal people who made the mountains their home, he had come up with a brilliant business plan to trade lumber for salt and bring prosperity to the *Viet Minh.* In the mountains, he had discovered the source of a river that flowed south and connected to tributaries all the way to his village,

Hoanh Nha. With the help of the *Montagnards*, he felled trees and then floated the logs down the river to his village, where they were chopped up and sold as lumber at a hefty profit.

Using some of the profits, he bought salt, a commodity that had been dried from ocean water on the flats near Hoanh Nha and was much in demand in the mountains. All the money he made from these ventures went straight into the coffers of the *Viet Minh* to purchase guns and ammunition. In effect, Phuong was a chief financial officer for the *Viet Minh*, and his wheeling and dealing eventually paid off.

When the Communists were consolidating their power in the countryside, Phuong's growing reputation in Hoanh Nha, and his fierce dedication to his comrades, made him a natural choice to become the political chief of the village. The village was now firmly in the *Viet Minh* camp, and more than anyone, he was responsible.

As he approached Uncle Qui's house, Phuong straightened out his shoulders and thrust out his chest. He knew he cut a dashing figure. He was taller than most Vietnamese, with high cheekbones and a wide, ingratiating smile. With his muscled arms and hardened body, he projected an aura of power and vigor that turned heads wherever he went. But there was only one head he wanted to turn: Nghia's.

They had never met face-to-face, and as far as he knew, she wasn't aware that he had made a marriage proposal to her father or for that matter, that he even existed. He was starting anew with her—and this time Phuong was determined to succeed. *She'll be impressed. She may not know who I am now, but she will know—soon.*

Phuong walked up the stairs to the house and stopped in front of the doorway, which was open wide to catch the breezes.

"Uncle *oi!*" he called out. No one answered. He tried again. Still no one came to the door. Then he heard the soft shuffle of feet, and a maid appeared.

"They're at the worship house," she said, nodding in the direction of the large rectangular building at the corner of Uncle Qui's property.

The worship house. Phuong grew pensive as he headed toward the whitewashed building. In most families, the building was set aside for ancestor worship, with a raised altar at one end lined with photographs of dead parents or grandparents and piled with offerings of fruits and joss sticks. But Uncle Qui's worship house was different. He used it for one purpose only: to worship this man-God, Jesus Christ. What's more, it had served that purpose for more than fifty years, starting with Uncle Qui's great-grandfather.

The way Phuong remembered the story, Uncle Qui's great-grandfather was a very spiritual man who, despite his wealth, was always in search of truth. One day a great storm blew up, with crackling bolts of lightning and deafening peals of thunder. To appease the "Thunder God," Uncle Qui's great-grandfather made his children put on their finest clothes and headdresses and go outside to bow down to this terrifying deity.

A week or so later, Uncle Qui's great-grandfather was in a boat, crossing a river to another town, when he met a Vietnamese man who said he was a missionary. The man asked him, "Do you know anything about God?"

For the first time, Uncle Qui's great-grandfather heard about the God of the Bible, and about Jesus, who the missionary said had risen from the dead and was alive today. As soon as the great-grandfather reached shore, he sent a messenger back to his son, saying, "I have finally found the God who made heaven and earth. Prepare for a great change in our household."

Upon his return home, Uncle Qui's great-grandfather turned the family's ancestral hall into a place of Christian worship, and it had been that way ever since. Now Uncle Qui was keeping the tradition alive.

Phuong knew that on many Sundays, whenever Uncle Qui couldn't make the trek to the Protestant Church in the nearby village of Hoang Nhi, he held services of his own at the worship house. Several times a week, he also sponsored Bible studies, which attracted people from nearby villages.

More than once, his uncle had urged Phuong to go to church or to join in the studies, but always he had demurred. He couldn't reconcile this religious belief with his growing involvement in the atheistic Communist movement. What would his excuse be now?

Phuong could feel his confidence flagging as he walked up the steps to the worship house. He moved to the side of the open door and peeked in.

There she is! He couldn't take his eyes off her. It almost seemed a case of déjà vu, a repeat of the first time he had seen this striking, delicate vision—and that had also been a church service. Was there some omen here?

Nghia was sitting with four other women, listening in rapt attention to Uncle Qui. A Bible lay open on her lap and every now and then, she looked down and leafed through its pages.

What purity, Phuong thought. *What a treasure.*

Phuong didn't dare disrupt them. Clearly this was a women's Bible study, and he had enough sense to know that his presence would be inappropriate. Before anyone could discover him, he slipped away from the door and out the gate. His mind was spinning as he calculated his next move.

Uncle Qui will know exactly what to do, he thought. *He always does.*

Uncle Qui did know what to do. He invited Phuong to a prayer meeting.

Nghia

Nghia was startled to see the handsome stranger walk in the door with Thay Qui.

"This is my nephew, Mr. Phuong," Thay Qui said. "I've invited him to join us for prayer."

The statement was as much a request as an introduction. After all, Nghia was the hostess—the meeting was being conducted in her house. Also, group prayer was an intimate event, and in these troubled times, one had to be careful about sharing hidden thoughts and concerns with just anyone. But Nghia didn't hesitate. Though she averted her eyes shyly, she immediately nodded.

"Please sit down," she said, motioning him to a tiny bench in the middle of the room. "Any relative of Thay Qui's is welcome here."

Nghia owed a great deal to Thay Qui. Without his help, her family's future might have been futile. After more than two years of hardscrabble trading, she had begun to despair of any kind of normalcy. After the French had forced them to flee across the river to

Hoanh Nha, they arranged to move into an uncle's worship house, which was located near Thay Qui's lodgings.

Immediately after they arrived in Hoanh Nha, Thay Qui had invited Nghia and her family to his Bible study. Then when they had become better established in their new home, they reciprocated by inviting him over to their house for prayer every night. The new friendship revived Nghia's spirits. And now, it seemed she might be on the verge of making still another friend. . . . "Where two or three are gathered in my name," Nghia thought, smiling as she looked at Phuong.

After a few brief formalities, Thay Qui invited them all to pray. Nghia didn't feel the least bit self-conscious about opening up in front of this stranger. It was the Lord she was speaking to, after all, and if this man, Phuong, was so willing to be part of their little group, she would accept him gladly as a brother in Christ.

When the prayers were over, the two men left. But Nghia couldn't get Phuong out of her mind. He seems so self-assured. So strong. Yet there was a nagging concern. Thay Qui says he's the village's political chief. She knew the Communists were opposed to religion, and in these times, one couldn't be too careful. Still. . . .

Phuong returned for prayer again and again. Some nights, Thay Qui left immediately after the prayers. Phuong always seemed to find some reason to stay longer. Other nights, Phuong arrived early—so early that Nghia invited him to dinner.

"Can I help you?" he would ask. "What can I bring tomorrow?"

Still other nights, Thay Qui wouldn't come at all, but Phuong would show up with his uncle's Bible—and, on occasion, he would actually lead the Bible study and prayers himself.

One moonless night after the Scriptures were finished, Thay Qui attended, but complaining of fatigue he excused himself early and headed down a narrow path that bordered a pond near his compound. All of a sudden, there was the sound of a splash and a scream.

Phuong sprinted out the door and down the dirt path. A few minutes later, dripping wet, he returned with Thay Qui slung over his shoulder. He laid the old man on a reed mat as Nghia rushed over with a blanket. It seemed that Thay Qui had slipped into the water on his way home and had almost drowned.

"He was about to go under," Phuong said to Nghia. "I got there just in time."

"You're drenched," Nghia said to Phuong. "Please, put on this shirt. It belongs to my uncle."

Phuong turned his back and started taking off his soggy shirt.

Out of modesty, Nghia tried not to look but she couldn't help herself. *His shoulders are so broad. Broad enough to support me?*

She couldn't believe she had dared to think such a thing. She didn't love Phuong, at least not in the way she had loved Minh. She had never dreamed of his voice whispering in her ear . . . or reading poetry with him . . . or feeling his kiss press against her lips with exquisite urgency.

That kiss! Stolen in the shadows of the poets' gate! At the time, she had pushed Minh away, fearful of abandoning herself to their passion. Yet the kiss would linger on her lips forever as a testimony to their abiding love. Her first love.

It was true she hadn't seen Minh or heard from him since she had left Hanoi. But even if Minh was gone forever, the memory of his love would never leave her. To have loved and been loved so rapturously was any woman's dream. She suspected that never again could she know a love as pure as hers and Minh's. But in a strange sort of way, the power of that past love gave her the courage to venture forth toward love once again.

Nghia had seen the way Phuong looked at her. She understood the secrets in his eyes, the burning desire that lay just beneath the surface of his skin. Could she return that love?

She knew it was time for her to marry. At age twenty-four, she had been feeling the pressure to fulfill her duty and assuage the family honor.

"It's not right to stay single," her mother kept telling her. "You'll be an old maid. Your sisters will be old maids."

But here in the country, Nghia had encountered no realistic prospects—no one with the stature and ability to support a family, and no one with the requisite Christian faith. At least not until now.

Perhaps she could learn to love again in another, quieter way. Perhaps she could open herself up to someone who loved her and was strong. Certainly he professed a belief in Jesus, and he had shown a willingness to pray with her. But Nghia had her reservations.

She wondered if his expressions of faith were as much designed to win her heart as to worship Christ. Also, with his *Viet Minh* connections, many of which he kept to himself, he remained a rather mysterious figure. And she knew that he had been in prison and that the Communist cause had hardened him.

Still, Phuong was in many ways a highly eligible bachelor. And Nghia needed a husband. Perhaps she would indeed marry him—provided they could arrive at a clear understanding about certain matters.

Phuong must have sensed her receptivity because the very next day, Thay Qui returned to Nghia's house in remarkably good health, with his usual energy restored. He was there, he told Nghia, not for a Bible study, but to deliver Phuong's marriage proposal. "He may be a new convert, but he has demonstrated his commitment. I know your father would approve," he said simply.

Nghia said she was inclined to accept, but first she had to talk with Phuong. Later that evening, when she saw Phuong in person, she looked him straight in the eye and put aside any pretense of womanly meekness. In clear terms, she laid down her conditions: "I will never renounce my God," she said emphatically. "And I will never divorce you. But if you ever harm me physically, I will leave you immediately."

15

TWO COWS, FOUR PIGS, AND THIRTY CHICKENS

On the morning of her wedding, Nghia awoke as dawn was breaking to the sound of the rooster crowing in the next yard. Usually the familiar sound was welcoming, as though it heralded a new beginning, a new chance to break free of the burdens of the past and move forward with hope and expectation.

But on that March morning in 1948, the rooster's cry filled her with a sense of foreboding. As Nghia lay on her mat, she looked across the room at her wedding dress hanging from a peg on the wall, and she could feel her chest grow tight. *Such a beautiful dress*, she thought. *Yet such a sacrifice.*

The pale pink satin *ao dai* shimmered as it caught the rays of sunlight breaking through the open window. Her mother had brought the heavy white satin fabric from their home in Hanoi and had kept it hidden for just a moment as this. Even when they were down to their last *dong*, Grandmother Nhu had given up Grandfather's watch rather than part with the precious silk that would pave the way for her daughter's future.

Nghia remembered how she had barely announced her wedding plans when her mother had pulled out the fabric from its hiding place and dyed it a delicate pink to echo the bright red color of celebration. Then Nhu had hired a seamstress to sew the *ao dai* and added a dainty undergarment in the palest yellow silk. To complete the outfit, Nhu had bartered with another evacuee from Hanoi for a pair of tiny shoes made of golden velvet and smothered in intricately embroidered beadwork.

The gown, the undergarment, the shoes—they were trappings fit for an empress. But Nghia was too caught up in her own misgivings to grasp the joy in her mother's loving gift. Images of Minh still drifted into her mind. Questions about Phuong and his background continued to nag at the back of her consciousness.

Nghia got up slowly from the floor and went out back behind the house to make her morning ablutions. She drew a bucket of water from the well, and as she poured it over her head the cool water ran over her skin, invigorating her body and renewing her sense of purpose. By the time she squeezed the last drop of water from her hair, she felt braced for the task ahead. *I can do this, and I will do it.* "God, give me strength."

Inside, she rolled her hair in a soft bun, the fashionable "onion style" that rested low on her neck, and then, too nervous to eat breakfast, she stood quietly as her mother helped her dress for the wedding. At ten o'clock, she and her family walked along the pond to Thay Qui's house to await her groom

In her father's place, Thay Qui was playing the role of father of the bride, and he had offered his house as her home for the occasion. By the time she arrived, more than one hundred guests had already gathered in the courtyard.

Nghia had been at Thay Qui's for only a few minutes when the boisterous sounds of Phuong's wedding party broke through the air. The gate of the compound flew open, and Phuong's family and friends poured into the courtyard in a joyous procession, led by men carrying tray upon tray piled with gifts wrapped in bright red paper. Nghia saw a dizzying display of gifts—packages of fruits, candles, and incense; envelopes stuffed with money—that belied the war that raged outside the village gates.

Most extraordinary of all were the cakes. Hoanh Nha was famous for its *xu xue* cake, a clear confection made of cornstarch mixed with finely chopped coconut and filled at the center with sweetened mung-bean paste. Not only were the groom's gift trays overflowing with paper-wrapped *xu xue*, but also they carried rare treats such as *banh gai*, a black rice cake, and *banh com*, a grainy pastry made of young wheat kernels that few villagers could afford anymore.

From the looks of the trays, Phuong's relatives must have

brought two hundred of the delicacies—four times what Nghia's mother had requested as customary gifts for her far-flung family. "Please let me bring more," Phuong had said. "Otherwise people will think I'm being greedy."

As guest after guest passed by, Nghia sat regally at Thay Qui's house, watching the proceedings in amazement. Phuong's mother and sisters came to the house, and then his cousins arrived. Finally Phuong entered, walking proudly at the rear of the procession in a crisp new gray suit and white shirt. The smile on his face was so broad that Nghia thought it almost unseemly.

Phuong motioned for Nghia to join him, and together they led the procession to Thay Qui's worship house for the ceremony. Flowers blanketed the floor—white jasmine, purple orchids, and fuchsia bougainvillea—and stretched up the steps and down the aisle, perfuming the air with a sweet aroma.

Nghia and Phuong picked their way up the steps and into the worship house, where they took seats across from each other facing Pastor Hoang Trong Nhat. The Protestant clergyman had risked his life to travel from French-occupied Hoanh Nhi to officiate.

Three months after Thay Qui introduced them, Nghia and Phuong—the guerrilla fighter and *Viet Minh* leader who would one day become my father—said their vows in a Christian ceremony, a curiosity that the village had never witnessed before. Dozens of guests, including friends, family, and even peasants from surrounding villages, spilled out the door of the worship house and into the courtyard, where they jockeyed for a view of the celebrated couple and clucked about the lavishness of the affair.

"He bought her a gold necklace," someone whispered.

"Did you hear about her earrings?" asked another.

"This wedding is the glory of the village," said an elder.

But the glory was lost on the wedding's most important participant: the bride. As the music of the harmonium rose with the opening hymn, Nghia felt an overwhelming rush of sadness. Ironically, it wasn't just because the event marked her final loss of Minh. She had resigned herself to that fate when she accepted Phuong's proposal of marriage.

No, her heart ached mostly for her family. Once the marriage vows were sealed, she would belong to Phuong's family. She could no longer help her mother, brother, and three younger sisters. They would be on their own to eke out a living as best they could, and there was nothing she could do to save them.

She thought of her vow to her father: "I will take care of them as you would," she had told him on his deathbed. Yet now she was leaving them to an uncertain future. Her mother had wanted her to marry. The commitment was expected of her—in fact, it was *demanded* of the eldest. Otherwise her younger sisters would have had to remain spinsters. Still, she couldn't forgive herself for leaving them.

"Love is patient and kind," she heard Pastor Nhat read from the thirteenth chapter of 1 Corinthians. "Love does not insist on its own way."

The love chapter. Nghia could barely bring herself to focus on the words, which seemed strangely hollow.

"Love bears all things, believes all things, hopes all things, endures all things," intoned the pastor.

Nghia had borne so much already. *Can I bear more? Can I believe that my family will be all right? Can I hope for a future for myself? Can I endure?*

"So faith, hope, love abide, these three; but the greatest of these is love."

As Pastor Nhat closed his Bible, Nghia shut her eyes and let the words linger in her mind. *The greatest . . . is love. Father Tieu. Minh.* She had known the sweetest of human love. That had been God's gift to her. Now she would ask for divine favor to be able to give back the gift of love to her husband, Phuong. With God's grace, she would love and honor him as a devoted wife, and she would make him proud.

Nghia looked at Phuong. His love for her was transparent. Although his face looked serious, she could see his eyes shining in anticipation as he awaited the words from the pastor that would seal their vows.

"Do you, Phuong, promise to love Nghia in sickness and in health?" he asked.

"Yes," Phuong said boldly.

"Do you, Nghia. . . ."

The vows seemed to fly back and forth with dizzying speed, and quickly the service drew to a close.

"Do you, Nghia, promise to love, honor, and obey, as long as you both shall live?"

She paused for a brief second. Then she softly said, "Yes."

Pastor Nhat ended by pronouncing Phuong and Nghia man and wife and said a final prayer of blessing. It was finished. The worship hall swelled with music. The newlyweds led the procession out the door, through the courtyard, and down the street to Phuong's family compound for the reception.

❖❖❖❖❖

The party was the biggest Hoanh Nha had ever seen. Two cows, four pigs, and dozens of chickens and ducks were sacrificed for a feast so grand that people still talk about it to this day. There was so much food that all the ponds in the village were slick with grease from the scores of dishes that had to be washed afterwards.

The kitchen was in constant motion, with ten ladies cooking and twice as many ferrying the food back and forth to the waiting crowd, which numbered more than three hundred by nightfall. Because Phuong was Hoanh Nha's political chief, people kept coming in waves from villages two or three hours' walk away and from distances as great as Hanoi. The gifts from relatives on both sides of the family were stacked up so high Nghia could barely see the top.

Children such as Nghia's cousin Tuan and Phuong's cousin Chau eyed the bounty and stuffed themselves with *xu xue* cake until they nearly burst. Nghia's fourteen-year-old sister, Bay, who was sick with the chicken pox, had to watch from a distance so as not to infect the guests.

The scene swirled around Nghia as though she were the center of the universe. But she felt no genuine joy. Dutifully, she nodded and smiled, asking about the welfare of a sick relative, or giving condolences on the death of a grandparent. By late afternoon, as some of the guests began to leave, Nghia busied herself saying good-bye to one of her husband's relatives. That was when she heard the voice of cousin Dan.

She hadn't seen Dan all day, and she had assumed he had failed to make it to the event. Yet there he was, speaking to her mother as he took his leave. She and Dan had shared so much: he had introduced her to Minh, and years later, he had evacuated to Hanh Thien around the same time as her family. As Dan began to relate something about Hanoi, Nghia strained to pick up what he was saying—even as she pretended to be interested in the guest in front of her.

"We're leaving in two days," Dan said to her mother. "My friends and I are going back to Hanoi. Why don't you come with us? We will take care of you. Let me know."

He's going back to Hanoi! Not now! Why didn't he tell me sooner? Nghia had never wanted to leave Hanoi in the first place—never wanted to leave the trading, or the house on Rue Duvillier, or her chance for happiness with Minh. If her brothers-in-law had not prevailed on her mother to leave, Nghia would have insisted that they stay in the city. She might have even gotten a teaching job once the French brought things back to order.

Now Dan was going back, and he was promising to take her mother and younger siblings with him and watch over them! Could this really be happening? *What about me?* she wanted to shout. *Don't leave me behind!*

But as the well-wishers flooded by, Nghia steeled herself and kept smiling. Cousin Dan held back until he found a discreet moment to talk to her. Then, when no one was nearby, he approached her and whispered in her ear. "Do you have anything for me to tell Minh?" he asked.

Nghia could feel her heart drop and her muscles tighten as she girded herself to say the fateful words. "Please tell Minh to forget me and have a good life," she said, and then she added irrelevantly: "And by the way, tell him he can get his duffel bag at Pastor Diep's house."

The sky rumbled in the distance as cousin Dan hurried through the gate. A storm was brewing, and soon the village was shrouded in darkness. It was time for Nghia to go home—to Phuong.

16

BETRAYED

Just days after the wedding, the accusations started bubbling to the surface.

"Nghia's a city woman," Phuong's mother said to him. "She doesn't understand our ways."

"We warned you not to marry her," his comrades complained. "She's bourgeois. And a *Christian*. She brings shame on the Party."

Phuong had heard the litany before: Nghia's family was too poor, her education was too lofty, her will was too strong. Before the wedding, he had listened politely to the objections of his family and friends and had summarily discounted them. *How could my marriage to the most beautiful woman in Tonkin possibly be a liability?* he had wondered.

He had wanted Nghia too much to let anyone stand between them. She was his prize, his conquest. For years, he had dreamed of her almost to the point of obsession. Then, just three months after they met, he had won her. Now she was his, forever. She had vowed it to him from her very own lips, and nothing anyone could do or say would take her away from him.

"She is my wife," he told his mother emphatically. "I'm willing to sacrifice everything for her if I have to."

Phuong never expected to have to make good on his pledge so soon. Four weeks after their wedding, Nghia discovered she was pregnant with their first child. Two weeks after that, she begged him to let her study in Kha Phong, a village more than one hundred kilometers away, where the Communists had recently instituted a "reeducation" class for French-trained teachers.

"I want to be certified by the *Viet Minh*," she told him. "I want to have a profession."

Phuong was in anguish. How could he let his precious bride, the mother-to-be of his firstborn, leave him for six months of training? There were so many arguments against it.

The trip alone was dangerous. The countryside was aflame, as village after village fell to the French and then to the *Viet Minh* and back again, like a bloody seesaw that never seemed to rest. To reach Kha Phong, Nghia would have to travel on foot and by boat, first through a French-occupied area and then through *Viet Minh*–controlled territory, flashing falsified "official" papers at each checkpoint. One misstep and she could be arrested—or even shot—if either side questioned her credentials or allegiance.

As if his worries about the potential physical dangers to Nghia weren't enough, Phuong had to contend with his mother's mounting ire. "How can you let her leave you for six months?" she said, nagging him until he felt numb. "She's going to have morning sickness. She might lose the baby. What if it's a boy?"

Phuong knew that his mother had little interest in Nghia's welfare. All she cared about was the family's future, or more precisely, the condition of the family heir. His elder brother's son might have borne the family mantle, but the boy was virtually an outcast. Elder brother had been forced to wed in an arranged marriage, but he had so despised his wife that a month after their wedding, he had left for the jungle to fight with the *Viet Minh*. From that moment on, the family had treated his wife as one of the servants and the son he left behind as a slave.

With the discovery of Nghia's pregnancy, Phuong saw that his mother was intent on exercising absolute control over the couple's relationship. She carped at him relentlessly to assert his leadership. "Tell your wife no!" she said. "Don't be so weak!"

Phuong found he couldn't stand up effectively to Nghia, who had at least as strong a will and personality as his mother. So he fell back on logical arguments and cajoling in an effort to convince her to stay home, but she remained adamant.

"This training will endear me to your comrades," Nghia retorted. "I'll be one of the first with the official *Viet Minh* certificate. Don't you see, I *must* go."

Phuong looked at his wife and nodded with a grudging smile. She looked even more beautiful when she had her mind made up. He loved the way her eyes burned with fire and how she thrust out her chin with just a hint of defiance.

Such a woman might emasculate any other man. But Nghia's petulance energized Phuong, and secretly he was proud of her abilities and aspirations. There wasn't a male teacher for the *Viet Minh* in the whole province, and yet his own wife would soon be qualified to fill that important role.

Besides, he reasoned, her arguments made sense. *After the training, she will have the "correct" teaching. My comrades will be won over.*

"You can go," he said finally. "But please . . . come back."

Nghia

Six months later, with her belly blossoming, Nghia returned to Hoanh Nha. The training had been rigid and tedious. But now she was prepared to contribute more significantly to her family's income and also to enhance their status in the new Communist society.

As Nghia turned off the main road onto the village's green-tiled footpath, she saw Phuong rushing toward her. At the sight of him, she softened and felt infused by a new sense of possibility for their marriage and for their future.

"Welcome home," he said, smiling tentatively as he drew up next to her.

She smiled back and nodded a greeting, and together, they started to amble home. Nghia waited for Phuong to speak further, but only the sound of their footsteps broke the silence. They passed the village school, and then the pond where Phuong had rescued his uncle Qui, familiar sights that should have triggered animated conversation. Still Phuong said nothing.

What could be wrong? Nghia wondered. In the past, Phuong would have prattled on self-importantly about his work. He might have boasted about his success in settling a dispute or about some special deal he had wrangled for the *Viet Minh*. But today, he was uncharacteristically quiet.

"How is your family?" she asked, straining to make conversation. "The baby is kicking constantly. It is a good sign."

Phuong just nodded and responded with that same uncertain smile.

Later, as they sat sipping tea in his mother's house, Nghia's mother-in-law broke the news. "He's been kicked out!" she said bluntly, glaring at Nghia as though she were to blame. "He's not the political chief anymore."

Nghia was too shocked to speak. She looked at Phuong, who sat coldly erect, staring passively in front of him. In Nghia's absence, Phuong's comrades had turned against him. Despite his family's support for Ho's cause, Phuong's lavish wedding and his connection to the Christians in the local community had stigmatized him among his fellow operatives. Ironically, while Nghia was hard at work learning proper Communist doctrine, Phuong's comrades had stripped him of his power in the village and left him without any political status in the Party. Now he had little to do but sit home, nurse his wounded ego, and hope that the political tide would change.

Nghia couldn't help but pity him. She understood her husband's fierce pride. She also knew that she was the only thing he had left to hold on to. He looked at her almost reverentially with the same longing, the same proud possessiveness, as though she were some rare object that only he deserved.

Perhaps she could be his rescuer. She reasoned that if she worked hard in her new job as the village's only teacher, educating students with nationalistic dogma, she could bring a modicum of honor back to him. She would be a perfect wife, love him, care for their baby, and support them financially. Surely his comrades would take notice and approve.

So, armed with her newly earned certificate, Nghia went to work immediately in the village school, where the *Viet Minh* had assigned her to teach all of the grades single-handedly. For several months after the birth of their daughter, Tram, it seemed that life was almost back to normal. During the day, Nghia taught school, leaving Tram in the care of a servant. In the evenings, she and Phuong read the Bible and prayed, just as they had before their wedding. In the circle of their little family, Phuong seemed almost like a lamb, soft and tender and gentle, and for the first time in years, Nghia felt content.

But before long, Nghia sensed that Phuong was drifting. He didn't smile as much, and soon his loving gazes came further and further apart. During Bible studies his mind seemed to wander, and during the daily routine he became annoyed over little things that had never bothered him before. "The baby's crying too much," he said one night. "Why can't you take care of her?

"The *pho* needs more basil," he said the next night. "Have you forgotten how to cook?"

Then one day, without any warning, Nghia came home from school to find him packing his things.

"I'm going up north to the *Viet Bac*," he said. "My only chance is to prove myself again. If I stay here, I will die."

Phuong

The letter from his mother lay open on the reed mat where he had thrown it in disgust. Phuong picked it up and read it again and became even angrier than the first time.

Con:
Your wife is making life miserable for us. She refused to let us have any of the rice you left in the storehouse for her so that we could pay our laborers. She claims she was giving it to the *Viet Minh*, but I know better. She's hoarding it all for herself. She makes 1,700 *dong* as a teacher—more than enough for any woman.

How can you let her be so independent? She is not the least bit obedient. Because she's a teacher, she thinks she can walk around with her nose in the air as if she's better than the rest of us.

Do something, before she ruins the family name!

Me

Phuong crumpled the letter in his fist and threw it against the wall.

His mother had been right. His comrades had been right.

Nghia had been trouble from the start. First her constant arguing and insistence on her own way. Then the six-month separation for "reeducation"—of which he had disapproved. And now this. Here he was living a bare-bones existence for the sake of the cause, and she was lording over his family with her superior lifestyle.

Giving grain to the *Viet Minh*—ha! She was undoubtedly building up the wealth of her own impoverished family right under the nose of his ancestors. Could anything be more shameful?

Phuong sent back a letter immediately with a courier, giving his mother permission to give Nghia a scolding. "Tell her I won't tolerate this behavior. She is a disgrace to the family."

While Phuong was stewing over his wife's alleged obstinacy, his courier returned to the mountains a few weeks later with even more disturbing news: the French had attacked Hoanh Nha. The soldiers had stormed into the village one noontime, sending the entire populace into hiding in the rice fields. Children ran from their lunches of *rieu*, tiny crabs and rice, wondering if they would ever be able to return. By late afternoon, the French had retreated, but the village was preparing for another round of attacks.

The minute he heard the report, Phuong's fighting spirit took over, and his anger at Nghia took a backseat to the pending crisis.

I have to protect her and Tram, he thought. *I have to get them to safety.* He knew how the French operated. The villains would tear through house after house, looking for *Viet Minh* sympathizers. To ferret out information, they were known to tie people to posts in the river and wait until the water rose after a torrential rain. Men, women—it didn't matter to the French. They would stop at nothing, not even when it came to Nghia.

Just the thought of his wife and child falling victim to his enemies was enough to mobilize Phuong into action. Immediately he sent the courier back to Hoanh Nha with orders to sneak into the village in the middle of the night and evacuate his wife and daughter by boat to the *Viet Minh*-held village of Thai Binh.

"Hurry," said Phuong. "Get her out of Hoanh Nha before the French come back."

Nghia

Nghia and Tram's evacuation from Hoanh Nha went smoothly under cover of night, and for several months the two were safe in Thai Binh. Then the French swept into Thai Binh, and the terrors started all over again. Was there no safe haven, no way to escape the ravages of war?

Once again, relying on his *Viet Minh* contacts, Phuong got wind of the French troop movements in advance and moved swiftly. Whatever his failings, Nghia's husband at least gave his family's security a top priority. Before long, Nghia found herself back with her mother-in-law in Hoanh Nha, which was now a peaceful enclave, though the village was firmly under French control.

"Better to be safe with my mother—even under the French—than alone in a war zone," Phuong had told her through a courier.

He obviously was well aware of Nghia's problems with her mother-in-law, and she could detect a note of sympathy for her plight. But she also had to agree that he was right. It was better for her and Tram to be safe, even if that meant moving back in with the mother-in-law.

By the time Nghia returned, life in Hoanh Nha had settled down to a fairly regular routine. Because the school had been closed during the troubles, Nghia couldn't teach, and so she had no choice but to live by her mother-in-law's rule. Although Nghia dutifully obeyed, she chafed under the woman's strict control and looked for ways to break free.

Should she start trading again? Should she find someplace else to teach? Should she and Tram just move to get out from under her mother-in-law's thumb?

Nghia despaired of an answer until one day, when she was out in the courtyard, she looked up to see a tall, angular woman walking through the gate of her mother-in-law's compound. Usually a stranger would call out at the gate and wait to be received. But this woman had walked through boldly and was now striding down the path at a determined pace. She was wearing a cone hat tilted down to shield her face, along with a pair of baggy black pants and a white cotton blouse that didn't quite seem to fit over her bulging arms. And her feet were remarkable. They seemed to be extraordinarily large.

Even a peasant wouldn't have such feet, Nghia thought.

The closer the woman got to the house, the more intrigued Nghia became. She stood transfixed until the stranger was right on top of her. The woman lifted her head, and Nghia let out a gasp. "Phuong!"

His face broke out into the wide toothy grin that was his signature, and then, without saying a word, he nodded his head toward the house. They slipped off their shoes and walked into the foyer, where his mother was waiting for them. After an hour or so, they retired to Nghia's room, where for the first time in months, they were alone.

Two days later, Phuong left as surreptitiously as he had come. A month later, Nghia awoke nauseated. Her breasts were sore, and she was so exhausted she could barely get out of bed.

I hope it's a boy, she thought. *We'll call him Phong.* The name was close in sound to that of her husband, but by custom—and as a matter of good luck—a Vietnamese son could not bear his father's name.

But nothing she could do seemed to make Phuong happy, and their relationship deteriorated even further during their next extended separation. Even after the birth of a son—an event that every Vietnamese family longed for—Phuong became increasingly demanding, almost irrational, it seemed to Nghia.

First, he wrote to her, insisting that she and the children join him and his comrades in the rugged *Viet Bac.* "It's too dangerous," she wrote back. "The French are bombing everywhere. I can't risk the lives of our children."

Finally, thoroughly frustrated with her mother-in-law's dictatorial manner, and also in need of extra money, Nghia decided that the time had arrived for her to find a better place to live and raise her children. She managed to use her impeccable French to land a plum teaching job in the French-controlled village of Bui Chu.

But Phuong, whose mother had notified him, immediately complained in a letter about Nghia's independence.

"I thought you would be happy that I was taking such good care of our children," she wrote in response. "Instead, you are making my life more difficult."

But for Nghia, her ongoing difficulties with Phuong were just the beginning of her problems.

※ ※ ※ ※ ※

"This Territory Under French Protection." The sign on the gate at Bui Chu village was meant as a warning to the *Viet Minh*. But from the moment she arrived in the village, Nghia didn't feel safe—not from anyone.

Nghia hid the gold and money she had saved under her blouse and slipped into bed, exhausted. On the other side of the room, the children were already asleep next to *Chi* Mao, the maid she had hired. It was nice to be on her own again, but she also was realistic about the situation. Nothing was stable, not in this environment. On a moment's notice, they had to be ready to run. Tonight? Tomorrow night? Peace eluded them.

Any night, without warning, the *Viet Minh* might sneak past the barbed wire that surrounded the village to terrorize anyone who worked for the French. She had heard the shots ring out in the darkness and had seen the blazing fires of houses burned to the ground, but as yet the dangers had not come near her or her children. But there was always tomorrow. And when the trouble came, she needed to be ready.

Even as she ingratiated herself with the villagers and with the Vietnamese soldiers who worked for the French, she lived in constant fear of being found out. *What if the French discover Phuong is Viet Minh?* she wondered.

Fortunately, she managed to evade suspicion. For more than a year she successfully carried on a double life in Bui Chu. By day, she witnessed an answer to her prayers that her secret life as the wife of a *Viet Minh* cadre would remain hidden from the French. By night, she prayed that her work for the French wouldn't make her a target of the *Viet Minh*. Again, God protected her.

Nghia found she wasn't the only one who was caught in the

middle. One day, as she was about to write on the blackboard of the one-room schoolhouse, she looked out the window to see a man peeking in. "Who are you?" she demanded, alarmed at first, and then curious. "You look familiar."

Before he had a chance to reply, the memories came flooding back. "Are you brother Quoc?" she asked in astonishment. "The rickshaw driver?"

"Yes, little mistress," he said. "I am Quoc. I was walking by your school and I heard your voice through the window, and I had to stop to see if it was you."

Nghia told the class to work on some exercises and then she hurried outside to greet the old family servant. "I'm so happy to see you!" she exclaimed. "How did you get here?"

As they stood in the dusty courtyard, Quoc explained how a year or so after her father died, he had evacuated from Hanoi, according to Ho Chi Minh's directive. But a few years after he arrived in his ancestral village, the French army raided the hamlet, and he found himself conscripted into service. Now he spent his days carrying munitions from village to village along with the French army. "The trucks can't drive along the muddy dikes between the rice fields," he explained, "and so they make us carry all the weapons.

"It's been two years," he said. "I haven't heard from my wife and children. I don't even know if they're alive. I would try to escape, but if I do, the *Viet Minh* will shoot me because I helped the French. I have no life, no future. It is out of my hands."

Nghia could feel herself choking up as she listened to brother Quoc's story. Their lives were so different, yet underneath it all, so much the same. He was like a reed blown in the wind, tossed to and fro by forces raging beyond his control. *Beyond anyone's control*, she thought, *except God's*.

"I have to leave now, before they see me," he said.

Nghia ran back into the school for her purse and took out all the cash she was carrying. "Please, take this money," she said. "Maybe it will help."

Quoc nodded and took the gifts. "*Tu biet*," he said. "Farewell forever." Then he turned and ran down the dusty road until Nghia lost sight of him.

What will become of him? What will become of any of us?

The message from her mother-in-law was rolled up like a cigarette in the middle of the fruit basket.

Your husband will be at home with us in Hoanh Nha on Wednesday, between 9 A.M. and noon. Please bring the children home to the village to see their father.

Mother-in-Law

Nghia was beside herself. Although she hadn't seen her husband in nearly two years, she knew it was her duty to meet him. But he and his mother didn't know what they were asking. She would have to take off several days from her teaching job in Bui Chu, which she could not easily explain. Then she would have to bundle up the children and pass through checkpoint after checkpoint, praying that the little ones wouldn't betray their mission.

But she would do it. She had to do it. For the sake of her marriage, she would do what she was asked.

The next week, Nghia and the children arrived in Hoanh Nha the night before the appointed rendezvous and stayed in her uncle's worship house, where she and her mother had lived before her wedding. Happily, her mother was now safely in Hanoi, living in *Giao Si* Cadman's apartment at the mission compound.

The church had been burned to the ground—no one could say by whom, the French or the *Viet Minh*—and Cadman had since died of a heart attack. But before he passed away, the blessed man had helped Nhu sell her house on Rue Duvillier and then opened his door to her family. Cousin Dan had been good to his word and was now looking after her as though she were his mother.

Nghia was so grateful that God had provided in ways none of them could have anticipated. And how she wished she could be with them. But her life had taken a course that prevented any such reunion, at least for now, and she was determined to make the best of it.

The next morning, as soon as she awoke, Nghia bathed the children and dressed them in their finest outfits. She tied a pink bow in Tram's hair and made sure that two-year-old Phong's hair was trimmed just right. Her husband had never seen his son before, and Nghia wanted everything to be perfect.

They're so fat and healthy! she thought smugly. *Compared to other children in the village, they look like royalty!*

As a final touch, she swept her hair back in the onion bun that Phuong loved so much and put on her yellow silk *ao dai.* Then she waited for him to arrive. *I want him to be proud. I want him to understand how well I am taking care of our children.*

At the appointed hour, Phuong slipped in the door. But instead of a warm welcome, he got a shriek. As Phuong walked over to embrace his young son, the two-year-old pulled back from the rugged stranger and started screaming uncontrollably.

"This is your father," Nghia told the toddler. "He has come back to see you."

But nothing seemed to console little Phong. He kept howling and screaming so much that his father finally bade them a reluctant farewell. "I'm sorry," Phuong told Nghia sadly. "I had wanted things to turn out better."

"I'm sorry too," she said. "He's too young to understand."

With that, Phuong turned his back on his wife, walked out the door, and headed for his mother's compound. The family reunion, after two years of separation, was over.

The next day, Nghia returned to Bui Chu.

◆◆◆◆◆

The bicycle turned down the path and stopped in front of Nghia's house in Bui Chu. Through the window, she watched as the rider twisted open the handlebar and pulled out a long paper tube.

"Teacher *oi!*" he called out to announce his arrival.

Nghia invited the courier in and grabbed the tube from his hand. It was a letter from her husband.

Phuong! He hadn't forgotten her. Even though she hadn't heard from him in months—and their last meeting had been less than ideal—Nghia was hopeful that things between them could be patched up. Eager for some positive word, she unrolled the paper and scanned the page. The few words that registered set the accusatory tone: "We need a family meeting . . . your disrespect . . . my mother says. . . ."

Nghia couldn't believe what she was reading. She had barely had any contact with his family or mother. What could they be thinking? Struggling to maintain her composure in front of the courier, she continued reading.

> Come at once to Hoanh Nha next Sunday. Because of you, I have to risk my life to settle this family dispute. I will be waiting.
>
> Phuong

Nghia could feel her jaw tighten. *Sharp fingernails, thick orange peel.* The old Vietnamese saying summed up her relationship with her in-laws. Her mother-in-law might have sharp fingernails, but her own skin was thicker than an orange peel's. She would have the last word, no matter what the consequences.

"Please wait," she said to the courier. "I have a letter for you to take to the person who sent this." Quickly, Nghia scribbled a response to her husband:

> *Anh* Phuong:
> I was so excited to see your friend riding his bike down the lane, because my heart told me there would be good news from you. But as I read the letter, my heart became very bitter, because this was not a letter of kindness and love from husband to wife. It read like the letter from a stranger.
> I am sorry, but I will not be able to make the family meeting in Hoanh Nha. Because of the war, I do not want to endanger our two children or myself. If anything happened to me, the children would be orphans, because you are not here to provide and take care of them. Also, I do not believe I have made any mistakes with your family. I have done no wrong. I have only tried to take care of our children as a good wife should.
>
> Nghia

From that moment on, any relationship that Nghia might have had with her in-laws was completely severed. And predictably, the relationship between Nghia and Phuong grew colder. The war, the constant separation, and the frequent misunderstandings had conspired to drive a wedge between them, hardening their hearts toward each other. There were no more rendezvous, no more letters—at least not until the summer of 1953, when my father's younger sister, Diem, turned up in Bui Chu.

"Phuong is ready to leave his comrades," she said. "The *Viet Minh* are taking over the land in their villages and giving it to the peasants. There are rumors that Hoanh Nha may be next. Phuong needs you to help him escape to Hanoi."

As Nghia got off her bike and wheeled it through the small gate that had been cut in the barbed wire, she couldn't believe she had agreed to do this. She was an unarmed woman, the mother of two small children. Why should it be her responsibility to arrange this escape for a tough guerrilla fighter—who already had plenty of experience ducking encounters with the French and breaking out of leg irons and prisons? But he was still her husband, and he had asked for her help. So she felt she really had no choice.

She flashed her ID to the Vietnamese sentry, and to her relief, he nodded for her to pass. *First test.* Luckily, he didn't pay any attention to the bulging package behind the seat of the bike, where she had wrapped up a pair of men's slacks and a western shirt as a change of clothes for Phuong. More than likely her husband would show up dressed in brown pajamas, the trademark of the *Viet Minh*, and she wanted to be prepared.

Near the gate was a small café where the soldiers often stopped for tea and water. Feigning fatigue, Nghia parked her bike and sat down at a small table. "Tea, please," she said to the girl.

Her eyes darted back and forth, surveying the scene. Soldiers were everywhere. French. Vietnamese. The French had enlisted scores of Vietnamese into their army to legitimize their claims to power. Now they were as ubiquitous as the Europeans.

Was she crazy? Did she really think she could get away with helping Phuong defect from the *Viet Minh*? But she had to try. Wasn't she partly to blame for his predicament?

After the wedding, his comrades had stripped him of his power in the Party. Even after he had rejoined them in the *Viet Bac*, they had never fully accepted him again. Five grueling years had left him with nothing. What's more, now that Ho Chi Minh was giving the peasants control of the land, Phuong might not have a life

to come back to. Tired, frustrated, and demoralized, he had decided to defect and rejoin her and the children.

Through his sister, Nghia had sent Phuong a message setting up
the rendezvous on the outskirts of Bui Chu, a hair's breadth from
Viet Minh territory. Nghia reasoned that at least in Bui Chu, where
she was known and respected as a teacher, he might have a chance
to escape. But the plan was risky for both of them, so risky that several days earlier, she had taken the children to stay with her mother
in Hanoi in case she and Phuong were discovered.

"God, show me what to do," she prayed. "I beg you, please protect us."

Nghia was still sipping her tea when she saw her sister-in-law
Diem striding through the gate, with Phuong close behind her.
The plan was that if the *Viet Minh* captured Phuong, Diem could
help him talk his way out of it; if the French captured him, she
could report the news back to his mother.

"Halt! Where are you going?" the sentry yelled. He hurled
Phuong to the ground and put a gun to his head.

Nghia bolted from the table and ran to his side. "This is my
husband," she said. "He was in the *Viet Minh*–occupied area and
he wants to be with me. Here's the paper from the mayor of Bui
Chu, explaining everything."

She pulled out a large, official-looking document, which the
mayor had signed. A few days earlier, Nghia had gone to city hall
and used her prestige as the teacher of the vice-mayor's son to get
the signature.

"This teacher is a very good woman, very trustworthy," the
vice-mayor had said to the mayor, when he introduced her.
"Could you please write a letter to help her husband?"

Without further questioning, the mayor had signed a letter that
read: "If anyone from the French or the Vietnamese military
meets Vu Duc Phuong, please provide security for him and bring
him to the Bui Chu city hall."

"See!" said Nghia. "See what it says! The mayor said my husband needs security."

The sentry called for reinforcements. "You're lying," he said.
"We'll see what the officials have to say."

With Nghia and Diem following behind, the soldiers marched

Phuong to a nearby office, where a man named Viet was in charge. As it happened, Nghia knew Viet from countless village meetings that she had attended as the town's highly visible and respected teacher.

Viet looked from Phuong to Nghia and back again. "Aren't you from Hoanh Nha?" he asked Phuong.

"Yes," said Phuong. "My family name is Vu."

"Vu, is it?" said Viet. "I grew up in Hoanh Nhi."

Nghia could tell from the look in Viet's eyes that he was frightened. *He must know that my mother-in-law supports the Viet Minh*, she thought. *Perhaps he's afraid of reprisals from the Communists.*

Whatever his reasons, Viet immediately offered to help. "What do you need?"

"Please give us an ID that says we are residents of Nam Dinh," Nghia said. "We are trying to reach Hanoi. Without official papers from Nam Dinh, we won't be able to travel past Bui Chu."

Viet signed the documents, and then, perhaps wanting to complete this questionable, touchy matter as quickly as possible, he put my mother and father on a plane for Nam Dinh that very hour.

◼◼◼◼◼

But in the unsettled milieu of Vietnam in the early 1950s, passage from one region to another was highly unpredictable. The balance of power was constantly shifting back and forth between the French and the insurrectionist *Viet Minh*.

"Why do you want to defect?" the officer in Nam Dinh said brusquely, looking Phuong straight in the eye. My parents had reported to the office of the French *Résident* as soon as they had arrived in Nam Dinh. Now they were being grilled to see which side they were on.

"I want to be with my family," said Phuong. "It is too difficult living apart."

The officer raised an eyebrow and sneered. "*Deuxième Bureau*," he said to an aide. "Take them to the *Deuxième Bureau*."

The soldier hustled them out the door and down a long, narrow corridor. Nghia was terrified. The *Deuxième Bureau*, or *Phong Tra Tan Cong* as it was known in Vietnamese, was notorious for interrogation and torture. Now they were headed there with a mustachioed guard who didn't look the least bit accommodating. If they had any hope of wriggling out of this one, Nghia would have to think fast.

"*S'il vous plaît,*" she asked before the soldier could separate her from Phuong. "May I translate for my husband?"

The minute Nghia started speaking French, the soldier's demeanor softened. "*Bien sûr, Madame,*" he said. "Of course. Whatever suits you."

He opened the door and ushered them into a room that was empty except for two wooden chairs and a map rolled up on the wall. Moments later, an officer appeared, and the aide whispered something in his ear. The officer nodded to Nghia.

"*Madame,*" he said. "You are welcome to translate." Then he turned his attention to Phuong. "Why did you come back from your post?" he asked sharply.

"Because of my wife and children," said Phuong.

Nghia jumped in with her own translation. "My husband is not *Viet Minh,*" she said insistently. "He is just a very patriotic person. He worked as a merchant, not as a soldier."

"But Madame—" The officer tried to interrupt, but she continued.

"We are Christians," she said, looking him in the eye. "We want to keep our religion. My husband was forced to collaborate with the *Viet Minh* in the jungle. We have not seen him for five years. He wanted to come back to be with his family and practice his religion."

Nghia sensed that she was making some inroads, but from the look on the officer's face, she could tell he still wasn't entirely convinced.

The interrogator pulled down a map of Indochina.

"Where were you on this map?" he asked Phuong, trying to trap my father into a confession.

Phuong pointed out a few spots, recently abandoned, that had once been *Viet Minh* strongholds. He mentioned a few others that had fallen into French hands. With those tidbits of information, the interrogator seemed satisfied for the time being. Then he directed his attention to Nghia. "Where did you live? What did you do? Where are you going from here?"

The questions were relentless, but Nghia answered everything with such supreme assurance that the interrogator finally gave in. "All right," he said, bowing curtly to Nghia. "I have heard enough. You can go now."

A few days later, my parents arrived in French-occupied Hanoi where for several weeks they stayed with Grandmother Nhu. But still, the little family couldn't rest. Nghia and the children had to leave again for Bui Chu so that she could resume her teaching job and keep the family afloat financially. My father, Phuong, without a job and shorn of his identity, walked the streets of Hanoi trying to find direction.

But in the far north, off in the northwest corner of the Tonkin region, a battle was taking shape that would decide not only my father's fate, but also that of Indochina. After nearly eight years of war that took the lives of ninety thousand men, the French would face General Giap's army in a valley known as Dien Bien Phu. There, encircling the French with artillery from the high ground, the *Viet Minh* were prepared to fight to the death.

The French forces at Dien Bien Phu fell in May 1954, a cataclysmic event that sent my family, along with many other Vietnamese, into a tailspin. Elsewhere in the north, the French were still holding on, but the *Viet Minh* were moving quickly to subdue as many villages as possible. With the withdrawal of the French imminent, the rumors flew—and the fears mounted.

"Collaborators will be killed," those supposedly in the know warned. "Christians will be destroyed. Landowners will be turned out."

In Bui Chu, my mother, Nghia, knew one thing for certain. If she remained in the village when the *Viet Minh* took over, she would never be able to leave. She would be stuck in Bui Chu with her children and would be separated, perhaps permanently, from her husband and mother in Hanoi.

Acting quickly, she devised a ruse to be dismissed from her teaching job and gain passage to Hanoi. She reasoned that if she could convince the French military doctor in Bui Chu that she had tuberculosis, perhaps she could find a way out.

So as soon as she could make arrangements, she dropped by the French military post, and using her most ingratiating French, she talked her way in to see the doctor. "I am a public servant, a teacher," she told him. "But lately I've been very tired."

Knowing the disease intimately from her experience with her father, she carefully enumerated the symptoms: low-grade fever in the afternoon, no appetite, insomnia, weight loss. "I don't know what's the matter," she said.

The doctor put her on a table and examined her. "I suspect you have TB, but we can't take care of you here," he said. "I'll have to put you on a French military plane for Nam Dinh, where you can get an X ray."

Nghia tried to appear devastated, but inside she was overjoyed. A plane to Nam Dinh! It was nothing less than a miracle. Under normal circumstances, she would never have been able to leave her teaching post at such a critical time. Examinations were coming up, and teachers needed to be on hand to grade papers and prepare students for their tests.

But as soon as she told the officials at the school the probable diagnosis, they asked no questions. The very next day, she and the children were on the plane heading for Nam Dinh.

As it turned out, the X ray did reveal a spot on her lung. She actually did have TB. But that didn't matter to Nghia. She took her life one day at a time. She had escaped from Bui Chu, and that was all that counted at the moment.

The following morning, she and the children boarded a ship for Hanoi. In time, she would confront her health problems. Two days later, the ship forged up the Red River and into Hanoi Harbor. Phuong was at the dock waiting for her.

"We have to flee to the south," Nghia told him. "Whatever we do, we cannot remain here."

My mother's words were prescient. Over the next few months, events snowballed, forcing people to make life-and-death decisions at a moment's notice.

Back in the village of Bui Chu, the *Viet Minh* swarmed in as my mother had anticipated. Some of her fellow teachers, not wanting to be caught as collaborators, jumped into the river with the *Viet*

Minh on their tail and swam to a French landing craft that carried them to safety. Others were not so fortunate.

The Indochinese war ended on July 21, 1954, with a cease-fire agreement hammered out in Geneva. But the cease-fire marked only the beginning of new turmoil for individual Vietnamese. Under the shaky political terms of the agreement, the country was temporarily divided at the seventeenth parallel, with one government in the north under Ho Chi Minh, and another in the south headed by Emperor Bao Dai and his designated prime minister, Ngo Dinh Diem. Ostensibly, the national elections in the summer of 1956 would decide the country's ultimate fate.

Soon after Geneva, there was a brief window of opportunity when citizens on both sides were free to flee north or south as their consciences dictated. Nearly one million people, mostly Vietnamese Catholics, ultimately fled south.

But on a personal level the choice to go or to stay was agonizing. Although the Communist propaganda machine painted a rosy picture of what life would be like under the new regime, many people, especially Catholics and Protestants, were skeptical. Besides the political uncertainty, there were more practical questions for families like mine: Where would they live? How would they survive? Would they ever see or hear from their loved ones again?

Entire families were at odds over the decisions, and the growing family of Nghia and Phuong was no different. The couple argued constantly.

"We must go to Saigon," Nghia said. "I need freedom to worship, and also freedom for myself. I won't feel safe until I'm there."

"Why are you so afraid of the Communists?" Phuong parried, seemingly oblivious to the humiliation he had suffered at the hands of the *Viet Minh.* "My old comrades assure me everything will be fine. They say I might even become a big boss in the new order."

The tug-of-war went on endlessly. My father wanted to stay; my mother was inclined to leave. Nghia's older sisters and their husbands pressed her to remain in the north; despite their compelling arguments for the status quo, she still had a nagging feeling that she and Phuong and their children should head south.

Yet when she put the matter before God in prayer, she met silence. She could identify no clear divine guidance about what they should do. As a result she was immobilized by indecision. *Has God forgotten to be gracious? Has he forgotten his tender mercies?* She prayed constantly: "Show me what to do!" But still no response.

Then one day, my mother found out she was pregnant with her third child, and her doubts disappeared. The new life within her abruptly silenced the outside noise and provided her with clear direction: "Go to Saigon! You've got to leave—now!"

Without telling Phuong, Nghia slipped into a French government office and forged his signature on an official application for a flight to Saigon. A week or so later, a letter arrived, setting the time and date of the family's departure from a French military airport.

"We're going to the airport," she announced to Phuong on the morning of their scheduled flight. "We leave for Saigon today—or never!"

Phuong grimaced, but he followed Nghia out the door.

A few weeks after my parents evacuated, the door to the south slammed shut for good. The French sanctioned no more flights to Saigon; there were no more quick escapes from the *Viet Minh* juggernaut, which moved into Hanoi in October 1954.

But as one of nearly a million Vietnamese who had managed to flee to the south, Nghia considered herself blessed. Although her older sisters had stayed behind, her mother, younger sisters, and brother had made the journey along with her. Happily surrounded by her little family, Nghia felt a surge of optimism.

We are free, she thought as she walked toward the river down Saigon's great thoroughfare, the *Rue Catinat*. When she reached the harbor, she looked out over the river, the *Song Saigon*, and patted her bulging stomach.

God is good, Number Four, she said to her unborn child. *You will be born in Saigon. You will be born free!*

❖❖❖❖❖

But as it turned out, this new freedom came at a terrible emotional price. A letter arrived from the north, and Nghia eagerly tore it open, hoping against hope that all her relatives and Phuong's were well. They needed good news. Phuong especially needed to have his spirits lifted.

As she read, however, her heart plummeted. She was petrified to tell Phuong the latest news because she feared this might be a final blow for him. Ever since they had arrived in Saigon, he had been disconsolate. He had no job. He had no status. All he did was mope around the house all day long with a wistful look in his eyes, dreaming of returning to some grand life in Tonkin that had never existed—and never would.

He'll never recover from this, she thought, the letter hanging limp in her hand. *How can I tell him about Hoanh Nha?*

Before Nghia had time to come up with a plan, Phuong walked into the room and looked from her face to the letter in her hand. "What is it?" he asked.

"It's from your friend Ha—about your mother and sister," Nghia said. "You read it."

Bac Phuong:

　All is lost. Your mother has been ruined—denounced as a landowner in front of the whole village. I saw it all—it was horrible. People were jeering at her. Shouting epithets. It was a witch hunt, by a group called the Agricultural Reform Tribunal. They are all from Hoanh Nha.

　Your family has been stripped of their land, and now they are living in a one-room house in what is left of your family compound. Your mother's former tenants took over her fields and divided up the property. The scum didn't even leave her the worship house to honor your ancestors.

　But that isn't even the worst of it. Your sister, Diem, went out on the streets, screaming for justice and threatening retribution from the gods. She carried on like a crazy woman—pointing at people, and shrieking in anger. Some thugs—you know them, but I don't dare mention their names—retaliated by locking her up in jail in a psychiatric wing. They said she died there. A heart attack, they said.

　Be glad you didn't stay to see it. Your mother and younger sister are alive. But beyond that, there is nothing left. Please, try to forget Hoanh Nha. I can only hope you have a better life in Saigon. I hope that for all of us.

Your comrade, Ha

The letter fell from Phuong's hand, and he dropped into the armchair in anguish.

Nghia didn't know what to do. Should she run over and comfort him? Leave him alone? Nothing anyone could do or say would change the terrible truth.

She had never loved her mother-in-law. The woman was a tyrant who had tried to ruin her marriage. But as she pictured the small, frightened figure standing alone in front of a kangaroo court, she could only pity her and weep for her country—and this so-called revolution that had gone terribly awry.

What had happened was unthinkable and so unfair. Her mother-in-law had actually supported Ho Chi Minh! She had bankrolled the *Viet Minh* with thousands, perhaps millions of *dong* and had given her sons to the Communist cause. Then, in the name of the revolution, her neighbors, the people she had lived with her whole life, had turned on her. Overnight, the Vu family, and by implication Phuong, had become the enemy.

Nghia looked at Phuong, who was slumped in the chair, staring blankly into space. "I'm sorry," she said. "I'm so very sorry."

※※※※※

A few weeks later, on March 24, 1955, a daughter was born to Nghia and Phuong. They named her Ngoc Anh, or "precious stone flower," a name whose Chinese characters juxtaposed the flinty toughness of a jade stone with the tender innocence of a blossom. In a way, the name symbolized the yin and yang of their lives: their hard times of deprivation in the north, and their fragile new life of hope in Saigon.

But my name also had the ring of prophecy. I'm not sure my parents meant it that way. But as a child growing up on the streets of war-ravaged Saigon, I would need all the hardness of stone and the innocence of a flower to be able to hear and heed God's song, which was playing in my heart.

PART II

The Call

17

LITTLE NUMBER FOUR

I always hated my nickname, *Be Tu*, "Little Number Four." It never made any sense to me, especially since I was the third child, not the fourth. But in Vietnam, there is no escaping superstition, and in the southern region people lived in fear that jealous gods would steal their firstborn child. In order to fool the gods, parents called their first child "Number Two" instead of "Number One," and the rest of the children fell in line accordingly.

So, I was stuck with *Be Tu* instead of my real name, Ngoc Anh, a lyrical phrase that my parents had taken from an ancient Chinese poem. To make matters worse, I was the only one of my siblings they called by a number name, and that made the moniker rankle even more. Growing up, I was sick of hearing my unglamorous nickname yelled on our street as if I were a servant.

"*Be Tu*, open the gate!" a relative would shout on arrival at our house in Saigon.

"*Be Tu*, time for dinner!" my nanny, *Chi* Huong, would call out.

Everyone in the neighborhood, including the poor folks who lived a hand-to-mouth existence in the lean-to shacks in the alley next to our house on Vo Truong Toan Street, knew me only as *Be Tu*.

But my nickname wasn't the only thing that set me apart in my household. From an early age, I was trouble—not the kind of trouble that brings eternal shame on a family, but rather the sort generated by a rebellious and inquisitive streak, an irrepressible quest for freedom that led me always to break the rules.

Typical was the time my parents put my elder sister, *Chi* Tram, in charge of me and my younger siblings while they were out doing errands. By then, I was about twelve, and there were six of us children in the house. Along with me there were elder sister Tram, elder brother Phong, younger sister Diep, and my two younger brothers Hai and Khanh.

On that particular day, I wanted to visit my aunt, who lived a few blocks away. But my sister refused to let me go. "*Me* doesn't like you to cross that big street!" she said, invoking my mother as a threat.

Undaunted, I headed for the door. Within seconds, *Chi* Tram was on top of me. She grabbed my arm and I pulled back in a furious tug-of-war that left my two younger brothers and younger sister rolling on the floor with laughter.

Chi Tram was so incensed at my insolence that she locked me in the living room. It didn't take long for me to plot my escape. "I have to go to the bathroom," I shouted after a few minutes in confinement.

Reluctantly, *Chi* Tram let me go into the lavatory, where I engineered the next part of my plan. Feigning an "accident," I poured water on the floor and called *Chi* Tram to look through the slats in the door. "See, I told you it was an emergency!" I told her.

With that, she opened the door to clean up the mess, and I darted past her and out the front door. When I returned, I got my usual beating from my father for disobedience. But that was a small price to pay to behave as I liked.

My quest for freedom didn't stop at home. At Le Van Duyet Girls High School, where I was a student from grades six to twelve, I was always looking for ways to escape the drudgery of routine and let my spirit soar, even if it was just for fifteen minutes at recess. Usually during break time, the girls in my class would wander, two by two, around the school courtyard or outside the front gate, holding hands and whispering secrets. Often I chose to wander alone, dreaming of swimming in the ocean somewhere, or flying high in the sky with the birds.

One glorious October day, I found a perfect outlet for my mental meanderings: a small "lake" that had been created just outside the school from a random rocket attack by the *Viet Cong*, as the Communist guerrillas were then called. The rains over the past few weeks had filled the crater to overflowing, and as I watched the sunlight flicker on the water, I couldn't resist the temptation to play out my fantasies.

In the corner of the bicycle rack, I found a huge, discarded cardboard appliance box, and I immediately dragged it over to the water and climbed in. Two sticks became my oars, and before I knew it, I was in a "boat," floating on the ocean.

Bobbing happily in my cardboard boat, I saw a few little fish swimming by, and I reached out my hand and caught one. *How wonderful to be alone at sea!* I thought, imagining myself in a Hemingway novel. Like the fisherman in *The Old Man and the Sea*, which we had just read in school, I visualized myself pitted against the elements, daring to capture something big and bold, risking everything to do the impossible.

I was so caught up in my reveries that the fifteen-minute recess flew by. Suddenly I heard the gong summoning us back to class. I looked up to see my girlfriends running toward the classrooms like a flock of white butterflies, with the long, silky front and back panels of their *ao dai* uniforms fluttering like wings behind them.

No one would dare be late. Vietnamese teachers were so strict that even a minute's delay would have incurred a swift slap on the hand with a wooden ruler.

Desperately I tried to get my boat to shore, but with "oars" that didn't work, I was stuck in the middle of the water going nowhere. I rocked my body back and forth, hoping to generate some forward momentum. But in my haste, I only succeeded in putting my foot through the box, and soon water was seeping in and I began to sink.

"What do you think you're doing?" yelled Mr. Khang, the janitor, who saw me struggling and ran over to the edge of the crater. He didn't appear to be the least bit sympathetic to my plight. I could see his face contorted with anger as he screamed something about not wanting to get wet. "You could drown!" he yelled, obviously torn between soaking himself and saving me.

By then, Mr. Khang had shouted so long and so loud that the teachers were pouring out of their classrooms and were ringing the crater, joining in a chorus of accusations.

"Ngoc Anh! What's the meaning of this?" yelled my mathematics teacher.

"Are you crazy?" cried another.

As for my classmates, they stuck their heads out of the big classroom windows, screaming and laughing with delight at my predicament.

Finally the janitor gave up and waded into the water. He reached for the box and pulled me toward the edge. I emerged, somewhat chagrined yet triumphant, with my white *ao dai* clinging to my body and mud all over my feet.

Immediately, my mathematics teacher hustled me to the principal's office.

"You're expelled for a week," the principal said. "When you come back, bring me a note from your parents acknowledging the punishment."

I never told my parents, of course. Every morning during my expulsion, I would awake in time for school, put on my white *ao dai*, and head straight for the shelter of Grandmother Nhu's house. It was a marvelous holiday with *Ba Ngoai* as I called her. We talked for hours, had nice little lunches, and took naps together. In the afternoons, I headed home as if it were a normal school day.

One week stretched into two, and I suppose I might have stayed at my grandmother's house forever if fate hadn't intervened. As it turned out, my mother ran into the principal at a teachers' conference. When the woman asked where I was now going to school, my mother quickly figured out my scheme.

That afternoon, I was swinging with *Ba Ngoai* in her hammock when we saw a *cyclo*—the pedal-driven rickshaw—drive up in a cloud of dust. "Hide behind the chair," *Ba Ngoai* told me.

I ran behind the big chair in her living room while *Ba Ngoai* continued to swing in the hammock as though nothing had happened.

My mother came charging up the path like a thunder goddess, hell-bent on punishment. "I know *Be Tu* is here," she said to my grandmother. "She must come with me right now!"

"*Be Tu?*" my grandmother said innocently. "You're looking for her?"

My mother knew *Ba Ngoai* was covering for me. "If you don't come out, I'll make you starve for a week!" she yelled through the doorway.

Sheepishly I came out from behind the chair. My mother grabbed my ear and pulled me to the *cyclo* without even giving me a chance to say good-bye to *Ba Ngoai*. As an extra measure of punishment, she made me sit on the footrest of the *cyclo*, where chick-

ens and market purchases were usually kept, so that the world
would know how low I had become. She sat above me on the seat,
berating me nonstop until we got home.

The school eventually reinstated me and, for a while, I tried to
behave. But if I had learned anything from my rebellious adventures at school and at home, it was that I needed my freedom—no
matter what the consequences.

◈◈◈◈◈

My naughtiness would have been laughable except for the reper-
cussions. More often than not, I would get a thrashing from my
father with his hand or a bamboo cane, whatever he had available. Most days, cane marks and bruises covered my body, from
my face to my back to my arms. I had so many welts that when I
was bored I would study the marks just to see the design: two parallel red marks, with a streak in the middle that was whiter than
my own flesh. Over time, the marks progressed from red to purple. Then they disappeared, only to reappear after a new round of
beatings.

No one protected me except my elder brother, Phong. When the
beatings became unbearably harsh, he took the bold step of chal-
lenging my father, an act of insubordination that is unthinkable in
a Vietnamese family. "You are going to kill her!" he would shout at
my father, stepping between me and the cane. For his efforts,
Phong was beaten too.

But no one in the family was pummeled the way I was. *"Tui bui"*
is how my sister Tram described it. "Like dust. You were beaten so
hard you could have turned into a cloud of dust."

Although I was certainly a handful, I have no idea why my father
was so severe with me. Maybe it was because I looked so much like
him, with high cheekbones and a wide mouth that stretched from
ear to ear. Perhaps whatever anger he felt toward himself he leveled
at me. From the time my family evacuated to Saigon, my father was
a shell of a man whose wife supported him by working as an ele-
mentary school teacher and a currency and commodities trader.

Among other things, in her spare time, she watched the shifts in
the foreign money and commodities exchanges and became quite
adept at predicting highs and lows. She seemed to know instinc-

tively whether gold was going up or down, or when to buy or sell dollars or *deutsch marks*.

As for my father, he dabbled at an occasional job but for the most part, he relied on my mother's income just like the rest of us. Usually he hung around the house with nowhere to go and nothing to do but remember in silent agony his glory days in the north. The war had broken my father's spirit. An intelligent, handsome and capable man now became bitterly disappointed with life and sadly disillusioned. I sensed that he constantly wept deep inside.

Although I became the brunt for all my father's troubles and unhappiness, I never let his anger stop me from dreaming—or from doing whatever I pleased, especially around siesta time. Every day, right after lunch on a break from school, I took a siesta with my family. When lunch was over and all the dishes were cleared and taken down to the washing area in the courtyard, my nanny, *Chi* Huong, would bring out a teapot with fresh green tea leaves and boiling hot water. My father loved the ritual of drinking the hot tea and then cleaning his teeth with a toothpick as a prelude to the daily nap.

To me, taking a siesta was a complete waste of time. With my day filled with school, and my evenings crammed with tutoring classes, the lunch break was the only precious time I had for myself. If I had my choice, I'd rather climb the *oi* tree outside our house, or read a book or two. But my parents believed that a nap would help all of us children be smarter when we went back to school in the afternoon. With our minds rested, my parents reasoned, we would pay perfect attention to our teachers, whose wisdom would stick to our brains like glue. And so we went to bed.

I would wait until I was sure everyone was asleep, and then with a book in my hand I would crawl on the floor past my father, who was sleeping on a divan in the next room, and slip out the door. Then I'd climb the *oi* tree and lose myself in my book. More often than not, my father would catch me, and then he would beat me roundly, not only because I had escaped from the siesta, but also because I was spending time reading. To him, it was a waste of money to educate girls. It was my mother who fought for her daughters to be able to study and who made sure that our spiritual education was solid as well.

Despite the risk of punishment, I kept slipping out, again and again. Then one day, in midsummer, my siesta excursions came to an abrupt end. Because it was summertime and beastly hot, my parents took even longer naps, and they expected us children to do the same.

As usual, on that particular day I had no intention of napping. I lay on my bed pretending to sleep, but my mind was spinning with excitement over our new neighbors, whose dog had just had puppies. Just the day before, the woman, Mai, had dropped by for tea at the invitation of my mother and brought her two little children along. Mai and I had hit it off instantly. She was in her mid-thirties and had an easygoing air that I found enormously appealing. She obviously felt the same about me because before she left, she extended an invitation for me to drop by and see the puppies and play with her children.

"Come over anytime," she said. "You're always welcome."

As I lay awake in the still, warm air, I couldn't get her and the puppies out of my mind. *I have to see them*, I thought. *This would be a perfect time.* From the snores in the next room, I could tell that my parents were in such a deep sleep that I might be able to sneak over to the neighbor's house and return to bed before my father even knew I was gone.

Holding my breath, I crept quietly off the bed. Instead of putting on my sandals, I held them in my hands. Then, instead of crawling through my parents' room, I decided to climb out my window and over the low balcony to the street. That way I could avoid going through the kitchen where *Chi* Huong was taking her nap.

I climbed over the balcony and dropped to the ground in front of the house. *So far, so good*, I thought. No one was on the street, except a snack seller who was taking a siesta herself, resting on the front steps of our house in the shade of an overhang.

In only a few minutes I reached my neighbor's yard. As I stood in the shade of the *hoa lai* bush, enveloped by the sweet scent of jasmine blossoms and total quietness, I realized that I had overlooked something important. At that very moment on that sultry summer afternoon, everyone in the entire country of Vietnam was taking a nap—including my neighbor Mai. I didn't dare knock on her door or call out to her, for fear of waking up her and her children. But I didn't want to leave without seeing the puppies.

The puppies must be here somewhere, I thought. *I know Mai won't mind if I play with them quietly for just a few minutes.*

Mai had mentioned that they kept the dogs around the back of the garden, and so without thinking twice, I jumped over the green hedge into the garden. There, across the yard, was the box where the puppies lay sleeping next to their mother. I was so excited, I practically sprinted to the box.

I should have known something was wrong the minute I saw the mother dog baring her fangs and the hair on her back standing on end. Because I had never owned a dog before, I blithely ignored the warnings and reached my hands into the box for a puppy. The mother dog lunged at me and before I knew it, I was on the ground screaming as the dog dug her teeth into my arms and legs and shook me from side to side. Gobs of red flew in the air and splattered all over me, but I had no idea that they came from me. All I could do was keep screaming.

The commotion woke up Mai, who came running toward me with her hair falling around her face and down her back, instead of tied up in the neat bun she had worn when I first met her. Strangely enough, even in the midst of the frenzy, I could see that her face was beautiful. Mai was circling around me, trying desperately to pull the dog away. But the animal was so consumed by her anger that she wouldn't let go of my thigh.

Out of nowhere, a manservant appeared with a broom and started screaming at the dog and beating her. Finally he managed to pull the dog away, and I was free.

Still in a daze, I looked at my arms and legs and realized that the red stuff was blood, my blood. I was covered with it. The vicious attack left me too surprised and frightened to feel any pain, but suddenly I was seized with fear. It wasn't the dog I was afraid of, but my father. *How will I ever be able to sneak back home without his catching me?* I could see the cane now. I could see the fury in his eyes and hear the epithets on his lips. I was terrified. For a little while longer, I had a blissful respite from what I knew was waiting at home. While Mai gently cleaned my wounds and wrapped my arms in bandages, I looked around her house, intrigued by the beautiful surroundings. Light filled her rooms. Books and fresh flowers were everywhere. I yearned to be in such a place with such a friend, but I knew that because of what had just happened, my parents would never allow me to see her again. "Please forgive me for being so stupid," I said. "I must go now."

But Mai insisted that I stay and rest. "You're not strong enough to leave," she said. "Take a nap, and then I will take you home."

After about an hour, I woke up, ready to face the worst. And the worst did happen. Mai walked me home, but the minute my father saw me, he grabbed me and started to strike me before my new friend had a chance to say anything. He didn't stop to inquire about my bandages or to find out what had happened. He just slugged me once, twice—

"Stop! It's not right!" I heard Mai cry. After that, I don't remember much of anything. Maybe I passed out or blocked out the horror, but later, my brothers and sister told me that elder brother Phong had tried to rescue me, only to be beaten himself.

"You want too much freedom," my mother and siblings told me over and over. "You're a bad kid and really ask for it. You need to be tamed." It seemed that even they accepted the idea that my father had a right to dispense such violence.

From that day on during siestas, my father kept me by his side in bed, pinned between him and the wall. I made no more attempts to escape across the floor or out the window—the risks were just too great. In my mind, my father's bed became an island where I was exiled, and my way of escape was to dream great dreams and let my imagination run free. More often than not, I would dream of a place where I knew life must be perfect. It had to be. It was the home of the missionaries I knew in Vietnam. It was America.

❖❖❖❖❖

As the sun rose high above our heads, beating down so hard that even dogs and beggars sought shade to take their noon nap, I lay in the bed next to my father and daydreamed. In the background, the soft clinking noises of *Chi* Huong washing the dishes by the cement rain collector, the distant sound of a dog barking, and my father's regular breathing next to me, became a lullaby that carried me as far away from Saigon as my imagination could carry me.

My father's bed was next to a large window with wooden shutters that were always open to let in the few precious breezes. Beyond the window, behind a brick wall that separated our house from the neighbor's, was a giant milk-fruit tree, a *cay vu sua*. I couldn't actually see the tree trunk, but the tree's generous branches spilled over our property and cast huge shadows on my father's bed.

With my arms under my head, I looked out the window and fixed my eyes on the greenness above me, watching mesmerized as the breeze swayed the branches and shifted images in the leaves. Sometimes in those images I saw perfect profiles of beautiful princesses, fierce dragons, or smiling cats. At other times, when the wind was stronger, the images became the heads of people laughing, or the bodies of two dancers, dipping and swirling with delight.

Mostly, though, I saw images of America, a land of golden streets, abundant food, and infectious laughter. In this country where I imagined myself one day, the people were never touched by sadness. Instead, love filled their lives, along with warmth and friendship, as though God himself had prepared a special place for them—and for me.

My image of America came not from the raucous young soldiers I saw on the streets of Saigon, but from Mr. Titus and the other Mennonite missionaries I met at Vacation Bible School, which I attended summer after summer as a child. I can't remember the lessons we learned or the crafts we made or the songs we sang. But I do remember the love, a love that poured out of these simple, gentle people with such power that as soon as I walked through the gate to their compound, I felt enveloped in joy and peace.

The missionaries may have set the tone for my dreams of America, but it was the Christmas cards they gave us as prizes for memorizing Bible verses that fixed the vision in my mind. My friends and I marveled at each other's pictures: scenes of skaters on frozen ponds, of children opening packages under a sparkling Christmas tree, and of cute dogs tied at the collar with big red bows.

Of all the cards, the one I liked most was a color photograph of a house on a winter night, all covered with sparkling snow. Although the scene seemed very cold, the house beyond the driveway was lit with warmth and cheer. Through the yellow glow of the window, a Christmas tree twinkled with lights and ornaments, beckoning me inside.

To me, the utter vastness of the cold outside the house only accentuated the coziness inside, which seemed to glow with a divinely ordered life that was safe, comfortable, and filled with boundless joy. Like a child yearning for a toy in a toy store, I let my mind run wild with visions of what happiness the house might contain: what foods were being cooked, what games were being played, what books were being read, and what love was being shared by a family who knew only hugs instead of beatings. With all my heart, I prayed that someday that life would be mine.

My dreams were one way to escape the fear—not just of my father, but of the present darkness that engulfed us day and night during the war between the north and the south. In a way, I grew up with the "American war"—the long conflict between North Vietnam and South Vietnam, where we lived. By the time I was a teenager, the internecine bloodshed was as much a part of our lives as our school exams.

From the time I was born, Ngo Dinh Diem maintained a despotic grip on the government. After defeating Emperor Bao Dai in a national referendum in October 1955, he named himself president of a new Republic of Vietnam. From then on, he tried desperately to maintain power as the *Viet Cong* waged a slow and steadily escalating guerrilla war to wrest control of the country.

By 1961, when President John F. Kennedy took office, President Diem was holding the losing hand, with the *Viet Cong* dominating more than two-thirds of the countryside. To keep South Vietnam from falling to the Communists, Kennedy opted to throw the weight of the U.S. military behind President Diem, and soon bases sprouted up and sixteen thousand American soldiers were on hand to support the South Vietnamese army.

Living in Saigon, I knew the war only from random rocket attacks and reports of isolated insurgents throwing grenades in cafés or on the streets. But gradually the streets grew thick with soldiers, and on *Rue Catinat*, where I went with my mother to eat at the Brodard Restaurant, or near the Hotel Rex, the freewheeling young Americans seemed to be everywhere.

Ngo Dinh Diem's assassination in a military coup in 1963, followed by Kennedy's assassination three weeks later, set the stage for President Lyndon Johnson to act. In August 1964, in response to a North Vietnamese attack on U.S. destroyers in the Tonkin Gulf, the American president retaliated by ordering the bombing of

North Vietnamese targets. During that mission, Lt. Everett Alvarez Jr. became the first American pilot to be shot down over North Vietnam. Alvarez was incarcerated for eight years in Hoa Lo prison, the same prison that had once housed my father, Phuong, under the Japanese. Later, U.S. Senator John McCain was confined in the same place, in what became known as the "Hanoi Hilton."

A few days after the incident in the Tonkin Gulf, the U.S. Congress passed the Tonkin Gulf Resolution, which gave President Johnson free rein to wage war on the north. Before long, American planes were bombing the north without provocation. Within a year, the first U.S. Marine combat troops landed in Da Nang and the massive American troop buildup had begun.

By 1968, more than a half million American soldiers were fighting in Vietnam, and with Ho Chi Minh's *Viet Cong* guerrillas ready to ambush or attack without warning, any place could turn deadly, especially at night, when the rockets wailed like bloodthirsty ghosts soaring over our heads in the darkness.

18

"HERE I AM"

The night sky lit up like lightning as the flares of fireworks burst all over the city to celebrate *Tết*. It was January 31, 1968, and the noise from the festive explosions was so loud it was almost deafening. As always at the Vietnamese New Year, my sisters and brothers and I were so excited we could hardly contain ourselves. Hour after hour, we set off strings of firecrackers, sometimes adding huge "cannons" that went off in blasts so powerful I could feel the pressure pushing against me from the force.

Sometime after midnight, I put my very best *ao dai* under my pillow so it would be neatly pressed by morning, and I went to sleep, dreaming of the red envelopes of *li xi* money I'd be receiving the next day as a good-luck token from my parents. Since the first day of the New Year was reserved for elders, I was also eagerly anticipating spending the day with *Ba Ngoai*, Grandmother Nhu.

The next morning I arose before dawn, but the minute I left my room I sensed something was wrong. The house was heavy with a silence I hadn't ever experienced before at *Tết*. Usually *Chi* Huong was bustling around making breakfast, and my parents would already be dressed in their finery, ready for the holiday. But this morning *Chi* Huong was quiet as a mouse, and my parents were still in their cotton pajamas, the same clothes they wore around the house every day.

"Don't put your new clothes on," my mother ordered me and my sisters and brothers. "Wear your regular clothes." My parents kept talking in hushed tones as if a death had occurred in the family.

They were huddled around the radio, listening intently, with their faces illuminated by a tiny oil lamp instead of the electric lamp.

"The Communists are here in Saigon," my mother announced somberly. "I don't know how they could make it here. But they're inside the city right now."

The radio crackled with snippets of news. "Be alert," the announcer said. "There's a twenty-four-hour curfew. Stay in your homes."

Although I was nearly thirteen, I still didn't completely grasp the significance of what was happening. But when I heard the whirring of helicopters overhead and the regular boom of nearby explosions, I slowly began to realize that something in our lives had changed radically.

We had to evacuate from our house the next day after a rocket attack destroyed a neighbor's house a block away. Because we lived in Gia Dinh, on the outskirts of the city, we were more vulnerable to *Viet Cong* incursions. For months, perhaps years, the *Viet Cong* had been digging tunnels as a conduit to the city, and on the night before the 1968 *Tết*, groups of commandos had slipped through them into Saigon under cover of the massive fireworks. Around three in the morning as Saigon slept, the *Viet Cong* stormed the American Embassy, destroyed the central radio station, and threatened the Presidential Palace, leaving the city reeling from the surprise attacks.

As the explosions burst around us, my family jumped into my father's gray Peugeot 203, a huge car that looked like a gangster's, and headed for a friend's house in the center of the city. Our friend owned a three-story house, a rarity in Saigon in those days, and for some reason my mother thought we would be safer there. The only things we had time to take with us were blankets and pillows, the food we had made for *Tết*, and the small cache of gold and diamonds my mother had managed to amass in her currency trading business.

When we arrived at our friend's house, we found three or four families already camped out. The first floor looked like a hospital ward, with sleeping areas lined up for each family. We headed for the second floor, where we found an empty spot, spread out our blankets, and settled in for what turned out to be a three-week sojourn.

If it hadn't been for the explosions bursting randomly outside, I would have said we had a wonderful time. For me, it was like a nonstop party, a sleep-over, with nothing but leisure stretching out in front of us. The women chatted, the children played, the men drank coffee, and the nannies cooked. We ate in shifts to accommodate all the people who had crowded into the house, and we often shared whatever food we had.

I discovered that even more exciting adventures lay beyond our designated living quarters. Ever curious, I couldn't help wandering beyond the second floor to the third floor, which our friend had told us was empty.

One day, I tiptoed upstairs, quietly opened the door to the third-floor suite, and peeked in. There, at the far end of the hallway, I spied a young couple locked in a tight embrace as one lay on top of the other on a divan. I had never witnessed anything like this before and so, more fascinated than embarrassed, I stared wide-eyed for a few moments as they kissed passionately and grappled at each other's clothes. Then, afraid of being discovered, I quickly closed the door and ran down the stairs.

A few days later, the young couple emerged from their solitude to join the rest of the crowd, which by now had swelled to five or six families. I was delighted that I could now scrutinize them more closely. The man was incredibly handsome, with moves like a cat and clothes so elegant he could have stepped out of a 1930s movie. The woman, with her flower-covered minidress and long, straight hair that stretched to her waist, seemed like some sixties Cinderella.

Seeing that I had taken an interest in her, she showed me a photograph of her on a beautiful sandy beach near Da Nang, where she lay stretched out like a model in a bikini and sunglasses. In another picture, she was wearing a body-hugging miniskirt and sandals that revealed her pink-tipped toes.

My mother, of course, didn't want me going near the woman. "She and that man are not married," my mother whispered to me, after hearing the story from her friend. "She's the daughter of a colonel, and she ran off with the man a few days before Tết. If her father knew where she was, he'd shoot her."

The story only intrigued me more, and for the entire three weeks we were at our friend's house, I watched the woman and her movie-star-handsome lover and created romantic scenarios about them in my mind, just to make the time pass.

A few weeks later, my storybook illusions burst like a bubble when I learned that she had become pregnant by her lover—who had ungallantly run off and left her stranded. That wasn't the kind of romance I had dreamed about.

But romantic fantasies weren't the only illusions that those uncertain days in Saigon destroyed. Soon after I heard the truth about the woman on the third floor, I started to awaken to more devastating realities about the war that was exploding around us.

After three weeks of being cooped up in our friend's house, we finally heard a helicopter circling overhead with a loudspeaker, announcing that it was safe to go out. When we left our temporary haven to join others who had fled their homes but were now returning, it seemed at first that nothing in the city had changed. As we headed toward a familiar market along with the others in the swelling crowd, the near-party atmosphere that pervaded the streets buoyed our spirits.

"They're gone!" people said to each other, relieved that the Viet Cong commando attacks appeared to have been isolated incidents.

But something about my mother's attitude was different. For one thing, I couldn't figure out at first why she had decided to take us on a roundabout route to the market. Then several days later, I saw the pictures in the newspaper of what was now being called "the Tết Offensive." The paper was full of photos of buildings blasted apart, and bodies strewn all over the streets. Fortunately, I never saw the full, stark reality of the carnage. By carefully avoiding the streets and neighborhoods that had been destroyed, my mother had managed to shield me from some of the horror that was literally just around the corner.

It wasn't until we had settled back in our house and started watching TV regularly again that I understood what we had just experienced not only in Saigon, but all across the country. With the theme song from the film *Exodus* playing in the background, the TV showed film clip after film clip of the destruction of the ancient capital of Hue. Mothers cried uncontrollably as they identified the bodies of their sons, whom the Viet Cong had dragged out of their houses and shot. The camera showed bodies everywhere: floating like a logjam in canals red with blood; piled up on the side of the road; and in mass graves, where a telltale hand reaching out indicated the victims had been buried alive. Authorities estimated that the *Viet Cong* had slaughtered more than three thousand people in the attacks.

The numerous bodies reminded me of pictures I had seen of the Nazi concentration camps. To make matters worse, because the humid weather caused the bodies to decay quickly, the authorities moved hastily to burn them. At the same time, they put a great deal of pressure on surviving relatives to move with speed to identify the victims so that the disposal procedure could move forward, thus minimizing the public health risk.

Many families had time only to identify their children by their clothing. Then they were allowed to proceed with a hurried burial ceremony. Left unburied, Vietnamese tradition said, the souls would wander from place to place forever, and the mothers would never have peace. Some of the weeping mothers I encountered never found any of their sons' remains.

As I saw the bodies burning, and the smoke curling, and the mothers wailing bitterly, I finally understood the significance of what had taken place. We weren't dealing with just isolated rockets anymore. The ground war had come to the cities, and to Saigon itself, and our future—as a family, and as a nation—was very much in doubt.

Despite my youth, I was shaken by one ongoing, devastating thought: *A terrible thing has happened to us—a disaster that will change our lives forever.*

Later I learned that many of the people killed were professors and students. According to news reports, the *Viet Cong* had entered Hue and had taken over the ancient citadel, expecting the city to welcome them as liberators. Instead, the people shunned the insurgents, and in retaliation the *Viet Cong* wiped out anyone suspected of opposing them. A month later, in a bloody battle, U.S. Marines retook the citadel and liberated the city, but by then the heart of Hue had already been ripped out, and its mothers wept.

The TV images of Hue never left me. From then on, my light girlish fantasies dissolved in the face of questions rooted in deeper, more disturbing realities. Could we survive? *Would* we survive? What about God? Did he really have some plan for us? What did he want of *me*?

"God help us," I prayed. "You are our only hope."

I needed that hope and any confidence that it might bring me. Over the next few years, as I finished high school and entered medical school, the war escalated and fear reigned everywhere, not only in the streets outside, but also in my heart.

❖❖❖❖❖

During those days in Saigon in the late 1960s and the early 1970s, we accepted fear as a beggar accepts poverty or a patient with a terminal illness accepts impending death. Fear was just part of life.

Each night, my sisters and brothers and I approached bedtime with stoic apprehension and more than a vague consciousness of our own mortality. After *Chi* Huong set up the mosquito net, my sister Diep and I climbed into the bed that we shared and drifted off to sleep, comforted in each other's arms. Sometimes we'd make our confessions to one another.

"I had such a good day today," Diep said one night. "But I'm afraid that tomorrow something bad will happen."

"I understand," I answered, hugging her tight in acknowledgment that when morning broke, we might not be alive to see it. That's because as we waited for sleep, we also waited for the shelling. The rockets came just before dawn without fail, launched by *Viet Cong* who had slipped into the outskirts of the city. The rockets had not yet hit our street, but we both knew of areas that bombs had completely destroyed and of people who had been blown apart or burned to death in their sleep.

My male friends who had been spared from death after an attack never failed to boast about the experience, hiding their fear behind a facade of braggadocio. "If you hear this whistling noise, *zee, zee, zee,* you'd better jump into your shelter, because a big rocket is coming your way," said one guy with a swagger.

"If it comes your way, you won't hear a thing," corrected another. "It will be too late and you'll be with Buddha."

"One boy I knew jumped under his bed and was killed anyway," added still another. "His brother got shrapnel in his back and it got infected and turned smelly. It was so gross."

On and on the stories went. But even worse than the stories was the reality, which rocked our house more nights than I can even count.

"*Tu oi Tu!* I'm afraid," Diep said, clinging to me one night after a rocket burst not far from our home. Her sharp nails dug into my thigh or arm, whatever flesh she could reach in the darkness. The house shook, and then dust from the ceiling sprinkled through the mosquito net and settled on our skin, reminding us that death was only a few feet away.

Even more than the rockets, I hated the feeling of despair that hung like a cloud over everyone I knew. But I refused to surrender to the hopelessness. Something inside made me understand instinctively that there was a "peace which passes all understanding" and a reality that was greater than any obstacles the world could put in my path.

"Just go to sleep, Diep," I would tell my sister as she lay trembling after an attack. "If we're hit by a rocket tonight and blown to bits, when we wake up in the morning, we will be in heaven with God."

To me, this wasn't just a platitude meant to comfort my frightened sister. I fervently believed with all my heart what I told her. My determination to cling to God's promise that "if we die, we will be in heaven" became a sweet security that helped Diep and me sleep many nights, and also many years, as the war intensified.

❖❖❖❖❖

But I still had many other questions for God—some that remained unanswered—during those frightening nights. *What will happen to the people who were killed tonight? What will happen to the children who have no homes?* As I asked these questions, I imagined myself as one of these children, walking the empty streets of Saigon at night, feeling utterly abandoned and alone. The next day, I would walk home from school and see them begging in the market or napping on the streets, and my heart would break for them.

"Is your love real?" I asked God. "Show me. Let me see your face." Lying in bed in the darkness, I strained my eyes looking for him. I wanted to see him, to touch him, to have him hold and comfort me. I needed to feel the reality of God's love because what I feared most wasn't death, but a life devoid of his presence. In the deepest reaches of my heart, I knew that without God in creation, life wouldn't make any sense.

Night after night, as I came to God with my questions and petitions, he came to me and let me feel his compassion. Before long, my concerns dissolved into thin ribbons of smoke that curled up toward heaven, leaving me filled with an abiding sense of peace. As the months and years went by, I didn't need any more explanations. I just knew. I felt God's presence. Gradually I began to understand his plan, and my heart became his.

"Let me be your servant," I prayed as I grew into womanhood. "Let me bring your hope, joy, and peace to this dark world. Here I am. Send me."

As I prayed this prayer, a smile would creep onto my lips and I would surrender to a blissful sleep. In my dreams, I saw a light growing brighter and brighter, spreading out for all eternity.

▨▨▨▨▨

I didn't know at this early point, of course, exactly how I would fit into God's plan. But by the time I turned twenty in March 1975, as a second-year medical student at Minh Duc Medical School, an overriding sense of assurance emboldened me. I was certain that the war would not destroy my family. Week by week, the North Vietnamese army was drawing closer to Saigon, and yet even as rumors of a takeover mounted, I never doubted that God would act on our behalf.

During those unsettling days, I would sometimes think back to Hue and those terrible scenes on TV seven years earlier at *Têt*. But soon, the images of dead bodies floating in blood-red canals were covered by another image: the picture of Jesus, sweet and loving and tender. I could almost hear Jesus' words, "My peace I give to you. My peace I leave with you," and I pushed aside the voices of fear that echoed in my mind and kept my eyes fixed on God to redeem us.

I dared to hope for the impossible because I knew that when I committed myself to God wholeheartedly in prayer, he would act. And he did act, in ways I can only marvel at now.

All my hopes, my dreams, my faith, and my determination came together on the day that Saigon was falling in April 1975. Against all the odds, I found myself leading my family over the wall of the American Embassy and to the *may bay*, the flying machine. God had given me the vision of the *may bay*, but he also had put in my heart from a young age such a drive for freedom that I would take any risk to achieve it.

That is why on that fateful day, I, *Be Tu*, "Little Number Four," was able to do the impossible. With a clarity of purpose that could have come only from God, I took charge of my family as my mother, Nghia, had done nearly thirty years before after her father's death, and pointed the way to freedom.

Fear and urgency had severed all my senses and nerve endings, yet I boldly pushed through barbed wire, fought through crowds, slipped through a hidden door, and ran up the ladder to the roof of the American Embassy where the helicopter, my visionary *may bay*, was waiting for us.

I rushed into the chopper, acutely aware that my God had sent us his wings to transport us to a better life, a life where fear could control me no more.

19

FLIGHT TO FREEDOM

The noise of the chopper suddenly changed pitch, and I could feel the floor rumbling beneath me. By now, the bright streaks of bullet tracers, which had appeared like shooting stars outside the windows, had been replaced by total darkness.

I had no idea how long it had been since the helicopter had lifted off from the embassy rooftop in Saigon. But time didn't matter. The only thing that mattered was that we were finally safe in the reassuring hands of the Americans.

Thank God, we're free, I thought as I turned to look at my family sitting around me on the chopper floor. I could feel my little sister's hand in mine, and suddenly I was flooded by feelings of relief, gratefulness, and anticipation as I contemplated the unseen but exciting life that I was sure lay ahead of us. Although I didn't know the future, I did know one thing: I was no longer afraid. My heart was still, and I was waiting eagerly to see what God had in store for me.

The chopper droned along at a steady whir until once again I heard the pitch shift and sensed that we were descending. In the dark, I could see the shiny eyes of my family growing wide with anxiety as if to say, "What is going to happen to us?"

Finally, the chopper bumped against the landing pad and settled to a stop, though the blades kept rotating. I heard clinking noises and then grating sounds as the metal door swung open. It was still dark outside, but as I peered through the doorway, I could see the pale light of morning peeking through the profiles of helmeted soldiers.

"Everybody out!" shouted an American voice.

We all hopped up and one by one stepped out of the chopper.

Bent over with heads down to avoid the whirring blades, we followed the person in front of us as if in a dream. As I put my foot on the ground, I saw long white lines stretching out before me, and I realized we were on some sort of runway.

I felt a strong, fresh wind on my face and heard the steady clap of waves in between the roar of planes and helicopters taking off and landing at the same time. The fresh air, the noises, and the movements were bewildering, but also strangely exhilarating. Though I sensed we had landed on some sort of ship, I still had no definite idea about where we were. But in my heart, I was certain that we were headed for something good.

By now, the wind was blowing so hard that our clothes were flapping like flags against our bodies. In the semidarkness of early dawn, the figures around me appeared flattened and bent, almost surreal, as if in a Dali painting. Clinging close to one another, we hurried behind a soldier who led us to a checkpoint, where two young soldiers were frisking everyone in line. But when my sister and I got to the head of the line, the soldiers did more than just search us—they started groping and fondling us. The silly grins on their faces told the whole story.

As I felt the hands running over my body, something inside me snapped, and for the first time since I had left Saigon I awoke from my state of dreamy optimism. Embarrassed, I recoiled from the soldiers' hands and yanked my sister away from them. Then the two of us sprinted toward my family, leaving the soldiers laughing behind us.

Once we caught up with my parents, we continued in single file through a narrow door and down some stairs until we found ourselves in a long corridor. We went down one corridor, and then another, merging with other people coming from other corridors. The girl in front of me vomited, whether from fear or from the helicopter ride, I don't know. But she kept walking and we kept following, through corridor after corridor, as though we were on some alien spaceship. We had no idea what would come next. Finally, we came to a large mess hall, where a Vietnamese Red Cross worker asked our names. "Do you have any kind of official papers?" the woman asked.

As my mother fumbled for some documents, I glanced around at the people crammed into the room. Their faces looked worried, uncertain, but for some reason that I couldn't explain, I no longer shared their fear. I could feel my body begin to relax in a way I had not sensed in recent memory.

I don't remember how or when we fell asleep, but when I awoke, I found myself lying on a blanket on a concrete floor under the wing of an airplane. Daylight flooded the place, and when my eyes adjusted, I realized we were inside a hangar with a couple of small planes nearby. Other families around us started to wake up as well, and I could see from the looks on their faces that they were as puzzled as we were about where they were and what was happening.

It was still like a dream. Perhaps if I dared wake up completely, I might find myself in the middle of the nightmare in Saigon instead of in the bosom of safety, lying under an American airplane. Just knowing that the sturdy metal plane was above me made me feel so secure, as though the very wings of God were sheltering me.

A few moments later, a blond American soldier wearing a green jumpsuit appeared and walked over to us.

Immediately my parents jerked up from their sitting position, but then they relaxed and sat down as soon as they saw his warm, child-like smile.

"Hi," he said.

"Hi," we all replied in unison.

"Do you like the plane?" he asked.

We all nodded, still shy of saying much in English.

He seemed unusually gentle, not at all like the GIs I had seen in Saigon—or like the two whom my sister and I had encountered the night before. Back in Vietnam, the Americans always seemed to be aggressive, as though they were ready to pick a fight. Or they might be looking for a certain kind of Vietnamese woman. But this guy was incredibly calm and relaxed, so much so that I worked up the courage to ask him what I couldn't wait to find out. "Please, sir," I asked, using my best high school English. "Where are we?"

"We're on the *Midway* aircraft carrier," he replied. "Do you know what that is?"

When I shook my head and said no, he rambled on, gesturing with his hands in the motion of birds flying. Seeing that I didn't understand, he grinned and said, "I'll show you later." Then he motioned for us to follow him.

Like sheep, my family and the other Vietnamese lined up behind him and headed down another long corridor. Suddenly, the delicious smell of buttery foods reached my nose, and I realized we were about to have breakfast. We had not eaten since lunchtime the day before in Saigon, when *Chi* Huong, my beloved nanny, had brought us food as we waited at the American church for a miracle to rescue us.

In the mess hall, lots of families were already ahead of us, sitting at long tables. We walked through a line where we picked up trays, plates, glasses, and utensils. I sensed immediately that the atmosphere was very different from the night before. The urgency, the hurried movements were gone. Instead, people were moving through the line at a leisurely pace, looking around and taking time to think about what foods they wanted.

My younger brothers heaped up their plates with everything in sight: scrambled eggs, bacon, ham, toast, and small pieces of dried food, which we later learned was something known as "cereal." My father hardly took anything, while my mother, my sister, and I made a few cautious choices.

My father chose a table for us, but not before scanning the mess hall as if worried that some *Viet Cong* might have infiltrated. We were so hungry we didn't even look up from our plates until we had tried at least one bite of everything.

The food was rich and plentiful, but it didn't have much taste to it, at least by Vietnamese standards. Back home, because meat was scarce, mothers and nannies marinated small bits of meat in fish sauce and spices to make it stretch along with bowls and bowls of rice. Here was more meat than we had ever seen in one place, but without any flavor.

As soon as we had finished eating, my sister, brothers, and I looked at each other and grinned. We couldn't believe we were eating American food, in some sort of American place—and we couldn't wait for the adventures ahead of us. But my parents weren't smiling. In spite of the food in their stomachs, their faces showed worry, apparently over the prospect of a future they felt powerless to control and events they were unable to foresee. My mother looked especially distraught.

"Mother, we will be going to America," I said, trying to reassure her.

"Wherever we go, it doesn't matter," she said. "I'm worried sick for Phong. I'm afraid he's still stuck in Saigon." Then she started to cry.

I had never seen my mother cry before. She had always been so strong. When I thought of her, the images that came to mind were the stories I had heard about her adventures carrying goods on the monkey bridges when she was a young girl, or supporting our family by exchanging foreign currency on the black market.

At the sight of her tears, I could feel my own chest start to grow tight. Phong, my heroic elder brother who had risked his life to leave California and fly to Saigon in order to rescue us, might be in danger at this very moment. As far as we knew, he had escaped the day before we did, but still, we had no way of confirming this hope.

All at once, it seemed that everyone at the table was seized with fear. I shook my head, trying to convince myself that our new haven wasn't all a lie. "No," I said emphatically. "We have a new life now—we all do. And we will not get dragged back into a hellish way of life again. Phong is all right. I'm sure of it. We will not give in to this fear!"

Right then and there at that table in the American mess hall, I began to pray out loud. "God, please protect my brother. You have brought us out of Egypt. I know that you will not let him or us die in the wilderness."

A few minutes later, as if in answer to my prayer, the young American sailor who had led us to the mess hall reappeared. In his hand, he had a postcard depicting a very large vessel with many military planes parked at one end. On the bottom of the picture were the words "U.S.S. *Midway* Aircraft Carrier." He pointed to the picture, and then made a circle around the room with his arm. "This is the *Midway*," he said, smiling.

He gave the postcard to my sister Diep, who still has it to this day. Then he gave us a salute and walked away. By the time we lost sight of him in the corridor, our hearts were light and we were smiling again.

It was as though God had sent him as a herald of what was to come. From then on, Diep and I prayed for blessings for him and for us and asked that other gracious people like him would cross our paths.

A land of milk and honey *must* await us. I knew it in my bones.

❖❖❖❖❖

Our taste of life in the promised land was short-lived. The very next day, we were lowered from the *Midway* onto a small boat that shuttled us to another ship, which was teeming with Vietnamese.

As soon as the launch drew close to the ship, I could see my mother's anxiety starting to build. Hundreds of Vietnamese pressed together on the deck, hanging over the rails, and not one American was in sight. "Maybe they're taking us back to Saigon," she said fearfully.

I tried to ignore her concerns, but the minute I stepped on deck, I myself could feel the same fear. The *Midway* had seemed open and welcoming, but here I met hostile stares—not from the Americans but from my own countrymen. I shivered as I looked into faces of young and old, faces marked with grief, paranoia, and raw helplessness.

A sailor helped us onto the ship and then grabbed the bundle of blankets we had brought with us from the *Midway* and led us down some stairs to a deck two flights below. There, without saying a word, he flung the bundle onto the floor in an empty corner and left us.

Immediately, my mother set to work staking out our territory. She stretched a blanket out on the floor so close to our neighbor's pallet that the two nearly overlapped. As it turned out, this blanket was to be the home for our entire family for the next ten days.

Eager for information, my mother started plying the neighbors with questions: "Do you know where they are taking us? How long have you been here? Is there enough for everyone to eat?"

Some people had been on the ship for two days; others, for a week or more. But everyone showed signs of strain, and no one seemed to give my mother answers that could satisfy her. Even my brother's announcement that he had found one of my mother's former students—a sixteen-year-old who had escaped from Saigon by tagging along with a neighbor's family—didn't appear to cheer her.

Day after day, I found my spirit sinking along with my mother's. The tight quarters were starting to get to me. To make matters worse, we had no bathroom facilities. I'm not sure how we managed to control ourselves, but—as unbelievable as it may sound—I don't remember any of us going to the bathroom the entire ten days we were on the ship.

We didn't have any "accidents," but others weren't so lucky. With hundreds of people crammed into every square inch of the ship, on days when the sun was hot and the air was still the stench was almost unbearable.

Some days, as an escape, my sister and I would go to the upper deck, where we would lean against the rail and dream of America. But even there my mother's pessimism undercut our dreams. "Who said we would be allowed in America?" my mother said, trying to keep us from being disappointed. "Maybe we'll go to France, or to Germany to be with elder sister Tram."

Wow, I thought. *I'll be like a gypsy, wandering the earth.* The idea appealed to me because it sounded romantic and free.

On other days, my sister and I would take long walks, weaving in and out of groups of people who gathered to swap stories about their fate. One day, I stumbled onto a group of men huddled around a small radio. Their brown faces betrayed such pain I could almost reach out and hold the sadness in my hand. Every day after that, I found myself drawn back to the men to catch snippets of their conversation and try to understand the cause of their great anguish.

It soon became clear that these were South Vietnamese soldiers whom the *Viet Cong* had forced to retreat from their posts as the *Viet Cong* closed in on Saigon. One man had tried to go back to his village only to find his home burned to the ground and his family gone without a trace. "My wife was pregnant, and I'm afraid for her," he told his friends. "The village was like a ghost town. No one was there except some hungry dogs."

"The road to my village was blocked," said another. "I just joined with all the other people fleeing south. There were old men, mothers, and children. Everyone was running like rats, carrying everything they could. I thought heaven must be punishing us."

The stories were pitiful, but even worse was the sense of utter defeat I could see on the young men's faces. Back home they had left wives, children, and elderly parents. Yet there was nothing they could do for them. Racked by guilt, they despaired of hope and felt inadequate to meet the challenges ahead of them.

"How am I going to survive in America?" a wiry young man asked his friend. "I am a farmer."

"You're better off than your family," his buddy answered. "The *Viet Cong* will punish them for having relatives in the army."

Hearing the bitter truth, some of the young men wiped their eyes while others just looked away, staring off into the distance.

As I heard the young men's stories, my soul wept for them and for hundreds like them who were crammed onto every deck. No wonder my spirit had been sinking. The ship didn't just hold refugees; it also carried broken hearts.

Despite the stories of hardship and the heaviness inside me, I fought within myself to keep my eyes fixed on the promises God had written on my heart: "Be strong and of good courage, never be afraid, for the Lord your God is with you wherever you go."

With all the courage I could muster, I climbed the stairs to the ship's control area, hoping to find an American with a sympathetic ear.

I've got to do something, I thought. All around me, people were starving. The eggs and rice the Americans had given us weren't enough to go around, and on top of that, the children on my deck had been suffering from diarrhea for days. None of the Vietnamese seemed willing to take action, and so I decided to take matters into my own hands. To me the risks didn't seem too great. The missionaries at Vacation Bible School had always been open and receptive, why wouldn't these sailors be too?

"What do you want?" demanded a sailor standing at the door of the control room.

"Please, sir," I said sweetly. "Could we please have some extra food? The children are hungry and some got sick from the American food."

The sailor gave me a hard look and then he disappeared into a back room. A few minutes later, he returned with a large brown bag and handed it to me. "Here," he said. "I hope this helps."

"Thank you," I replied. "I promise to share it." With that, I ran down the stairs as fast as I could, ecstatic about my heroic victory. *I did it!* I thought. *Be Tu did it!*

As soon as I reached our blanket, I pulled my mother aside and opened the bag in front of her. Inside were dozens of little packages of crackers.

"How did you get this?" she asked suspiciously.

"I just asked a sailor—and he gave it to me."

"We've got to hide it immediately," said my mother, whose instincts told her to hoard the stuff in case we ran out of food for ourselves.

"No, Me," I said firmly, grabbing the bag from her. "I promised I'd share it." Before she had a chance to change her mind, I turned away and with my sister helping me, I started distributing the crackers, one packet to each family.

It was exhilarating to be doing something useful. With each outstretched hand and happy face, I felt the way Jesus' disciples must have felt as they gave the fishes and loaves to the five thousand. *What a blessing this is,* I thought, smiling to each family as I gave them the crackers. *God is so good.*

Most of the people on deck were munching on their crackers or had already finished by the time I came to the last family, a mother and a little boy who looked to be about five years old. The boy watched eagerly as I reached in the bag for his prize. But my fingers searched in vain for a packet, and I came up empty-handed.

"Where are my crackers?" demanded the mother.

"There are none left," I said. "I'm so sorry."

"Sorry!" the woman shrieked. She looked at her son, whose lower lip was stuck out in a pout, and then she started cursing at me. "Everyone else got one," she said. "Why not me?"

In a flash, my mother was by my side like some avenging angel. "No more," my mother said, staring the woman down.

"How did you get the food?" the woman demanded.

"We paid for it," my mother said, fudging the truth in hopes of dissuading the woman from pestering us any further. With that, my mother grabbed my arm and we headed back to our blanket.

I have to admit that the altercation left me feeling very unsettled. For hours afterwards, I tried to figure out what I might have done differently. I had only been trying to help, yet somehow it had backfired, and a little boy had been left out. But by the time I was ready to bed down for the night, I had put the matter behind me. Tomorrow would be another day, another opportunity. God would set everything right. I was sure of it.

I had just curled up on the blanket and was about to drift off to sleep when I heard the sound of heavy boots running down the stairs. The sound got louder and louder until suddenly I looked up to see the mother of the little boy leading three armed sailors toward our blanket. "There she is!" she shouted, pointing at me as though I were a fugitive.

"Get up," one of the sailors barked as he drew up beside the blanket with the other two. He aimed a rifle straight at my chest. "Come with me."

I was terrified, but I knew better than to put up an argument against three huge, weapon-toting Americans. Desperate for help, I looked at my mother, who seemed to have been struck dumb. I had no choice but to get up immediately and follow the sailors' orders.

By then, the entire deck was astir and every eye was upon me. As I walked meekly behind the sailors through the crowd, I could feel people recoiling as if to distance themselves from me and the cracker incident. What about the food I had given them? A few hours ago, these people had been happy to see me and to take my gifts. Would no one defend me now?

The sailors led me up the steps toward the control room and sat me down on the top step, which was open to the warm night air. The sky was dark and everything was quiet. If it hadn't been for the gentle lapping of waves against the ship, I might have thought I was in the middle of a nightmare instead of a horrible reality.

But it was real, and I was terrified. I could hear my heart thumping so hard I thought it might burst. *What will they do to me?*

"Where did you get the crackers?" asked a sailor, his eyes burning with anger.

"I came up here this afternoon and asked for some food because we were hungry," I replied as calmly as I could.

"Did you pay for them?" he demanded.

"No!" I said insistently.

"Are you sure?" another asked, pressing me for a confession. "The woman reported that you bought it. Any sailor caught taking money will be punished."

The questions were relentless. "Who gave it to you? How much money did you give him?"

I shook my head back and forth. "We have no money to give anyone. We lost everything. The sailor *gave* the food to me." I could hear my voice quivering as I tried to keep my composure. "I didn't do anything bad," I said with a sigh. "I only asked for food for all of us. Is there any crime in that?"

Something in my tone must have touched them because the three sailors put their heads together and began whispering. Then the one in charge said gently, "You can go."

As I rushed down the steps past the sailors, one of them held my arm and then released me. "Don't worry," he said. "Tomorrow we will be on land, and there will be a lot more food for everyone."

I barely heard what he had to say. I was shaking from head to toe, and when I got back to the lower deck, the hostile stares of the Vietnamese only made me feel more agitated. I felt dirty. Ashamed. Like a tainted woman, who was marked for life. All because of a few crackers. The realities of life on American turf weren't as pleasant as I had dreamed.

Suddenly, I felt tired—very tired. When I reached my family, I refused to answer any questions. I just curled up on the blanket and shut my eyes tight, pretending that nothing had happened. But I couldn't help remembering what my sister Diep had said earlier that day when she helped me pass out the crackers. "I had such a good day," she had said, echoing the words she used to repeat to me at night in our bed in Saigon, when the rockets wailed overhead. "But I'm afraid something bad is going to happen."

20

IS THIS AMERICA?

As the sailors had promised, the next day we saw land.

"Are we in America now?" Diep asked my mother.

"I don't know," my mother answered. "It doesn't look like America."

I had no idea what America looked like, but I did know that everyone around me was cheering and laughing as though we had reached the shores of the promised land. Eager to see the great country I had heard so much about, I pushed through the crowd to try to reach the railings.

Off in the distance, I could see some kind of port, but even from far away I could tell that it didn't seem to have the kind of hustle and bustle that I associated with big American cities like New York or Hollywood.

This is just a sleepy place, I thought, not wanting to dash my sister's dreams. *We can't be in America yet.* Deep inside, I sensed that we still had a long journey ahead of us before we reached the freedom I was yearning for. But I also sensed that we were getting closer. Much closer.

I could see that longing for freedom written all over the faces of the Vietnamese who were waiting for us on the dock behind the guard barrier. As we walked down the gangplank, they smiled and waved at us as though we were celebrities on a holiday instead of a ragtag group of smelly refugees.

Even more welcoming were the American nurses, who were so exuberant I felt as if I had encountered a host of angels. The minute we stepped foot on the sandy beach, they ran over to us with big smiles on their faces. "Hello!" they shouted. "Welcome!"

America or not, this place was a paradise, and I loved it already. I felt like soaring with the seagulls that were dipping in and out of the sky overhead, as if they too were joining in my celebration. Somewhere along the way I had lost my shoes, and as my bare feet sank into the fine, soft sand, my toes wiggled with a delicious feeling of liberation.

I wanted to kneel down and kiss the ground like some character I had read about in an American novel. Instead I restrained myself and skipped along with my family as we followed the crowd to a table where juice and water were waiting for us.

"What's the name of this place?" my father asked a Vietnamese man standing nearby. "Are we in America?"

"No," the man said, laughing. "We are in Subic Bay. The Philippines."

"The Philippines?" my father repeated.

My brothers looked at each other in shock. "This isn't America?"

The nurses led us down a long dusty road, and eventually we arrived at a large hall where a Vietnamese volunteer recorded our names and addresses. Someone handed us blankets, towels, some soap, and a number with our new "address." The walls of the hall were covered with sheets of paper listing the names of hundreds of people who had already come through this place ahead of us.

"Ngoc Anh! Ngoc Anh!" I heard someone shouting my name. I turned around to see Phuc, my classmate and lab partner from medical school. He grabbed me by the shoulder. "We are very lucky to have made it," he said. "I've been here four days, and I know every inch of the place. Let me see your number."

I flashed our number, and Phuc immediately led us to a huge tent with twenty or thirty cots lined up on the sand. As soon as we found our assigned area, my brothers jumped on their cots and started giggling.

I suppose you could say that our new lives began that very moment. At least mine did. Whatever had gone before—all the fears, all the burdens, all the feelings of being trapped and toyed with by forces beyond our control—were wiped away, replaced by an overriding sense of possibility.

In this new realm where hope and optimism ran rampant, it was fitting that the very first thing we did, even before eating, was to take a shower. I lined up with my brothers and sister in an orderly line and thought about the kindness of the Americans who had organized these things for us. These people didn't even know us, and yet they were making everything wonderfully easy, giving us a schedule of when to eat and when to take showers, imposing a gentle order that made life simple and calm. It was a striking contrast to the chaos we had just endured.

I stepped into the shower fully clothed, and as the cold water rushed over my body I felt reborn, as if I had been baptized into a new life that was fresh and clean and good. I was Ngoc Anh, a precious stone, a flower. God had given me the gift of life and with his help, I could be anything and do anything that I desired. The old life of fear in Saigon was miles and oceans behind me. A new life of endless beginnings stretched out ahead of me as far as my dreams could take me.

" 'Let me dwell in thy tent forever!' " I prayed, remembering Psalm 61. " 'Oh to be safe under the shelter of thy wings.' Thank you, God."

I emerged from the shower feeling three hundred pounds lighter, with my clothes dripping wet and a big smile on my face. Within an hour in the hot Philippine sun, my clothes were dry. But the smile stayed with me, marred only by a lingering sadness over my aunts and cousins and the thousands of unnamed Vietnamese we had left behind. "Please let them not be afraid," I prayed to God. "Give them the same peace that I have now."

Forever after, that sense of peace was a plumb line, an inner guidepost that would help me gauge the direction and rightness of the choices I was making in my life. Whenever I had that peace, I knew I was on God's wavelength. Whenever I didn't feel right inside, I knew it was God telling me no.

Over the next few weeks, my life seemed to be on fast forward. After a few days at Subic Bay, a plane transferred us to a refugee camp on Wake Island.

"Is this America?" we asked upon arrival at the military base.

It still wasn't America, but to me it seemed like heaven on earth, with endless food, free American movies, games at the beach, and even live entertainment at night by top Vietnamese singers.

For my mother, though, I could tell that these endless days of almost decadent pleasure seemed like a living hell. She was growing more and more anxious about our future, and most of all, about the whereabouts of my elder brother, Phong. Every day she would pay a visit to the large hall to check the list of names of refugees coming through. And every day, her search came up empty. "If the *Viet Cong* catch him, I pray death will come quickly and that he will not suffer," she said in resignation.

I wanted desperately to encourage her and to remind her of my prayers for him, but I was afraid even to discuss the matter with her. Her despair seemed even more powerful than my hope. Whenever I was with her, my emotions were on a roller coaster, with my joy and sadness colliding with each other mercilessly.

So, to keep my mind focused on the assurances God had given me, I tried to stay occupied with the dozens of activities that were provided for us, and by volunteering at the medical clinic.

Our time on Wake Island stretched from days into weeks, but eventually we found ourselves on yet another military plane, heading for yet another unknown destination. This time the flight was long, so long that we even had some real meals on board, instead of just bags of nuts.

But I didn't think anything of it. After so many false expectations, I just drifted off to sleep, certain that wherever we were headed, the military plane would deposit us someplace safe in the arms of the Americans.

I never imagined it would be in Arkansas.

◼◼◼◼

We landed at night and a van immediately shuttled us to our new home, a barracks filled with Vietnamese. It wasn't until I woke up the next morning that I found out where we were.

This is America? I thought as I looked around the spare landscape of the military base at Fort Chaffee, Arkansas. I was a little disappointed. I had expected to see tall buildings, lots of cars, and big, burly Americans. Instead, I saw rows and rows of army barracks and thousands of my countrymen, who were wandering around as aimlessly as they had been on Wake Island.

But something was different about this place, a bigness that smacked of American expansiveness and soon began to feed my spirit. There our family had our own room that we didn't have to share with anyone else. We had access to a telephone, which connected us to the wider world outside the camp gates. Most of all, we had real hope.

At Fort Chaffee, hope wasn't just some vague expectation, but rather a tangible reality that we witnessed daily as one by one, families found sponsors and left the camp to start new lives. We put our names on a list for sponsorship and waited.

Our first personal ray of hope came with a telephone call to California, where we found my brother Phong very much alive and very worried—about *us*. "I was afraid you were dead!" he said. "I called everywhere but couldn't get any answers."

As Phong explained it, the day before we escaped he had run back inside the embassy, where he had managed to spend the night. The next day, he scaled two fortified walls to reach a helicopter, only to be jumped by four U.S. Marines who dragged him outside the embassy again. Just as things were looking hopeless for him, an officer appeared, and Phong flashed his proof of American residency and a marriage certificate. Immediately he was put on a helicopter out of Saigon.

On the phone, he explained to us how for several days after his flight out, he had volunteered as a translator on three different ships, hoping to find our lost family. From there, he had flown to Subic Bay and then to Guam, where he volunteered again and continued to search in vain for our names on a refugee roster. Finally, despairing of ever seeing us again, he flew home to his wife in San Francisco.

Our spirits soared still higher when we got a phone message from a man in Illinois named Mr. Billings. Hearing from him at that point seemed one of those divine coincidences that aren't really coincidences. Just the day before his call, after weeks of waiting in vain for a sponsor, my mother had suggested that the family split up. "We have such a big family, it will be hard for anyone to want to adopt us unless they are millionaires," she said.

"Millionaires—that would be nice!" we joked, but we knew she was probably right. So we divided our family into three groups, one with my father and brothers, another with my mother and sister, and one with me by myself. "*Be Tu* is older and brave enough to go alone," said my mother.

With our new plan in place, we went to the sponsoring office and reapplied. The very next day, we heard from Mr. Billings. "I want to sponsor Ann Vu," he said unequivocally over the phone.

Clearly he had made up his own pronunciation of my name. "It's Anh, like Ein-stein," I said, correcting him.

After speaking with me briefly and finding out about my background as a medical student, he immediately offered to help. "I'll help you go back to medical school, Ann," he said, ignoring what I had told him about the pronunciation of my name. "As soon as you're in Illinois, I'll see that you get into college."

Everything was happening so fast that I felt dizzy. Mr. Billings sounded so nice and sure of himself, and his promise of college and medical school was incredibly seductive. These Americans seemed more kind and generous than I had ever imagined.

After I hung up the phone, a thrill of anticipation went through me and for a moment, any worry I might have had over being separated from my family was pushed aside.

My mother's enthusiasm only underscored my excitement. "It's good that he's willing to put you through medical school," she said, accepting the offer as a *fait accompli*. "Education is the most important thing."

I could see that she was pleased with herself that her plan to separate us appeared to be working. With my offer from a sponsor in hand, the rest of the family was sure to follow close behind. Could I be any happier?

Yet over the next few days, I could tell that something in my spirit was blocked. As wonderful as this opportunity was, I didn't feel that sense of peace, the overwhelming assurance inside that this was the direction I should take. But the deal was done. The paperwork was being processed, and as soon as it was in order, I would be separated from my family and on my way to Illinois—to my new "father," Mr. Billings.

I could feel the smile on my face getting a little bit smaller. But a few days later, that smile brightened once again when my parents got word from my aunt, *Co* Bay, who was a missionary in India, that a church in Illinois had agreed to sponsor the *entire* family.

With great trepidation, I headed for the camp's pay phone to call Mr. Billings and tell him the news. *He's been so kind*, I thought. *I hate to disappoint him.*

21

THE DARK SIDE OF HOPE

W hat do you mean, you have another sponsor?"
Mr. Billings sounded agitated and even a little angry, exactly the reaction I had hoped to avoid. I had been so worried about his response that I had even rehearsed what I would say on the way to the pay phone. More than anything, I didn't want to hurt his feelings.

"I'm so sorry," I said in halting English. "But today we received a letter from my aunt. A church in Illinois, Christ Church in Oak Brook, is willing to sponsor my entire family. My mother asked me to let you know that I'll be going with them. She wanted me to tell you how much we appreciate your kindness."

"But we really want to have you here, Ann," he said insistently. "Are you sure you should go with your family? I'll help you go to medical school. Can the church promise you that?"

I could feel my stomach tightening as I tried to come back with an answer. Maybe he was right. Maybe the church wouldn't help me.

"Churches have expenses of their own," he said, sensing my hesitation. "They can't take care of you like I can.

"Besides," he said, pressing his case. "I've just picked out a medical textbook for you from the library. I'll send it to the camp."

"I'll have to discuss this with my mother," I told him.

"Call me back after you two have talked it over, okay?" he said.

"Okay," I said.

After I hung up the phone, I was torn. Should I grab the chance to be a doctor and bring honor to my parents, even if it wasn't my deepest desire? Or should I take the simple, safe route and follow my heart to Oak Brook with my family?

It didn't take long for me to make up my mind. The thought of flying away from Fort Chaffee and being free to live and pursue my dreams was happiness enough. I didn't need medical school. Thanks to Christ Church, I had my family and the enduring testimony of God's faithfulness. "Thank you, God," I prayed. "Thank you for keeping us together."

A few days later, we received a letter from Christ Church informing us of our departure date and letting us know that a couple named Mr. and Mrs. Kieft would be meeting us at Chicago's O'Hare Airport.

I couldn't believe it was really happening. Chicago. An American "family" to take care of us. It was a dream come true.

My mother immediately set to work, wheeling and dealing with other refugees to trade some of her jewelry for fresh clothes, *ao dai,* and shoes so that we could look presentable. We ended up with two flowery *ao dai,* one for my mother, and one for me. Mine was made of sticky synthetic material with a gold background and red-and-white flowers. I wasn't crazy about it, but it was the best we could find. I also got a pair of platform sandals, and my sister got a blouse.

When my father complained about all the money my mother was wasting on clothes, she put her foot down. "We may be refugees and we may need help, but we have to look respectable," she insisted.

The night before our departure, I was so excited I couldn't sleep. In a few hours, we would be flying to Chicago, where America and all its promise would be at our doorstep. But even as I exulted in our good fortune, I couldn't help but grieve for those we had left behind. As I lay on my cot in the darkness, the high-pitched hum of the cicadas outside the barracks' window reminded me of Vietnam and the song of the crickets that came just before the rains.

My mind flooded with images of my aunts, cousins, nanny, and friends. In my dreams, I saw them running scared through the streets of Saigon, and my body tightened up as I felt their fear.

For the past few months, ever since we had landed in Subic Bay, I had been totally at peace. But now, on the eve of my greatest opportunity, the fear returned. I was overcome with grief, not just for my loved ones, but for the children of American GIs and ladies of the night who had been left behind. Why God put them on my heart, I don't really know. But as I lay on my cot in the darkness, I wept for them and prayed. "Please, God, protect all your children who are suffering. Free them from fear, and give them hope and peace that you will come to save them."

With my spirit calmed, I fell asleep, dreaming of that glorious new world: Chicago.

◼◼◼◼◼

"I hope Chicago is more interesting than this," said my brother Khanh, pressing his nose against the window of the bus that was taking us from Fort Chaffee to the airport. After three months of being cooped up in the refugee camp, we were getting our first taste of what America was like outside the gates, and so far the picture wasn't too compelling. I saw nothing but field after field of farmland, bisected by miles of almost deserted highway.

"Look! Look!" One of the Vietnamese men traveling with us pointed to a billboard emblazoned with a picture of a short-legged dog, whose long body was drawn to look like a sausage.

"Eat hot dogs!" the billboard commanded.

"They eat dogs in this country too," said the man happily. "I can't wait to eat some good Vietnamese food." Then he and his friends laughed with relief, confident that America wasn't so different after all.

At the airport, the soldier who drove our bus got us boarding passes and took us to the gate. Then a pretty young woman came toward us with a big smile on her face and gestured for us to follow her through a door. We dutifully walked behind her through the jet-way and onto the plane, where she ushered us to our seats. Once we were settled in, she turned around and left. We were completely on our own.

I felt incredibly insecure. More and more people, mostly Americans, were taking seats all around us. Now we really were in America. I couldn't stop staring at the Americans, who were also looking curiously at me. I was feeling more than a little self-conscious. *How strange we must look*, I thought. I looked down at my shiny gold *ao dai* and realized that it screamed for attention.

Right then and there, I started dreaming about what I would do to fit in. I would look for a college. I would make many friends. I would dress like them.

"Did you see that lady with the bare back?" my sister whispered to me.

I looked over at my brothers to see if they had caught a glimpse of her. They had. Their cheeks were red and their eyes were turned toward the ceiling as if they hadn't seen a thing.

"I would never wear that!" I said indignantly. Little did I know that a year later I would also be wearing a halter top and not giving it a second thought.

⬧⬧⬧⬧⬧

"Ladies and gentlemen, welcome to Chicago." The sweet voice of the flight attendant over the loudspeaker sounded like heavenly music.

I was here! I was in Chicago of America! Quickly we followed the passengers out of the plane to the main concourse, where the noise and the crowds were so bewildering we didn't know what to do. Everyone around us was so big and tall we walked right past a man holding a sign that said "Vu." Even if we had seen him, we might not have stopped, since we were used to calling people by first rather than last names.

"Vu! Vu!" We turned to see a man with a sign calling out to us as he and a lady with two young girls ran toward us.

"Are you Mr. and Mrs. Vu?" he asked my parents. He had a huge smile on his face and kept speaking rapidly.

"What is he saying?" we asked one another. All we could do was stare at him.

The beautiful lady stepped closer and spoke more slowly. "We are from Christ Church of Oak Brook," she said.

"Ah, Christ Church," I said. We were so relieved we smiled big smiles and nodded as if our necks were made of springs.

The lady proceeded to hug us. We cringed, especially my father and brothers, since Vietnamese aren't accustomed to hugs, particularly among strangers.

"I am Barbara Kieft, this is my husband, John Kieft, and these are our daughters Anne and Kathy," the woman said.

"Kieft," we all repeated. Again, we smiled big smiles and bobbed our heads up and down. I felt so lucky that these nice people were responsible for us. By now, any lingering thoughts I might have had about Mr. Billings and his promise of medical school had completely disappeared.

"Such a beautiful family!" I whispered to my sister Diep. The Kiefts had the bluest eyes I had ever seen. Mrs. Kieft looked like a movie star, with stunning blue eye makeup and frosty pink lipstick. The girls had fine blond hair and adorable smiles. As for Mr. Kieft, he towered over us, yet he was so warm and caring I felt an instant sense of security.

With Mr. Kieft leading the way, we made our way through the busy airport to the huge parking lot, where I saw what seemed like millions of cars arranged in an orderly fashion.

This is America! I thought, marveling at what was in front of me. It was just as I had always thought: so overwhelmingly big, so clean, so new, so modern, and so full of life.

Once we got on the highway, I grew dizzy watching all the expressways crisscrossing each other. I could never have imagined so many cars with so many colors and shapes, and even in the fast-moving cars, I could see that everyone looked sharp and self-important.

"Anyone hungry?" Mrs. Kieft turned around in the front seat to ask us.

I translated for my family. We all nodded.

"Let's go to McDonald's," Mr. Kieft said.

His daughters squealed with delight. "Yeah!"

"Americans love this restaurant," Mrs. Kieft explained.

"See there," said Anne, pointing out the window. "That golden arch is the sign of McDonald's."

We pulled into the parking lot and piled out of the car. The first thing that hit me was the delicious smell of meat being grilled, and I felt as though I were already in paradise. Inside, we let Mrs. Kieft do the ordering, and before long Mr. Kieft left the table and came back with a tray piled with Quarter Pounders and something called French fries. Even though Saigon had many French influences, we had never run into anything quite like this before. Not wanting to make any mistakes, we let the Kiefts start eating first.

"Notice that the Americans don't use chopsticks or any other utensils," my father marveled.

We watched Anne and Kathy squirt some kind of red paste on their French fries, and then the rest of us kids followed suit.

"Look at all this meat—just for one meal!" my mother said, sounding annoyed. "I could make three meals out of this."

"*Be Tu,*" my father said, "could you see if they have any fish sauce or soy sauce? The meat is not seasoned."

"What do you need?" asked Mrs. Kieft solicitously.

When I told her, the entire Kieft family burst out laughing. "I'm sorry, but we don't use fish sauce or soy sauce. Can your father use some salt?" Mrs. Kieft said.

I regret to say that neither of my parents seemed to enjoy the meal. From their comments, I realized that they were preoccupied as they compared the extravagances of America with the scarcity of things back home. Clearly it would take time for them to adjust.

But for my brothers and sister and me, the transition had already begun, and we immediately warmed to the new American names the Kiefts christened us with: I became Ann, my sister became Debbie, and my brothers became Mark and Kenneth.

As we stood up to leave, Mr. Kieft noticed us looking curiously at the change he had left on his tray. He passed out a coin to each of us. "As a souvenir," he said. By the time he got to me, there were no coins left, and so he handed me a dollar bill. We admired the shiny coins, but as I looked at the dollar bill, I saw a phrase that caught my eye: "In God We Trust."

"Look!" I said to my siblings, marveling at the fact that Americans honored God even on their money. "No wonder God has blessed Americans so richly."

We left McDonald's feeling very rich indeed, not just for the food in our stomachs or the money in our hands, but for the sense of peace and freedom we now felt, which were the most precious blessings of all.

Later that night, after the Kiefts had left us in our new "home," a second-floor apartment that a member of the church had donated, I snuggled in my bed, letting the coziness of the place consume me. Feeling totally safe and protected, I drifted off to sleep.

I had been sound asleep for an hour or more when a loud rumbling noise jolted me awake. It sounded like something big and terrifying was coming right toward us. Was it a fighter plane, flying low? A rocket attack?

I bolted out of bed and ran to the window. As soon as I saw the bright white streetlights and the other apartment building across the courtyard, I remembered where I was. I wasn't in Saigon anymore; I was in our new home in La Grange, Illinois.

As my ears attuned to the new surroundings, I realized that the noise I had heard was just a train. I sat very still, listening to the rumble of the train on the track and letting the gentle rhythm soothe and comfort me. War was very far away, and there was nothing to fear. *Nothing at all.*

❖❖❖❖❖

The next morning, I had been up for only a few minutes when I heard a knock at the door. "It must be Mrs. Kieft," I said, running to the door. "She promised to take us grocery shopping." I opened the door to find a tall, skinny man I had never seen before.

"Are you Ann?" he asked, smiling broadly.

"Yes," I answered, surprised that he knew my American name.

"I'm Mr. Billings."

"Mr. Billings?" I said, puzzled. I shot a glance at my mother, who looked extremely worried. Before I had a chance to figure out what to do next, I heard the thump of footsteps coming up the stairs to our floor. *It's the Kiefts*, I thought. *Thank God! They'll know what to do.*

Mr. Kieft came up to the door, where Mr. Billings was still waiting to be invited in, and gave us a nod. "You have visitors already?" Mr. Kieft said warmly. With that, he introduced himself to Mr. Billings, and the two Americans came inside and took a seat with my parents in our tiny living room.

My sister and brothers and I slipped into the kitchen to prepare tea for our guests, leaving the men under the watchful eye of my mother. While the tea was brewing, we strained our ears to hear what was going on. From what I could tell, Mr. Billings was trying to explain to Mr. Kieft why he had come.

"I had offered to sponsor Ann and send her to medical school," Mr. Billings said matter-of-factly. "I just wanted to let her know the offer still stands."

Even though I didn't understand everything Mr. Billings was saying, something put me on my guard. I found it odd that he had somehow managed to track us down, and I couldn't understand why he would go to all this trouble to pay for medical school for someone he didn't know. It just didn't make sense. But even more unsettling was the thought that I might have to leave. I had already grown extremely fond of the Kiefts, and I certainly couldn't bear to leave my family. *Why is he really here?* I asked myself.

I put the tea on a tray and set it on the table in front of Mr. Billings and Mr. Kieft.

"This is for you, Ann," said Mr. Billings, pulling out a medical text and laying it on the table. "I checked it out of the library, and you can keep it for several weeks."

"Thank you," I said, flushing in embarrassment. Again, I looked at my mother, searching her face for a clue for what to do. My sister Diep rushed over and clung to my arm, as if she feared we would be separated that very day.

Mr. Billings and Mr. Kieft kept talking so fast I couldn't catch the drift of their conversation. But I could hear the tone shift, and before long they raised their voices and were practically shouting at one another.

Mr. Kieft motioned for Mr. Billings to go outside, and when the door closed behind them, we could hear some more shouting and then some scuffling of feet. The next thing we heard was the sound of heavy footsteps running down the stairs.

A few minutes later, Mr. Kieft appeared. He looked a little strained, but he was smiling. "Don't worry," he said. "It's all settled. I think you should all stay together. The church wants to take care of you."

We were all thankful that the decision had been taken out of our hands. But no one was more grateful than I. Although I didn't know it then, Mr. Kieft's intervention was a turning point in my life, an act of divine providence that was to shape the direction of my future in ways I could never have predicted.

At the time, though, I was simply relieved to be rid of Mr. Billings and the whole peculiar business and to start my new American life. By the next day, I had put the episode behind me.

With my family and the Kiefts by my side, I felt more at peace. *I am safe,* I thought. But now something in the back of my mind made me question my sense of security about America.

The next few months were like a whirlwind as the Kiefts jumped in to help us get settled. First Mrs. Kieft enrolled my sister and youngest brother in the local high school.

Then she ferried us to the church's English classes at night and helped us find jobs. Soon other people in the church pitched in to help, and before long we were surrounded by a circle of new friends, whose kindness and energy never seemed to stop.

It wasn't long before we all had jobs. My sister and I baby-sat for other families and earned real American dollars, which we turned over to my parents. A few months later, my father found work in an Elgin watch factory, my brother Mark worked for a moving company, and I got a job in the cafeteria at Hinsdale Hospital.

To make things easier for us, Mrs. Kieft found us a townhouse in nearby Western Springs, which was near the train station and also within walking distance of a quaint shopping center. One day, just before we moved in, I discovered her down on her knees, with her hair tied back in a scarf, scrubbing the floor to get the place ready for us. But she did even more. Since we didn't have a car for those first few months in Illinois, she drove us everywhere, along with taking her own children back and forth to school.

Another woman befriended my mother and taught her American cooking. Still another, a nurse, bought bicycles for Diep and Khanh to ride to school. She even took them to a bicycle shop and let them pick out what they liked.

These new friends showed us a very different side of Americans than we had ever seen before, with the exception of the missionaries at Vacation Bible School. The movies we had watched and the books we had read projected an image of Americans as completely materialistic, self-absorbed, and spoiled. But these people from Christ Church seemed different. They might have had abundant resources and their own family commitments, but they willingly included us in their lives and shared what they had.

These people didn't appear to be spoiled at all by their material possessions. They merely seemed to be enjoying their lives and the gifts God had given them. Was that so wrong?

As I watched these Americans up close, enjoying the fruits of their freedom, I gained a new respect for them and their way of life. But it was the women who impressed me the most. Whether they were on their hands and knees scrubbing a floor or in their Sunday best, American women always seemed so "put together." I could see from the way they carried themselves that being a woman was special, and that they thought themselves worthy to be respected and well treated by men. Even more important, I learned from watching them that, as a young woman, I had all the right in the world to dream big dreams and be whatever I wanted to be.

But for the time being, my dreams of going to college and having a profession would have to wait. I had a job to do, as a kitchen worker in the hospital cafeteria, and I had little time to spare for studying or dreaming.

Every day I caught an extra-early train in order to get to my shift on time. As soon as I arrived at work, I stood at my assigned station by the conveyor belt and set up trays for breakfast. One by one, trays would come by my station, and I would put the food on the tray according to the order listed on the patient's menu. After breakfast was over, I took the dirty trays from another moving belt, scraped the plates, and popped the dishes into the dishwasher.

At first I enjoyed my job, but gradually the hot steam from the giant dishwasher and the strange, unpleasant smell of old Jell-O, prune juice, scrambled eggs, and other leftovers started to get to me. I came home each day smelling like the kitchen.

But it wasn't the hard work that bothered me. What I craved most was companionship. During lunch, I tried my best to make friends with my fellow cafeteria workers, but they didn't seem interested. I couldn't relate to what they were talking about, and I hated their crude jokes. As the weeks wore on, I got more and more depressed, feeling that I would be stuck forever in a dead-end job and that my hopes of college were fast fading from my grasp.

It wasn't until I gave up eating with the kitchen crew and started volunteering to help the cooks during lunch that I got a new infusion of energy. The two African-American cooks, Mary, who oversaw special diets, and Mrs. Ritchie, the salad lady, immediately took me under their wings. Mary even offered to let me stay in her apartment so I could avoid waiting two hours for a train after work. But even more important, she gave me a pep talk about college. "Honey, you need an education," she said. "Get yourself to college as soon as you can."

Mrs. Kieft must have heard Mary's message because one day she dropped by our house, picked me up in her wood-paneled station wagon, and took me to a small college I had never heard of.

"What's its name?" I asked.

"Wheaton College," she said.

"Is it a good school?" I asked, thinking of Yale or Harvard, schools I had heard about in Vietnam.

"Yes," she said. "It's an excellent Christian college."

I didn't quite believe her, since I had never heard of the school, but as I looked around the campus I immediately felt drawn in by its warm spirit. The place was small, yet pretty and comfortable, with charming old buildings dotting its well-kept grounds. Young people were everywhere, greeting each other on their way to classes. They seemed friendly and approachable. A few even walked past us and said hello.

All of a sudden, I realized how much I missed being in the company of people my age and how desperately I wanted to go to school. Without any hesitation, I told Mrs. Kieft, "This is where I want to go."

Mrs. Kieft was delighted, but my parents dismissed the idea. They had never heard of Wheaton, and on their meager salaries, the costs seemed beyond their reach. Since they had never borrowed money in their lives, the idea of my taking out a student loan was unthinkable. They relented only when Mrs. Kieft assured them that along with taking out a loan, I could apply for a scholarship.

In September 1976, barely a year and a half after escaping from Vietnam, I entered Wheaton College. My room was in Elliot, a girls' dorm named after a martyred missionary, Jim Elliot, and I immediately made friends with everybody up and down the building. From the outset, my classmates called me "Anh." Even though I was in a new country, at school I was able to be completely myself.

I was in my element. I was so happy I even sang in the shower. The girls on my floor shared a big bathroom with five or ten shower stalls, and I kept forgetting that others were in the bathroom when I showered. Every morning I would stand in the shower stall and shamelessly belt out a song in Vietnamese or English. I even made some up. I forgot how awful my voice was. One of my brothers once told me I sounded like a broken muffler.

"How can you stand being that happy in the morning?" one of my dorm friends asked me one day.

"I'm sorry," I said. "I'll try to control myself." But I couldn't do it. I was so overjoyed at my life as a college student that my heart just couldn't keep still.

What more could I want out of life? I had everything. There was even a Mission Barrel in the basement of the science building that supplied all my clothes. That was where I found the halter top that I had no problem wearing. The first time I saw the mountains of clothes the students gave away to the Mission Barrel, I went crazy choosing my wardrobe. I picked whatever I liked, whether the clothes were too big or the colors clashed painfully. I'm afraid this kaleidoscopic sense of fashion has followed me to this day.

If my clothes clashed, my room was even more of a disaster, with my new clothes strewn all over the floor. I had never owned so much before, and I had no sense of organization. More than once, my friend and classmate, Linda, said with a sigh, "I'll have to tidy up your room for you." Reluctantly I solved the problem by washing the clothes and donating most of them back to the Mission Barrel.

For weeks at Wheaton, I lived like a songbird, luxuriating in a single room filled with sunlight on the top floor of Elliot. Every morning, the "bird" woke up with a new tune in her head. She flew, she danced, she saw goodness in strangers and friends. She fell in love with everything that crossed her path and believed that life was a garden of roses without thorns. Then, one day in late fall, a chill settled over the rose garden.

I had just returned to my dorm from the dining hall with my friend Nancy, who was legally blind, when I heard the phone ringing in my room at the other end of the floor. "Good-bye, Nancy," I said, sprinting down the hall. "I'd better get the phone."

I burst into my room, lunged across the bed, and picked up the phone on the other side. "Hello," I answered. "*Be Tu!*" said my mother. From the urgency in her voice, I immediately sensed trouble.

"Mr. Billings just called and demanded to see you. I made something up about your working at the hospital with Mrs. Ritchie. Please be careful. He sounded angry. If you see him, try to hide."

I could tell that my mother had gone into her survival mode. Since we didn't yet know about our rights in this country, we had to rely on our instincts to get by. More than anyone, my mother played the game like a veteran.

"I don't know what he's up to," my mother cautioned. "But I sense danger. Be careful."

"Yes, Me," I said. "I'll be careful."

I hung up the phone, but before I had time to think about the news my mother had delivered, the phone rang again. It rang and rang, and for a few seconds I just watched it, wondering what evil lurked inside.

Suddenly, my once-sunny little room seemed huge and cold, and the darkness outside my window loomed pitch-black and forbidding.

The phone stopped for a few minutes. Then it started ringing again. *Maybe Me has something else to tell me,* I thought. I grabbed the phone and held my breath, listening intently.

"Annie! Annie! Are you there?" The voice on the other end sounded as worried as my mother's had been.

"Mrs. Ritchie!" I answered. "I am so happy to hear your voice."

"Listen, Annie, and listen carefully," she said. "An American man called and asked for you. I told him you were at college. Now I'm very worried that I said the wrong thing. He sounded angry and drunk. Please be careful."

"Did he tell you what he wanted from me?" I asked, hoping to solve the mystery.

"No, but I think you should call the police."

The police. This sounded too serious. I remembered the police in Vietnam, soldiers with guns and iron faces, whose very presence invited dread instead of hope for any kind of assistance. How could I possibly call the police?

"I'll be careful," I said, trying to reassure her. "Don't worry." I hung up the phone and sat on my bed, bewildered. Then I heard a knock on the door. I froze, terrified that Mr. Billings had found me.

The knock came again, this time, more insistently: *tap, tap . . . tap, tap.* "Are you sleeping already?" I heard a girl's familiar voice.

"Nancy!" I said. I jumped up and opened the door. I pulled Nancy into the room and locked the door behind us.

"What's going on?" she asked. She pressed her eyes within an inch of my face to be able to see me. "You're white as a sheet."

I told her about the calls from my mother and Mrs. Ritchie, but like me, she seemed skeptical. The whole story sounded like something out of a Charles Bronson movie, and on one level it was hard to take it seriously.

"Tomorrow you'll go to classes with me," Nancy said, clutching my arm. "Then we'll walk back to the dorm together. I'll protect you."

I had to laugh to myself. If my blind friend wasn't afraid, why should I be?

The next morning, I sang in the shower as usual and afterwards Nancy, faithful as ever, showed up at my room to walk me to the dining hall. As we walked hand in hand, giggling and chattering away, I quickly forgot about Mr. Billings and the warnings of the night before.

After breakfast, Nancy left for class and I headed to the north side of the dining hall where friends were waiting for our weekly Bible study. "Hi, everybody!" I said cheerfully. I walked over to the big window to take a seat in a nearby chair when my heart stopped. Outside the window, where the long queue of students waiting for breakfast spilled out onto the sidewalk, I could see Mr. Billings walking up and down like a gestapo agent, scrutinizing every face in line. As he looked from one face to the next, his face grew contorted with anger.

With reflexes honed during years of war in Vietnam, I dove under the table, instinctively seeking cover.

"Anh, what are you doing?" one of my friends asked.

I whispered to them what was happening, and suddenly eight pairs of feet circled the table as my friends huddled together and started praying over me. They prayed and they prayed. And then they prayed some more.

By the time they were finished, I was filled with an overwhelming sense of assurance, and Mr. Billings was nowhere in sight. I never saw him or heard of him again until nearly twenty years later, when I visited the Kiefts in their new home out west.

As the story goes, sometime during the 1980s, the police in Illinois arrested a ring of prostitutes in a Chicago suburb. The men running the ring—who reportedly included Mr. Billings—had sponsored or adopted Vietnamese refugees and forced them to work as virtual slaves for years.

"Ann, you are very lucky, " said Mr. Kieft. "Do you remember how I had to muscle him out of your apartment the day after you arrived? We almost got into a fistfight."

I wasn't lucky. I was blessed by a Lord who had sent his angels to protect me. "He will give his angels charge of you to guard you in all your ways," the psalmist wrote, and I had experienced this promise as an extraordinary reality.

I had been guarded. Protected. It was a reason to rejoice. But still, I couldn't help feeling sad. Even in America, in this wonderful country, among the kindest people, raw evil still existed. It was hidden just beneath the surface, and Mr. Billings was one tangible symbol.

Because of Mr. Billings, I had lost some of my innocence and naiveté. But I never lost my song. Since that day, the little songbird hasn't stopped singing, because I know the power of God's all-encompassing love, which writes a new song in my heart with each new day.

Back at Wheaton College, as the late fall snow was descending on the campus, God was writing me a different kind of love song, one that would echo across oceans and memories to bring me the man of my teenaged dreams.

22

STRANGE HARMONIES

I couldn't drag myself out of bed. Outside of my dorm window, it was still dark and cold when I heard the chapel bell start to ring. With each stroke, I murmured: *One, two, three, four, five, six, seven. Seven o'clock!*

I jumped out of bed. My chemistry class would be starting in a half hour, and I had to take a shower and have breakfast. Fumbling through a pile of clothes on the floor of my closet, I grabbed a towel and raced for the bathroom. A tune was already running through my head: "What If You Fall in Love Again?" by the Carpenters. It was a rather silly song, but it stuck in my brain, and I started singing it at the top of my lungs in the steamy shower. Thank God for hot water!

My hair was still wet as I rushed out of the dorm to get to the dining hall in time for breakfast. It was so cold my hair was starting to freeze, and I could feel the droplets of water on my neck turning to icicles.

Why was I always late? I envied the girls on my floor who seemed to be able to obey the sound of the alarm clock. They were the kind who always had their clothes laid out on their beds the night before, and who stood in the communal bathroom with time to kill, calmly putting on their makeup. They never seemed to have to tear out of the dorm like I did.

As the crisp November air hit my nostrils, I was thankful for the big puffy coat I had found in the Mission Barrel. At first, I hadn't liked it because it made me look like a huge orange marshmallow. But now I appreciated its downy warmth, and I dug my hands deep into its pockets and hurried up to the top of the hill where a hot breakfast and good friends were waiting.

A line had already formed in the dining hall, but it was moving quickly. I skipped the cold cereal, which to my Vietnamese palate always tasted like sugar-coated, grated cardboard, and piled hot eggs and bacon on my plate. Then I walked over to the rack of glasses. I was just about to grab an orange juice glass when I saw him.

My heart started to beat faster. I had seen him around campus every now and then, and each time I couldn't get him out of my mind. With his long wavy hair draped over his shoulders and a big cross earring dangling from his left ear, he stuck out from everyone else on the conservative Wheaton campus. Something was strangely compelling about his radical style. His serene manner and gentle eyes touched my spirit. More than anything, I wanted to get to know him.

But this morning, with chemistry class looming before me, I couldn't take time for any introductions. Flopping down at a table next to my friends, I gulped my breakfast and then, with scrambled eggs still in my mouth, I hurriedly said good-bye.

I dreaded my classes. Since I was a pre-med major, my morning was filled with chemistry and biology, subjects that had once been my strong suits in Vietnam. But with my English still shaky, the sciences had become a nightmare. My chemistry teacher spoke in an Asian accent that was impossible to understand. As for biology, I could understand the teacher, but the terminology was over my head, and the student tutor who had been assigned to me spoke English with a heavy African accent. It didn't take long for me to realize that as an aspiring doctor, I was doomed.

My salvation was my friends, a circle of science and English majors from across America and all over the globe. They were young and fun, and although they were totally ignorant of the realities of my life, they loved me and accepted me as though I were one of them instead of as a refugee from some distant planet. It was obvious to me from everything they did and said that they were serious about their beliefs, and that they were trying to model their lives on Jesus.

One afternoon when the weather turned unusually warm for early November, we all congregated on the steps of the Memorial Student Center with dozens of other students craving the sun.

"Look—the homosexual!" A girl I didn't know whispered so loudly we all turned our heads to see who she was talking about.

It was the mystery man with the flowing hair and earring. "What's a homosexual?" I asked.

"Shhh, not so loud," someone said.

"It's very bad," said another girl. "You don't want to know."

Their discomfort made me even more curious, and I looked at him more closely. The way they talked about him, it sounded as though he were stricken with a contagious illness. But he didn't look sick. In fact, to me he looked incredibly dashing, as though he had stepped out of the pages of *The Three Musketeers*, one of my favorite novels. With his long brown hair flowing in the breeze and his rakish handlebar moustache and goatee, he cut a swashbuckling figure. His clothes—a billowy shirt with beautiful lace at the collar and cuffs, atop flared pants and boots—only accentuated his intrigue. From the looks of it, he even had red fingernail polish on one hand.

The rest of the students tried desperately to conceal their gawking, but I couldn't keep my eyes off him. This flamboyant character truly impressed me. He seemed to be a real adventurer, a man who dared to be himself no matter how outrageous his behavior appeared.

I recognized him instantly as a potential soul mate. As I watched, the independent young woman inside me—who for years had suppressed her true spirit in an attempt to be a "proper" Vietnamese young lady—felt gripped by overwhelming desire. Like this daring young man, I wanted to break out of my cage of conformity and soar to the heights of personal freedom. Just the sight of him sent me into an intense reverie that forced me to reexamine who I really was, and what I wanted out of life.

◆◆◆◆◆

All my life, I had felt boxed in by the pressure to conform, and I had lost a little of myself each day because of it. In Vietnam, my daily life had been ruled by fears rooted in an ancient culture that was steeped in superstition. According to Vietnamese thinking, the world was an incredibly dangerous and cruel place. The only way to escape the danger and ensure peace and security was to live strictly within the bounds of tradition. Anything that didn't fit the mold—any pastime, or friend, or aspiration that didn't conform to a rigid notion of right and wrong—was anathema.

Although both my parents professed a belief in God, they were also captive to these ancient fears, which they had passed down to us as an inheritance that dominated our lives. Whatever understanding they might have had of God's mercy and grace—a grace that allows for differences, mistakes, and the forgiveness of sin—never reached our ears. Instead, what they communicated to me most of all during my childhood was fear. This fear was a kind of parasite that thrived in the destruction of all good things, especially relationships.

In these pensive moments I recalled my friendship with my Saigon classmate Phu, who was so beautiful that all the boys flocked around her and wrote her love letters. Phu had long flat hair parted in the middle, and when she got on her bike, she would sit on one flap of her white *ao dai* and hold the other in her hand by the bike handle so it wouldn't get caught in the spokes.

She's so elegant, I would think, watching her as she rode confidently away from school. *No wonder the boys like her.* But to my mother and the parents of the other girls in the class, Phu was *too* attractive.

"You are forbidden to talk to her," my mother said.

To keep me separated from Phu's "evil" influence, my mother went to my teacher and requested that I be seated next to the class brain, a girl whom I regarded as obnoxious and arrogant. My mother's implicit message to me was "If you're beautiful, you're in trouble."

Despite my mother's warnings I found myself drawn to Phu, not only because she seemed so secure in her own beauty, but also because of her interest in photography. Whenever I could, I would chat with her at the bike stand outside the school gate to hear more about her hobby. She explained the technique of developing, and how she had to wait expectantly for the paper to emerge from the chemicals with a picture that was all her own. She even took photographs of our classmates one day during a party at school.

I longed for a print of one of her photos, if only as tangible evidence of her boldness in trying to carve out an independent life for herself, separate from the rest of us. Through her photography, she was making a statement about what women could do and could be, and I respected her greatly for it. To me, Phu was the embodiment of freedom, and I yearned desperately to know her better.

But I never did get to become a close friend because of the strictures that my family had placed on me. I could only admire her from a distance and hope for a few chance conversations after school.

I don't know what ever became of Phu, but I sense that life might have been hard on her. Her beauty had made her the object of scorn, and her photography marked her as a rebel. In wartime Vietnam, that was a dangerous mix.

But something always drew me to these "dangerous" types, the people set apart from the crowd. It wasn't that I wanted to live on the edge, but rather that I saw something rare and beautiful in people others would consider imperfect. That's why, when I was a schoolgirl, I felt compelled every now and then to visit my schoolmate Vinh, who lived in a house so small my mother was ashamed for me to set foot in it. "You must never go there," mother said. "They are not our kind."

Yet I did go, many times, because Vinh's family always seemed so delighted to see me. It didn't matter to me that Vinh's father was always lying on his pallet, immobilized by his opium habit. Nor did it concern me that Vinh's mother slept most of the day and arose at five in the afternoon to put on heavy mascara, circles of pink rouge, and long, dangling earrings before going out to work. Vinh's family members opened their hearts to me, and that was all that mattered.

I knew that an opium addict and a lady of the night might not be the kind of people I should consort with. Yet God had given me a heart of compassion for such people, and my spirit burst with the desire to share his love with them in any way I could.

But always I felt restrained, held back by the need to do what was "right." The right people; the right professions. These biases, which controlled much of Vietnamese culture, grated on my spirit.

My parents expected my siblings and me to make our marks in science, medicine, engineering, or pharmacy. My elder sister Tram had set the pace by going to Germany to study chemistry, while my brother Phong had ended up in California, studying engineering. These were all acceptable careers that would guarantee a respectable future. Poets, artists, or philosophers didn't fit into the neatly ordered world that my parents had carved out for us.

Down deep, though, I understood that God could surmount all these boundaries, and as a young woman in Saigon, I had prayed for the courage to be set free. Most of all, I had prayed for love. "Someday, somewhere, give me a husband who loves you very much and who loves me with complete abandon. Give me a kind and romantic lover who isn't afraid to be what he is, and who cherishes me for who I am."

That prayer was still on my lips at Wheaton College. On that sunny fall day on the steps of the Memorial Student Center, as I looked at this striking young man, this American D'Artagnan rushing by in a blaze of passion, something stirred inside me. Perhaps the answer to my prayers was right in front of me.

❂❂❂❂❂

"Who is he? What's his name? What is his major?" I wanted to know everything I could about this intriguing fellow. From that day on, I secretly looked for him on campus whenever I had the chance. I noticed that he was always by himself, walking the campus grounds or eating in the dining hall. There was an air of solitude about him that touched me deeply and made me want to reach out to him. I was only a refugee, and yet I already had dozens of friends. He was one of "them," the American majority, but the other students seemed to shun him. I yearned to be his friend.

I got my first chance one Saturday evening in the dining hall on Steak Night, a weekly event that I never missed. I suppose the lack of meat back home prompted me to crave red meat, and I couldn't seem to get enough of it. On the food line, I eyed the steaks, hoping that the server would give me the juiciest piece. He did, and with a fat portion on my plate I moved to the next line, where I was happy to see French fries and okra. Chocolate milk was last. The ice cream would have to wait.

With my tray overflowing, I joined my friends at a long table. Everyone seemed to be talking at once. For once I didn't say anything because my mouth was filled with the tastiest steak ever. I had just finished my meal and was about to get up for a second helping of fries when someone came over and sat across the table from me. All of a sudden, everything became quiet.

A friend leaned over and whispered in my ear, "That's the homosexual guy." I forgot about the French fries and stared at him. *Should I say hi?* I wondered.

While my friends continued to whisper among themselves, my mind was racing with ideas about how to open a conversation. I had never had problems making friends before, but now, for some reason, I was speechless.

Before I could say a word, the "homosexual" guy stood up and left the table. As soon as I finished my dessert—two servings of Jell-O and ice cream—I raced back to my dorm to try to find someone to talk to. I couldn't contain my excitement. I hadn't even spoken to the guy, and yet I felt so close to him. I had to tell someone about this special encounter and automatically I thought of my friend Jackie. I ran to her floor and knocked at her door.

"Anh, what's going on?" she asked, eyeing me suspiciously.

"You won't believe it," I said, still breathless from running so hard. "I sat right next to the homosexual guy at dinner."

"Homosexual?" Jackie asked quizzically. "Anh, that's a very serious thing to call someone. What does he look like?"

As my calm and highly intellectual friend peered down her nose at me through her thick glasses, I described exactly who he was and what he was wearing, from the cross dangling from his ear to his silky shirt. I also didn't forget to tell her how kind and gentle he looked.

"Oh, that's Phil, my cousin," Jackie said. "He's okay."

Of course he's okay, I thought, not having a clue what she was referring to. I had no idea what the word *homosexual* meant. Even if someone had explained it to me, it would have taken a long time to digest since there was no comparable word in Vietnamese.

Blissfully ignorant, I fell asleep that night with many sweet dreams. The next time I saw Philip was after Thanksgiving break, when Jackie invited me to church. "Phil will give us a ride," she said.

When Sunday rolled around, I didn't need my alarm clock. Nor did I grab any old outfit from the pile in my closet. I pulled out my nicest dress and even took time to iron it.

I'm sorry to say that on the way to church, Philip didn't seem to notice me. After a few brief introductions, he and Jackie launched into a deep discussion of Kirkegaard and some other philosophers, which was way over my head. I just drank in the sound of his voice and dreamed.

If driving to church with Philip was ethereal, attending the service at Saint Barnabas Episcopal Church was close to ecstasy. All my life, I had gone to "no fuss, no muss" conservative evangelical Protestant churches, and I assumed that all Protestant churches were alike. But at Saint Barnabas, I was touched by a new sense of intimacy with God. I watched as Philip knelt and crossed himself, and the combination of the simple rituals and his sincere humility struck a responsive chord in my soul. Worshiping God had always been holy and sacred to me, but for the first time I found an overt expression that satisfied my deepest spiritual longings.

On a more earthly plane, as I watched Philip out of the corner of my eye, I also saw something that filled my inner feminine yearnings. With his flamboyant style, spiritual depth, and inner reserve, he set off an unfamiliar, explosive chain reaction of emotions inside me.

My mind raced back to Saigon, and to my fantasy American lover who had consumed my dreams during anatomy class at Minh Duc Medical School. My American was gentle and kind, with curly brown hair and a quiet confidence that swept me up in his aura. Could I have finally found him?

I didn't dare dwell on the thought; instead, I pushed it far to the back of my mind.

❖❖❖❖❖

Christmas break arrived and everyone had cleared out of the dorms except me and a handful of missionaries' kids who had nowhere to go for the holiday. Since my brother couldn't pick me up until the next day, after dinner I wandered back to my dorm all alone, wishing that one of my friends were around. In the light of the cold bright moon, my dorm looked strangely unfamiliar. All the windows were dark except one, and as I stopped to look at the inviting little window filled with light, I realized that it was my own room. Suddenly, I felt utterly alone.

I had no desire to go back to the big empty dorm where I would be the only one rattling around. The sound of the silence would be deafening. I decided to keep walking, and soon I found myself on a street of residential homes that were twinkling with Christmas lights. The warm glow of the houses reminded me of my favorite

Christmas card, the one the missionaries had given to me in Saigon, and I could feel myself begin to relax.

Up ahead of me, I noticed a large dorm, Traber, and with nothing else to do, I began to count the number of rooms that were still lit up. There weren't many, but at least there wasn't just one room, like mine. As I looked at the brightly lit rooms, I thought of the students who were inside and what they might be doing.

Then it hit me. One of the rooms belonged to Philip! He had pointed out his room to Jackie and me the Sunday he drove us to Saint Barnabas. But why was he still here? *Poor guy,* I thought. *He lives in the next town. Why isn't he at home?* I decided to ring him up from the lobby.

"Hi, this is Anh," I said brightly.

"Hi," Philip said.

Then there was nothing but a long silence.

"I just want to see your artwork," I said lamely. I was relieved that I had thought of an excuse so fast.

"Sure," he said. "I'll come down with my portfolio."

I went to the lounge, where a handful of students huddled around the TV. As soon as I sat down on one of the couches, Philip appeared and sat next to me. Without saying anything, he handed me a stack of artwork.

I flipped through his drawings and found myself especially impressed by his calligraphy, a series of letters whose lyrical lines evoked a certain freedom of spirit. When I was finished, I closed the portfolio, but still Philip said nothing. He seemed to be lost in the TV show, a program called *Monty Python.* Every now and then, he laughed uproariously with the rest of the group at some joke I didn't understand.

Instead of getting annoyed by his lack of interest in me, I started watching TV along with him. After a while, it didn't matter that I didn't get the jokes, or even that he was so quiet. I discovered that instead of feeling awkward, I felt very comfortable just sitting by his side, doing nothing.

Finally I decided it was time to leave and I thanked Philip for showing me his art.

"Let me walk you back," he said.

I didn't protest, and together we walked back to my dorm with barely a word passing between us.

The next day, I went home to share the holidays with my family, and a few days later, I received a Christmas card from Philip. He had signed it, "Love, Philip."

"What does this mean?" I said to my sister Debbie. "What does he mean by 'love'?"

I continued to ask myself the same question, day after day, but the answer eluded me.

❖❖❖❖❖

Back at Wheaton after the holidays, Philip and I were no longer strangers. We said hi to each other in passing, and every now and then Philip would even sit down with me in the dining hall.

One afternoon, my friend Claudia took me to the art department to show me around. She pointed to one painting and said, "My friend Philip Sawyer painted that one."

My heart filled with delight at the painting with its riot of colors. Despite Philip's quietness, I had sensed that a wellspring of joy and hope was in him, and I wanted to discover more.

The next day, I ran into my friend Eric, who announced, "Anh, Valentine's Day is coming. I have to find you a secret sweetie."

"What is Valentine's Day?" I asked.

"It's a celebration of lovers and romance," Eric said with an air of humor and drama.

"I guess I can't celebrate," I said, teasing. But secretly, I wanted to celebrate this holiday more than anything. I suppose it wasn't a coincidence that when I got back to my dorm, a note inscribed with intricate calligraphy was waiting for me in my mailbox. "Please come to a Valentine's party." Again it was signed "Love, Philip."

What could all this mean? My heart couldn't remain still.

The party was the beginning of our romance, if you could call it that. Philip called me often and took me out on dates, even though I still didn't understand the job description of a "date."

"Would you be my date?" guys would ask me.

"Sure," I would answer. I assumed a date meant that someone would pay for my ice cream. The idea of real romance was still very far from my mind. My parents had raised me to steer clear of it.

"Romance and happiness don't go together," my mother often told me, reminding me more than once of the young woman we had met at Tết, whose lover had left her pregnant and alone. I knew that Vietnamese literature, art, and music were replete with stories of hearts that had been broken for the sake of love. Then there was my mother's own testimony of her unrequited love affair with Mr. Minh.

With such a heritage, it was easy for me to believe that the safest way to avoid pain was to wait for a spouse whom my parents would pick out for me. "Romance must wait until *after* you get married," my mother advised.

When I was with Philip, though, my heart told me that something about our relationship was different. I never dared call it "romance," but everyone else I knew seemed to have an opinion about Philip and me. One of them was an older friend of mine, Christopher, who may have had a hidden agenda of his own.

❖❖❖❖❖

"Where is everybody else?" I asked when I walked in the door of Christopher's apartment. He was the only member of our crowd with his own place, and when he had invited me for dinner, I had assumed that all of our friends would be there.

"This is a treat just for you," he said, ushering me into the living room. I felt so honored. It all seemed so grown-up. He even had his own kitchen, cookware and all, and as it turned out, he was a great cook. I ate everything he put in front of me and almost licked the dessert plate. When I finally finished the delicious meal and started to leave, Christopher sat me down on the steps outside of his apartment. He looked unusually serious.

"Anh, I have something personal to ask you," he said. "Is Philip your boyfriend?"

I was shocked. "I don't think so," I answered. "Why would you ask?"

Christopher mentioned that a few people had seen Philip and me holding hands, and that it was rumored that Philip had invited me to a Valentine's party.

"It's true," I said, growing flustered, "but he never said anything about boyfriend or girlfriend."

Christopher leaned very close and looked me straight in the eye. "This may be serious," he said confidentially. "I have reason to believe that there's a homosexual in Traber dorm and that Philip may be the one."

"I know he is," I responded. "Someone in the dining room told me he is a homosexual."

"Then Philip may need help," Christopher said. "You have to ask him if he is a homosexual."

"What does that mean? Is it bad? The girls told me he could die forever."

"They just mean he will go to hell," Christopher said.

By now, I was getting fed up with the whole conversation. I didn't understand this homosexual business, and from what I had seen of Philip, I was certain that he loved Jesus and wouldn't get anywhere near hell, in this life or the one hereafter.

"If you're so worried about it, why don't you ask him?" I said.

"I can't," said Christopher. "Besides, he held your hand."

I went back to my room totally confused. I looked up the word *homosexual* in my tattered Vietnamese dictionary but couldn't find it. I checked for *homo*, which had something to do with human beings, and *sexual*, an adjective of sex. That one even I could figure out without looking up.

From what I could piece together, homosexual didn't sound like a disease or anything that remotely resembled Philip. But if there was any chance that he would die forever, I wanted to set him straight. Also I was perplexed about our relationship, and to settle the matter I asked God to show me what to do.

The very next day, I ran into one of my brainy chemistry friends whose advice I often sought out. "How do you know if someone is your boyfriend?" I asked her.

"When two people hold hands, like you and Philip," she replied.

I didn't know what to say. Everyone seemed to know about Philip and my relationship except me. I couldn't concentrate on anything, and as soon as my next class was over, I ran to the chapel. "Dear God," I prayed. "If you want me to talk to Philip directly, please bring him to me."

I was sure I was off the hook. I had a class in a few minutes, and if I ran as fast as I could, even if Philip saw me, he could never catch up.

I was wrong. As I sprinted to my class, I heard a calm voice behind me. "Anh! Why are you running so fast?"

It was Philip. I had no choice but to fulfill my end of the bargain.

"I'm running away from you," I confessed, "but I made a bargain with God that if he brought you to me, I'd have to talk to you."

I skipped my class and we went to a small chapel on the third floor of the student center. As soon as we sat down, I popped the question. "Philip," I said, "are you a homosexual?"

"No," he said. "And as a matter of fact, I like you very much."

"Oh, good," I said. I was glad I didn't have to tell him the part about going to hell. I looked out the window and saw pure-white snowflakes sparkling in the sun, reflecting back a chaos of tiny rainbows that seemed to be dancing and waving at us. For the first time in my life, I realized someone was falling in love with me. I knew it was a dangerous game, this romance, but my heart leapt with joy.

No one ever spoke to me about homosexuality again, not even Christopher. As Philip and I spent more time together, I began to understand the pain he went through each day on the Wheaton campus, as many of his fellow Christian students shunned him for the wrong reasons. It seemed odd to me that these were the same people who would quickly remind me about Jesus' love for sinners. Jesus loved sinners so much, people said, that he had to die and pay the debt for their sins, so that they could be forgiven and have life.

One day, as I waited for Philip in the dorm lounge at Traber, I recognized a poster of his on the bulletin board by the elevator: "Tickets for Sale. Queen Concert." But the letter n in Queen had been given an extra stroke to make it an r. When Philip came down, I asked him why someone would change his poster and what "queer" meant. He grew very quiet and pensive.

I never learned what it meant until almost a decade later, when I lived in New York City. By then, I had quite a few friends who were homosexual. Even though I knew from the Scriptures that my friends' way of life was wrong in God's eyes, I could never stop loving them. I prayed for them as I prayed for myself, that God would have mercy on each one of us.

Gradually I came to understand that we are all under the same condemnation for our sins against God. Whether it was my lack of faith, my friends' homosexuality, or the students' gossip about Philip, the conduct was wrong. I knew too that unless we confessed our sins and repented of them, we would continue to be separated from God, every one of us.

It wasn't easy to identify our sins, for me or for anyone else. But I grew certain of one thing: "We know that our old self was crucified with him so that the sinful body might be destroyed, and we might no longer be enslaved to sin."

AIDS took away the life of many of my friends, including Christopher's. From time to time, I still think of the special dinner Christopher had for me, and I wonder what it was all about. And I pray, *Lord, have mercy upon all of us.*

▦▦▦▦▦

The Lord did have mercy on me and Philip, but especially on me. By the end of my year at Wheaton, Philip and I had become very close, but I didn't have enough money to continue at the school. My brothers and sisters all had nearly full scholarships to major universities, and I was becoming a drain on the family. Everyone in the family agreed: "You must apply for a scholarship at another school."

My heart sank. I loved my friends at Wheaton, Philip most of all. But at the same time, I needed to be able to help my parents. With their poor English, they had found it hard to find good jobs. My father was still working at the watch factory, and my mother walked two miles in the snow and rain to work every day in the kitchen of Hinsdale Hospital. What's more, my brother Phong, who was now working in Michigan, and my sister Tram in Germany had been regularly supporting us. Now it was my turn to help.

I committed the decision to God, and soon a scholarship came through from Calvin College, a Christian school in Grand Rapids, Michigan. It was all decided. The week before school started, my mother had some other plans for me as well. "*Be Tu,*" she said, "be sure you take a shower and look nice. We're going to have some visitors."

To my surprise, they were some people from Canada, old friends of my parents who had children my age. *Male* children. The minute they walked in the door I sized up the situation. The families clearly wanted to set up a marriage arrangement for their children, and I was the number-one prospect.

But instead of acting like a shy, modest Vietnamese young lady, I proceeded to be myself. I ate like a tigress, shared my opinions like a man, and laughed with my mouth wide open like a monkey.

Needless to say, I didn't hook a husband on that visit, which was just fine with me since I was yearning for Philip. I sensed that he was yearning for me, too. Even though we both knew that my marital future was completely in the hands of my parents, just before I left for Calvin College, Philip gave me a pearl ring. I didn't need to ask what it meant.

The next three years at Calvin College were very different from my year at Wheaton. For one thing, I studied much harder. At Calvin, I switched from medicine to the engineering program, which pleased my parents, but not me. I yearned to be in arts or literature. One bright spot in my life during these years was my weekly letter from Philip. Always, he signed it, "Love, Philip."

I missed Philip often, but I was afraid of allowing myself to fall in love with him. I knew he was one of those my parents always warned me to stay away from. Artists, writers, and philosophers were not in their orbit of acceptable mates.

Sure enough, when my parents found out about our relationship, they weren't happy. "What is he studying?" my mother demanded.

"Art," I answered.

"He's a dreamer!" she exclaimed, shaking her head in disgust.

"So, what kind of a job is he planning to have?" asked my father.

"He's also studying Chinese philosophy," I said, hoping that Philip's intellectual bent would sway them. It didn't.

"He's not only a dreamer, but he's also impractical," my father insisted. "This is no good. He will be poor."

I tried to tell them that he came from a very good, highly educated family, one whose legacy at Wheaton College extended back for generations on both sides. Still that wasn't enough.

"Are they rich? What does his father do?" My mother's interrogation was relentless.

"They must be rich, because they have seven children," I answered.

"Seven children? And he's the first? His parents will have to pay for college for six more children. *Be Tu*, you can find a better husband than that!" With that, my mother walked out of the living room. The case was closed.

I have to admit that my parents got me thinking. How would I live with a poor husband? I'd be like Tevye's wife in *Fiddler on the Roof*, perennially worried about where the next meal would come from. I knew how hard my parents had worked to make it in this country.

Although they were rich by Vietnamese standards, they were poor compared to other Americans. They had managed to scrape together enough money to purchase a two-bedroom townhouse in the suburbs, but it was a tiny place, not anything like the mansions with rolling lawns that were all around us. I could see that the American dream was at my doorstep, but to realize it fully, I would need a lot more money than we had now.

Slowly I began to lose my focus. The innocent confidence I had gained at Wheaton dissolved into confusion and self-doubt. My spiritual life dried up, and instead of going to God for guidance, I began to worry more about school, about my future, even about Philip. Schoolwork became a burden instead of a challenge, and by my last semester at college, I was in such a stew that I developed sores all over my legs.

"Shingles," the doctor said. "It's caused by stress." The sores were so painful that I couldn't even put a sheet over me at night. If anything came in contact with the blisters, I was in agony.

As I languished on the top bunk in my dorm room, allowing the sores to heal, I had plenty of time to think, and after much contemplation I decided that I didn't want to be an engineer at all. I didn't know what I wanted to do; I knew only that I wanted the freedom to experiment and to explore.

Most of all, I wanted to marry Philip. He hadn't asked me, of course. In fact, during my vacations from school, it was Philip who often drove me to my house, where a prospective Vietnamese husband was inevitably waiting to "interview" me as a prelude to an arranged marriage. These men were usually older, and they were *always* successful doctors or lawyers or engineers.

On one particular holiday, there was even a Vietnamese doctor from Switzerland who had flown to Chicago especially to meet me. His rented Mercedes was sitting in the driveway when Philip and I drove up.

"Looks like you have quite a prosperous visitor," said Philip, giving me a knowing glance.

Embarrassed, I ran in the door to meet the latest prospect. He was about ten years older than I and extremely serious. I tried to be gracious, if only for my mother's sake. She had told me she would die with her eyes open if I put shame on her. According to Vietnamese custom, if your eyes are closed when you die, it means you're at peace. If they're open, it means you are unhappy for eternity.

I couldn't put such a burden on my mother; she had already sacrificed so much for me and for my siblings. The least I could do was play the role of the dutiful daughter and let fate take its course. If this man agreed to marry me, I would have no choice but to acquiesce and bury my dreams of a life with Philip. It was just the Vietnamese custom.

But no matter how hard I tried, I couldn't stop being myself. I don't know whether I talked too much or smiled too broadly. Whatever I did or said, the Swiss-Vietnamese doctor didn't stay very long, and soon the answer came back as it always had: *No.*

I was a rejected bride! To me, it was an act of God, and I couldn't have been more overjoyed. After several more abortive meetings with sons of my parents' so-called friends, my mother got the message. Inevitably the friends or the go-between simply never called back, and eventually the visits stopped altogether.

My parents finally gave up and granted Philip and me permission to get married. To their way of thinking, my marriage to anyone, even to an American dreamer, was a lesser evil than if I remained single at age twenty-five.

I still laugh at my wedding photographs. Philip's family was all smiles. "Maybe they were glad to get rid of him," was the way my mother interpreted it. My family, on the other hand, looked as if they were attending my funeral. The worry on their faces betrayed their deep concern for my future and my happiness.

"*Hai qua tim vang, mot lu nuoc la,*" my father was overheard to say as he saw us walking down the aisle. "Two golden hearts and an urn of water." The Vietnamese saying described two impractical, romantic lovers who have nothing to eat except for the water that they could freely collect in an urn from the rain—*if* it rained.

As it happened, this disturbing prediction came closer to the truth than either Philip or I could have anticipated.

23

NEW YORK, NEW YORK

We didn't have a honeymoon. Philip's father gave us two luxurious days at the Sheraton in downtown Chicago, and that helped me absorb the shock that I was no longer Anh Vu, but Mrs. Philip Sawyer. Right after that, with all of our possessions packed to the roof in our little green Opel station wagon, we drove east to Boston to find jobs and set up our nest.

I was deliriously happy traveling across country. Except for a few short trips around Grand Rapids when I was in college, I hadn't traveled anywhere in the United States. The road map on my lap became my teacher. I traced our route along the highways and marveled at the great American outdoors. Instead of staying in motels, Philip and I rented small trailers at different campsites. It was like playing house.

Underneath it all, though, I felt a nagging guilt because we had absolutely no worries. The sense of "daughter's duty" that had clung to me all my life no longer weighed on me. My mother had said that now that I was married, I had my own family to take care of and shouldn't worry about her and my father anymore. I suppose she figured that since we didn't appear to have enough money to even take care of ourselves, we had plenty to handle without taking on other responsibilities.

Perhaps as a harbinger of less-pleasant things to come, our car broke down in the middle of some farmland in upstate New York. But I was oblivious to any signs of impending problems. The area was so beautiful I thought I was part of a photo spread in *National Geographic*. Lush green fields and gentle hills, dotted here and there by sheep, cows, old farmhouses, and barns, surrounded us. Not very far from where we stopped, a white church with a tall steeple stood proudly against the blue sky, as if benignly observing the tranquil scene. It was so quiet, I could hear the breeze mingled with the chirping of birds, the barking of a distant dog, and the humming of a tractor motor.

"The car must have overheated with all these hills," Philip said with a shrug. "Let's go to that house over there and see if we can call Uncle John." We had planned to stop by Uncle John's place anyway, and it looked like we might be doing it sooner than later. Philip reached out his hand to hold mine. To this day, his big hands continue to be my comfort in uncertain times.

Hand-in-hand, we walked down the hilly street from our car toward a white farmhouse encircled cozily by a wide porch. The door was wide open and a cat looked out at us from the other side of the screen door.

"Hello!" Philip called out. "Is anybody home?"

We heard some noises inside the house and soon a lady appeared in the doorway wiping her hands on her apron. "Good morning," she said, smiling.

Philip explained that our car had broken down and asked if he could call his uncle who lived in town.

"Of course, please come in," she said, pushing open the screen door. "What's your uncle's name?"

"John Sawyer," replied Philip.

"Pastor Sawyer, isn't he?"

"Yes," said Philip.

"He's our pastor," said the woman.

We all smiled knowingly, certain that our meeting couldn't have just been coincidence.

As it turned out, Uncle John's mechanic also lived down the same road, and he quickly came over and towed the car away for repairs. For the next couple of days while we waited for the car, we stayed with Uncle John, luxuriating in the leisurely pace of our new lives.

To me, everything was like a dream. In just a few days, my life had changed radically. A few days earlier, I had been a single woman, a student, living a hectic life, wedded to a clock. Now I was married, and time stretched out before me like a gift to be enjoyed. Philip and I watched the sun rise and set every day. At night, we lay back on the lawn and counted the stars.

One afternoon, as I sat on the front porch watching my husband playing with Uncle John's new puppy, I realized how happy I was. Our future still remained unknown. We had to find jobs and a place to stay, but I had a sense that somehow everything would be all right.

Just like this trip, I thought. Life will have its troubles: cars will break down, and things won't go exactly as we had planned. But as long as we had God and each other, we could conquer the world.

❖❖❖❖❖

First we had to conquer Boston. Within a week of our arrival in Bean Town, we set up house in the suburbs in an apartment that was a block from the beach and just a train stop away from the city. Philip got a job with the State of Massachusetts as a graphic designer, while I worked in customer service at Lord & Taylor. We made new friends, threw ourselves into the life of the local Episcopal cathedral, and expected to settle down for the long haul.

Within a year, however, Philip found out that both he and his nice boss were out of jobs. "Budget cut," the big boss said.

In the meantime, I had been waiting to hear about a transfer to New York City to be trained as a buyer for the department store. Week after week had gone by without anything definite, and I was beginning to get impatient. One morning on my way to work, I emerged from the metro station at Copley Plaza and a sign in front of the nearby hotel caught my eye: "People Express Airlines Interview Today."

Immediately I called my boss to let her know that I would be late. Then I ran into the hotel to apply for a job with the brand-new airline. The following Saturday, we were still in bed asleep when the phone rang. "This is People Express," the caller said. "Can you report to work on Monday?"

I didn't hesitate a second. "Sure," I said. The only hitch was that the job was in Newark, New Jersey, in the New York metropolitan area. The very next day, we piled all our things in our little green beast, as we thought of our Opel, and after church we headed for New York City.

We hadn't exactly conquered Boston. Would we really be able to conquer New York, which posed much larger challenges? At that point in our lives, we were confident that we could do anything, and for a while it seemed as though we could. We were a team, but more than that, we supported each other's dreams.

"Marriage is a commitment to help each other grow," Philip once explained to a friend, and for me, he did just that. I was hungry to be free and he knew it. I thrived on being able to spread my wings to meet new people and to see the world, and Philip opened the door of my cage and let me fly—literally.

At People Express Airlines, my new job stretched me to my limits professionally, and I reveled in it. Because the company was a start-up, I found myself doing a little bit of everything. One day I would work in customer service. Another I'd be in accounting. Still another I'd be doing communications, training, or recruiting. Often I worked as a flight attendant. Whatever was needed, I did it, and so did my colleagues.

With my job at People Express, I became a different person. At college, I had hated to get up in the morning. Now I jumped out of bed before the alarm went off, eager to get ready for work. The days that I traveled were even more exciting. Although I always dreaded having to leave Philip to go on a long trip abroad, as soon as I was out the door with my suitcase in hand, I was a free spirit.

Wherever I flew, whether it was to Paris or London, during my off time I could do whatever I wanted and go wherever I pleased. More often than not, I would hop on a train to some little town, or visit an old castle somewhere, or see a museum. These excursions thrilled me with the privilege of being able to explore and make discoveries on my own, and I felt richer than any king or queen in the entire world.

What I loved even more were the times when Philip and I could fly off together for a romantic weekend in Paris or London or Belgium. Then, hand-in-hand as usual, we would walk the streets of the *Rive Gauche* in Paris, or sample chocolates at La Grande Place in Brussels. In London, we would pick up fabrics on Savile Row, have tea at Harrods, or see shows on the West End. It was a heady existence.

If my job afforded me the incredible luxury of travel, it also provided other blessings, including a floor-through apartment in a beautiful turn-of-the century brownstone in the Fort Greene section of Brooklyn, across from Washington Park.

"That's 'switchblade park'," someone at work cautioned me, but I blissfully ignored such dangers.

I loved the apartment with its window seat, where through the open shutters I could watch the vibrant street life below me. In the summers, when the neighborhood kids opened the fire hydrants, the street was like a water park, with water spewing out of the hydrant to the opposite side of the street and children running in and out, laughing and screaming as they got soaking wet. In the fall, the street turned into a town meeting, with neighbors, black and white alike, chatting on street corners on their way to and from work.

Before long, I became more than a mere observer. New York and its mix of people and cultures became my heartland, a place whose varied and exotic rhythms seemed to strike an inner chord that resonated with my truest nature. In the Pakistani cab driver, or the Korean greengrocer, or the Italian butcher, I saw a reflection of the beauty and mystery of God's handiwork.

"What plan do you have for us?" I asked God one day as I watched people pass below me from my third-floor window. "How do we fit into your creation?"

Even if some of the millions passing by me every day did not know God, I knew that he knew them, and that he had a plan for them. I yearned to plumb the depths of God's love by getting to know more of these anonymous New Yorkers face-to-face.

Although our brownstone had only three apartments, I had never taken time to meet our neighbors. When the second-floor tenants moved out, I determined to make friends with whoever moved in.

The next weekend, I was just returning from the neighborhood deli when I saw a moving van pull up in front of our building and begin to unload some furniture. Eager for the chance to put my new personal outreach effort to work, I ran up the stairs to see who was moving in. "Good morning," I called out at the front door, which opened, like ours, right into the kitchen.

"What do you want?" asked a female voice, somewhat suspiciously. A young woman appeared from between the boxes and furniture. She looked to be about my age, with bright red lips, jet-black hair, and skin as delicate as bone china.

"I don't want anything," I said cheerily. "We live upstairs, and I just wanted to say hello. Let me know if you need anything."

"Sure," she answered, seemingly unimpressed by my overture. Then she turned her back on me and continued working.

From then on, we often bumped into each other in the hall or by the mailboxes, but no matter how much I tried to start a conversation, she was cool and put me off. Still I was undaunted. One day, I made a big batch of egg rolls and brought some downstairs for her as a friendship offering. "What is this?" she asked.

"Vietnamese egg rolls," I said. "They're very delicious. I don't know anyone who doesn't like them."

"Do they have pork in them?" she asked.

"Yes, lots," I answered proudly.

"I can't eat it," she said bluntly. "I'm kosher. But thank you anyway."

She made a move to close the door, but I persisted. There was something in her big dark eyes, a certain sadness, which drew me to her and made me want to be her friend. "How about coming up for tea?" I asked.

Again she had an excuse. "I have to take a shower," she said.

"No problem," I said. "I will get the tea and croissants ready. Please come up whenever you are ready."

She was stuck. "Okay," she said with a sigh.

That was how Ruth and I became bosom friends. She did come up for tea that day and for many days and months afterward, despite the fact that she liked to say how my perennial cheerfulness grated on her nerves. "I'm glad you didn't give up on me," she admitted later.

Ruth didn't realize it, but she opened up the world of the Old Testament for me. She taught me about keeping kosher and about the rich traditions of Judaism, which I experienced firsthand during excursions like one we took to Flatbush, Queens, for Purim, a festival in honor of the biblical Queen Esther. As I ate the three-cornered pastry, *Hamantaschen*, I learned about how God had used Esther to save her people from the evil Haman.

Through Ruth, I also came to understand the evils of discrimination. Ruth lived with Jerome, a warm guy who was her polar opposite. She was white; he was black. She was Jewish; he was gentile. She kept kosher; he ate whatever he liked. She was serious; he was as fun as he could be. She was tiny; he was huge, with muscles that bulged under his T-shirts. But they had one important thing in common: they loved each more than any two people I had ever known.

But the more I got to know Ruth and Jerome, the more I came to understand that their love was the very cause of the sadness I saw reflected in her eyes. Because of Jerome, Ruth's entire family shunned her. Although Ruth loved her heritage and faithfully kept kosher, she couldn't participate in any family gatherings, including her nieces' bat mitzvahs or her cousin's wedding. She couldn't even maintain a relationship with her mother. Every time she tried to call, her mother hung up the phone without saying a word.

As I heard of Ruth's trials and watched her life unfold, I could see that life in America was as complex as it had been in Vietnam. I realized that behind each face on the subway or in the grocery store lay burdens that were often buried deep beneath the surface. But as I soon discovered, sometimes the burdens weren't hidden at all: they were right out in the open, if we only had eyes to see them.

One Friday evening, Jerome, Ruth, Philip, and I went to see a Broadway show in Manhattan. Because it was late when the show let out, we decided to hail a cab to take us back to Brooklyn. We were lucky to see several vacant cabs coming down Broadway, but for some reason they all passed us by. After six cabs went by without stopping, Jerome disappeared into a phone booth. Immediately, a cab slowed down and stopped for us. With that, Jerome emerged from the phone booth and hopped in.

"It happens all the time," said Ruth matter-of-factly.

I was dumbfounded. As a student in Vietnam, I had read books such as *Cry, the Beloved Country* about the hardships of blacks in South Africa. But I never imagined that I would find that kind of discrimination in America. Yet here it was, right in New York City, and my dear friends were its victims.

"What does all this mean?" I asked God. "How can you allow this to happen?" The more I saw in New York and the more I experienced, the more confused I became.

But for a time, I pushed my questions aside, throwing myself instead into the whirlwind of a life that Philip and I were creating for ourselves—or perhaps I should say, that I was creating for us. In my overwhelming excitement over reaching out to God's people—all the people of New York if I had my way—I began to see our apartment as a place of refuge for anyone who needed it. Often when a passenger was stranded at the airport with no place to go, I would call Philip and announce, "I'm on my way home with someone. Would you spread out the futon in the spare room?"

More often than not, Philip got the message on our phone answering machine, but always he obliged. Though once a complete loner, he quickly warmed to the idea of reaching out to others. Before long, our open-door policy became a pattern that would stay with us for the rest of our lives.

Most people stayed for the night and left the next day, but not Eddie. Eddie was a colleague at People Express who lived in Boston and flew back and forth regularly to Newark. One evening, as I was getting ready to commute home for the night, I saw him sitting in the crew lounge looking rather forlorn. "Did you get bumped?" I asked. "I thought you were trying to catch the flight to Boston."

"I made the flight," he said. "But when I got home to Boston, I couldn't get in the house. My wife had changed all the locks. I had to fly back here so I could get to work tomorrow."

Immediately I offered our apartment. "I'll call Philip," I said. "I'm sure you can stay with us."

Eddie stayed—for a couple of years! One day stretched into two until finally, he became like a third member of the family. He ate with us, cooked for us, and laughed with us.

Our lives were like a TV sitcom, with a round-robin work schedule that had us all coming and going. On a typical day, Eddie and I would have an early breakfast with Philip, who had just arrived home from his night shift as a proofreader at a law firm, a job he landed soon after we moved to New York. Then, while Eddie and I headed off to the subway to commute to Newark, Philip would go to sleep. Later in the morning, Philip would wake up and work on his clothing designs, which he was trying to sell on Seventh Avenue.

By the time Eddie and I were finished at work, it was long after eight in the evening and we were starving. I'd call Philip, and then Eddie and I would meet him at our favorite noodle shop in Chinatown on Mott Street, which was just a subway stop away from our apartment. After dinner, the three of us would head back home to Brooklyn, and an hour or so later, Philip would leave for work.

Day by day, our circle of "family" and friends widened beyond

Eddie, Ruth, and Jerome to include old friends from Wheaton and new friends in an Episcopal parish, Calvary-Saint George's, in the heart of Manhattan. Sundays would find us at church, followed by lunch at a Chinese restaurant around the corner with the vicar, Rev. Steve Garmey, and a hodgepodge of other friends. One Tuesday a month, we'd meet with another group of church friends for a potluck Bible study and prayer time in Murray Hill.

With these new friends at church, I felt totally comfortable and accepted, loved for who I was. And so did Philip. With them, we could dare to dream, dare to be vulnerable, dare to doubt. Our hopes became their hopes; our struggles their struggles. In the bosom of the church, Anh, the globe-trotting former refugee and Philip, the would-be clothing designer, were treasured children of God. Through these dear people, we sensed God's love being poured out, pressed down, running over beyond measure in our lives.

No one demonstrated that love more than the parish's rector, Rev. Tom Pike. Sensing that Philip was having a tough time breaking into the clothing industry of Seventh Avenue and wanting to encourage him, Tom offered to stage a fashion show of Philip's designs at the rectory on Gramercy Park. Tom even volunteered to be a model, an act of supreme sacrifice for a guy who was used to wearing gray suits with a clerical collar. For other models, we recruited a handsome lawyer and also Richard, another friend of mine from People Express. Philip was set to play the role of commentator.

In preparation for the big event, Philip spent hours measuring the models and tailoring the clothes just for them. They would wear jackets and slacks, all created in Philip's signature style, an avant-garde, unstructured look that was simple yet precisely tailored. Made of the finest fabrics, the designs presaged the haute couture elegance that would appear on Armani models five years later.

We scheduled the show for a weekday, when buyers from various boutiques in the area could come, and sent out dozens of invitations. As an added touch, I whipped up hundreds of Vietnamese egg rolls and threw together a festive fruit punch. With the models primed, the clothes perfect, and the food plentiful, we were certain it would be a day to remember.

Only two buyers showed up. The rest of the attendees were friends, including the vicar, Steve Garmey, and his wife, Jane. Altogether, between the buyers, the models, and Philip and me, there were about eleven people. But the show went on, and it was fabulous.

Philip stood at the base of the stairs of the duplex apartment, and as the models came down one by one, he described the outfits. There were unusual pants made of wheat-colored canvas that we had bought straight from a paint-supply shop. The pants were fitted at the hip but loose at the knee down to the ankle. Atop the pants, the models wore royal purple turtlenecks, the color of the Lenten season on the Episcopal calendar. But the *pièces de resistance* were the jackets: overcoats without lapels or with diagonal zippers that made a bold, if nontraditional statement.

My favorite was a seal-gray overcoat made of waterproof cotton in a gray-on-gray herringbone pattern. With its sturdy shoulder, stand-up collar that reached high up the neck, and daring diagonal zipper from the left shoulder to the center, it resembled a samurai warrior's armor. But what I loved best was the lining: quilted satin made of gold silk, which added a touch of hidden luxury.

I can't remember now who wore it. All I remember is the jacket, and the incredible feeling that came over me as I stood mesmerized by its beauty, knowing that my husband had created this magnificent work with his very own hands.

As my eyes feasted on the jacket and I listened to Philip describe each detail, I couldn't help pinching myself. Our lives might not yet be perfect, but in New York, we seemed to have found our niche. We were surrounded by friends who loved us, and we were bound by a love for each other that seemed unshakable.

Unfortunately, Philip didn't sell any of his designs. "Very good work," the buyers said one by one as they slipped out the door without ordering anything. Nevertheless, the day after Philip's fashion show, we decided to celebrate his first professional venture by going on our favorite cheap date. We took the subway to Battery Park, where, for a quarter each, we caught the Staten Island Ferry. As we always did when the weather was warm, we stood at the nose of the ferry, with our faces to the wind.

There, in the middle of New York harbor, under Lady Liberty's unchanging gaze, we kissed passionately. I felt as though I could live like this forever.

I couldn't have been more wrong.

24

A LITTLE CHILD SHALL LEAD THEM

My marriage almost fell apart over a three-hundred-dollar pair of Joan & David boots. They were gorgeous, off-white and buttery soft, made out of one continuous piece of leather with a slender heel three inches high.

I had seen them in the window of a boutique on Fifth Avenue, and it was love at first sight. I just had to have them. At People Express, I was required to wear uniforms, and so whenever I had the chance to dress up, I did so to the nines. But my biggest weakness was shoes.

"Even Imelda Marcos would be jealous of you!" Philip often said. Shoes were a fetish, and like the devil, they wouldn't leave me alone. I'm not sure why I latched on to that particular addiction. Maybe it was because years earlier during my escape from Saigon, I had lost my sandals and arrived shoeless in Subic Bay.

Whatever the reason, after we had moved to New York and I had access to free transportation on People Express, I became so shoe crazy that I would fly to Boston on my day off to shop for bargains at Filene's Basement. There I would satisfy my hunger for discontinued Chanel, Bruno Magli, Charles Jourdan, and Bally of England. On any given day, if I hit it lucky, I might even snare a pair of Pancaldi, the fancy Italian shoes worn by the likes of the Queen of Brunei. For a mere fifty dollars, I could walk away with a three-hundred-dollar pair of pumps.

My modus operandi on my day off was simple. Typical was the day in the fall of 1985 when I grabbed the car and headed for the Holland Tunnel and Newark to catch an early flight to Boston. On the plane, I started fantasizing about the shoes I would find. But since I always committed things to God, I took my passion one step further. "Lord," I prayed, as I looked out the window at the soft fluffy clouds in the distance, "please help me find some great shoes today."

It never dawned on me that it might be somewhat frivolous to ask God to bless my shopping spree. I just assumed that he automatically approved of everything I wanted to do—including the way I chose to spend my money.

As soon as I arrived at Logan Airport, I took the subway to Faneuil Hall and an outdoor mall where the revolutionary-era building stands, and then headed straight for the Steaming Kettle Restaurant. There, amongst the early morning breakfast crowd, I ordered a big bowl of clam chowder and a croissant. With my stomach full, I walked a few blocks to Filene's department store and its famous bargain basement.

I never bothered with the first or second floor. I always went directly to the basement and started with one rack at a time, first the clothes, and then the shoes. It was always hit-or-miss, like a treasure hunt. Invariably my eyes were drawn to the most up-to-the moment designer clothes.

As usual, on that particular day I pulled some elegant prospects off the rack and took them to my own private "dressing room," a tent I created at the end of one of the racks from the mountains of clothes I had selected. I tried on everything from a fur coat to a beautiful wedding dress by Nina Ricci, and some fabulous gowns by Oscar de la Renta.

By noon, I was exhausted and starving. I hid my finds in the coat section of the men's department under a size-fifty-two coat and then turned to the sales ladies who knew me by sight. "Please don't move these," I begged.

They winked, and off I went for lunch in Chinatown. An hour or so later, I headed back to Filene's Basement for a second round of shopping—this time for shoes. God was indeed good and as enthusiastic about my activities as I was—or so I thought. I ended up with several stunning pairs, including a black velvet, square-toed selection with red jewels on the toe by the Japanese designer Kenzo.

With my shoes under my arm, I grabbed the dresses I had left in the coat department and raced to the MTA station. From there, I caught the train to the airport and the eight o'clock People Express flight to Newark.

But I wasn't finished yet. On the plane, I refused to let the flight attendants put my purchases in the overhead bin. Instead, I pushed them under the seat in front of me, and the minute we were skyward, I pulled out the shoes and started trying them on. That was my routine on every trip.

Because I was the main breadwinner in the family at this point, I rationalized that I *deserved* to treat myself—as often as possible. This attitude brought me to a personal crisis the day I saw the off-white leather boots at the boutique in Manhattan. These certainly weren't Filene's Basement prices. But I was practically breathless as I rushed into our home to Brooklyn to tell Philip the exciting news.

"I saw the most fabulous boots," I told him. "You would love the workmanship. They're on sale for only *three hundred dollars*. You save fifty-percent!" I was sure that my appeal to high style and craftsmanship would win Philip over.

Instead he just looked at me in shock. "Anh," he said, obviously trying hard to be gentle with me, "we can't afford to pay three hundred dollars for shoes."

I was outraged. "What do you mean? I work for People Express. I have money in the bank. I can buy anything I want!" Then I stomped off into the kitchen and sulked.

As I sat there fuming, it dawned on me that my life wasn't as rosy as I had pretended. I had a husband who loved me, but the bald truth was that he couldn't afford to take care of me the way I expected. In fact, he couldn't take care of me at all. For the past few years, as he had earned a pittance at the law firm and struggled to make it as a designer, I had been the one taking care of him. *I'm tired of this*, I thought. *Why doesn't Philip get a real job?*

For a while I kept my thoughts to myself. But gradually, as I found myself spending my days off trying to sell Philip's trendy clothes to boutiques instead of taking myself on shopping sprees to Filene's, my frustration mounted. So I finally said it: "You've been doing this for four years and it's going nowhere. Give it up!"

Philip looked pained, but he said nothing.

The real source of my frustration had nothing to do with my shopping sprees. In Vietnam, the war had raged outside me. But now in America, and especially in New York City, the war had moved deep inside. At the time, I was pushing thirty, and I wanted to start a family. Working in New Jersey just aggravated this need. There, I saw many of my colleagues with a "normal" life: a traditional spouse, a couple of kids, and a house with a nice yard. My heart was yearning for this kind of stability even if Philip didn't appear to have the same inclinations.

As the weeks went by, I found myself dwelling on the difficulties of my life, and also more broadly on the injustices I observed around me. Increasingly the world seemed cruel and unfair, especially after I learned that a dear friend had been beaten by her husband. The story triggered something deep in my buried childhood memories, and without fully understanding why, I wept for her and for myself.

Soon after, following a particularly hectic day at People Express, where I was working with telecommunications vendors to develop a new reservation system for the airline, I happened to glance at a copy of the *New York Times*. A headline immediately grabbed my attention: "Drought in Africa." I scanned the article, which was about the ravages of hunger on the continent, and then turned to the jump page, where my eye drifted to a series of wrenching photographs. One showed bodies littering the road, where people had died of starvation on the way to a relief station. Another pictured a little child sitting on the ground with her head resting on her bony knees while a vulture waited a few feet away. According to the story, the photographer who had taken the photo had picked up the little girl and carried her to the relief station. But it was too late. The child had died in his arms, only steps from food and water.

"What sin did this child commit to suffer like this?" I asked God. "What about my friend? She loves you. All she wanted to do was go to church, and because of it, her husband beat her."

Still I wasn't finished with my complaints: "How about Philip? You've given him enormous gifts and he can't seem to make good use of them. It's so unfair!"

The more I ranted and raved, the more hardened I became. "All I see is sadness and suffering. Where is your mercy?"

My anger at God grew so intense that I stopped going to church altogether. It didn't take long for people to notice and try to intervene.

"My sermon this morning was for you, Anh," said the vicar. "But you weren't there."

"I'm praying for you, Anh," said Philip. "It's all I know to do."

I didn't care anymore about sermons, or prayers, or anything. "Get a job, Philip!" I kept insisting, and our arguments mounted.

Finally, I had had enough. "I want a divorce!" I announced one night after a particularly long day at work. I packed a small bag and headed straight back to the airport. When I arrived in Newark, I looked up at the departure screen and saw a light flashing for Baltimore. It was the only flight ready for immediate departure. I ran to the gate and climbed on board, and as soon as I hit Baltimore, I checked into the airport hotel and called Philip's father. Because this was such a devastating decision, out of respect for Philip's parents, I felt obligated to let them know. I secretly hoped that as the head of the family, Philip's father might say something to salvage the situation.

"I want a divorce from Philip!" I said. "Don't try to talk me out of it." I spewed out my anger into the phone, barely stopping to let Dad Sawyer have a word. If he said anything, I don't remember it. All I remember is hanging up the phone and crying myself to sleep.

The next day, after a good night's sleep and a big breakfast, I felt better and flew home. Philip was waiting for me, patient and loving as ever.

I had been blind to God's mercy. It was right in front of me in the loving, gentle embraces of my husband. But I couldn't see it; I didn't want to see it. I saw only a bleak future for me, for Philip, and for the whole wide world.

I wish I could say this was an isolated incident, and our marriage worked perfectly after my attempt to escape—but it didn't. I broached the *divorce* word many times and continued to wallow in my self-pity. On one level I loved Philip dearly, but on another I was so miserable about our circumstances that my body sometimes ached inside and out.

"O Lord, why do you cast me off?" I cried out with King David. "Why do you hide your face from me?"

In the darkness, I cried myself to sleep.

As it turned out, God's face was in the small things—eight first-graders, to be exact. Just when my life seemed to have reached rock bottom, Philip and I were asked to teach Sunday school.

"I don't think so," I said curtly, when the Sunday school director at Saint George's Church called us to help. "I'm much too busy."

I wasn't in the mood to get involved in anything at church—particularly with a group of rambunctious six-year-olds. I had pretty much given up on my own spiritual life, and the thought of spoon-feeding Bible stories into some overactive little minds wasn't the least bit appealing.

But the woman didn't give up. Whether it was because of God's mercy or simply out of desperation, she finally shifted her attention from me and called Philip to ask him to teach.

"You said *what?*" I asked when I heard he had accepted her offer.

I couldn't believe it, and I doubted that it would work. Philip was a loner, and even though he had embraced the guests in our house, he still managed to live a near-monastic existence. He loved nothing more than to settle back in his chair with a book, or work quietly at his sewing machine with a bolt of fabric. But children? I had never seen him show the slightest interest in making friends with a child, ever.

He doesn't even want to have his own child! I thought, fuming. *How does he expect to teach Sunday school?*

Philip was scheduled to start the very next Sunday, and reluctantly I agreed to help—provided I didn't decide to fly off to London or Paris, that is.

Sunday arrived, and we walked in to find eight boys and girls climbing all over the chairs and tables in the little room where we were to teach. I took one look at our charges and realized that they weren't just rambunctious, they were terrors! The whole scene reminded me of the mad crowd at the airport at Christmas: totally restless, impatient, and out of control.

To make matters worse, the room wasn't really a room at all, but rather a large entryway that opened into a hallway to the church. The minute we tried to get the kids to settle down, someone would come barging through the door, walk through our class, and go out another door to church. It was a recipe for total chaos, and for a while, chaos was exactly what we got.

The children were a bright but motley crew: six attended a nearby prep school and two came from a homeless shelter in Brooklyn. They all talked at once and vied for Philip's attention. Whenever they felt like it, they got up from their seats and roamed around.

I tried to get them to sit still, but nothing I said seemed to penetrate. It was Philip who got their attention. He spoke so softly that in order to hear him, they had to get completely quiet. Before long, he had them sitting like angels listening to the day's Bible story. I was flabbergasted.

I had expected Philip to be a nervous wreck. Instead, he was totally in control. In that tiny classroom, the spiritual leadership that had lain dormant inside him came to the surface with incredible force, quieting the storms of rebellion in the hearts of Michael, Cristofer, Alex, Anna, Susie, Adjua, Damien, and Letitia.

Week after week, as Philip unfolded the Bible to those now-eager little ears, something in me began to change. As I heard the old stories—of the miracle of the loaves and the fishes, or of Jesus walking on water, or of the healing of the lepers—I started to hear the voice of God calling to me afresh. In Philip's lessons, I heard the gentle voices of Mr. Titus and the missionaries who had ministered to me in Saigon as a child in Vacation Bible School, and my heart began to melt. Something in those Bible stories was true, and real and lasting. Each one resonated with God's love, a love that was so great and so powerful that nothing else in the world could compare.

These little children knew the power of that love. That's why they came back Sunday after Sunday. In that classroom, they saw and heard the love of Jesus not only in the Bible stories, but also in the faithfulness and patience of one man—my husband, Philip. Almost against my will, I found myself falling in love with Philip all over again.

As my eyes opened to the miracle in front of me, at first I felt humbled and ashamed. But soon I was swept up in the joy of God's awakening, and I felt a rush of thankfulness.

One morning I woke up and didn't feel angry anymore. I didn't blame Philip for the disappointments in my life, and I no longer blamed God. The outward circumstances in my life hadn't changed: People Express was falling on hard times, and Philip still hadn't sold any of his designs. But those things no longer seemed so important. What was important was my relationship with God.

For years in New York, I had buried the very thing that had brought me out of bondage and given me my freedom; now as I began to unearth the spiritual treasure within me, I began to feel the new power of God's promises. It didn't take long before my heart and God's were attuned again, and soon I felt the same sweet sense of assurance, the same overpowering conviction of God's eternal faithfulness that I had known intimately as a teenager in Saigon.

Overnight, our lives seemed to be on an upswing. Some friends invited Philip to join a weekly prayer group at the Harvard Club in Midtown Manhattan, and for the first time in his life, he had the support of a circle of strong Christian men. They became his mentors and kept him on a steady path when he had problems with his work or with me.

Before long, he decided to go back to school, and within a few months he was a student at Columbia University studying Chinese in a master's program in international affairs. Because his clothing design business hadn't taken off, he temporarily shelved his dream in order to earn a more marketable credential that might land him a well-paying job.

As for me, I kept working at People Express, but my focus had changed radically. No longer was I ready to head out the door and catch a plane to Paris or San Francisco at the drop of a hat. I still sneaked up to Boston to my beloved Filene's Basement every now and then, but even shopping had lost some of its allure.

Now I poured myself into the life of the church with an enthusiasm I had never felt before. I showed up at the Sunday school's Talent Night and helped get the kids dressed for the Christmas Pageant. I wept when I saw the baby Jesus, a plastic baby doll in the arms of a little African-American Mary. It was hard for me to express how grateful I was that this tender babe became my Savior, but the Spirit said it through my tears. Through moments like these, I became so committed to the Sunday school that gradually I moved into the role of assistant director.

Like Philip, I soon became involved in a prayer group. Mine was a quirky group of Christian women, including a sixty-something actress, a boutique clerk, and a writer who was also the Sunday school director. With these women, as I became more accountable for my actions, my spiritual life took on new clarity.

The blessings were pouring out so fast I could hardly keep up with them. Love, joy, peace, patience, faithfulness, self-control: these were some of the fruits of the Spirit, and they were fast becoming manifest in our lives. Then God gave us the biggest blessing of all. One morning, I woke up feeling nauseated. It happened the next day, and then the next. I was pregnant!

At that very moment, as I contemplated the miracle of the new life within me, I made a commitment to God. From that time forward, no matter what difficulties might come into our lives, I would never again consider divorcing Philip, and I would never turn away from the path of truth that God had laid out before me. "Forgive me, God," I prayed. "Forgive my faithlessness. I promise never to forget you again."

It wasn't long before I was put to the test. The attacks came in rapid-fire succession. Philip was the first to get hit. By this time he was fluent in Chinese and with his hard-earned master's degree in international relations from Columbia, he had hoped to land a plum job in Asia. After a very successful interview, he seemed like a shoo-in for a position with a multinational corporation. But within days of his interview, the stock market crashed and so did the job.

Next came the mugging. I was puttering around in the kitchen, waiting for Philip to return from a postgraduate Chinese class he was taking, when I heard the sound of his footsteps on the stairs. I opened the door and he practically fell into the apartment.

"What's wrong?" I asked, blocking out the horror that was right in front of me. "Is something wrong?"

"Can't you see?" said Philip in frustration. "I've been mugged! Four guys jumped me and stole my watch. When they didn't find any money, they beat me up."

Philip's face looked as though it had been smashed by a truck. His lips were as puffy as marshmallows, one eye was completely swollen shut, two teeth were chipped, and blood was dripping off his face and onto his shirt. Worst of all was his nose. It was completely off center.

For a few moments, I stood paralyzed. "What can we do?" I said helplessly.

Seconds later, Jerome and Ruth burst in the door, and I began to regain my focus.

"Who did it?" Jerome demanded. "I'm going after them." As Jerome raced outside in a vain effort to find the four teenaged thugs, Ruth and I helped Philip down the stairs and into a cab. Brooklyn Hospital was just a few blocks away, and a few minutes later, Philip and I were waiting in the emergency room.

It looked like a war zone. Shootings. Stabbings. Overdoses. For the doctors and nurses, it was triage, and Philip's face was at the bottom of the pecking order. A doctor handed Philip some pain medicine and sent us home. "Go to your own doctor tomorrow and let him align your nose," the doctor told Philip.

Philip's face was put back in order the next day, but my mind was in turmoil. "We can't stay in Fort Greene," I said to God. "It's too dangerous. I can't let my baby be born here. Please show us a way out."

But the attacks kept coming, and I was the next victim. People Express had merged with Continental, and although I still had my job, I discovered that because I had neglected to fill out some paperwork, I no longer had any medical insurance. I got the bad news, not from the airline, but from the doctor's office at my first prenatal visit after the merger.

"Your medical insurance isn't effective," the nurse told me bluntly. "The doctor can't help you."

I walked out of the office utterly shocked and scared. *Who will deliver my baby?* I wondered. Philip hadn't yet found a job, I was about to give birth, and we seemed to have no insurance. *Will my baby be born on the street?*

As I sat weeping on the subway back to Brooklyn, I thought of Mary and Joseph and the holy child who was born in a manger because there was no place to stay at the inn. Through my tears, I saw an advertisement lit up on the subway wall: "If you're pregnant and don't know what to do, call Planned Parenthood." I had never heard of Planned Parenthood, but the minute I got home, I dialed the agency.

"Do you intend to keep the baby?" the lady on the other end asked pointedly.

"Of course," I said, startled by her question.

Then, in a tone as matter-of-fact as if she were reading me a grocery list, she directed me to Gouverneur Hospital on Manhattan's
Lower East Side, a welfare hospital where I could receive free prenatal care.

The next day, while Philip was out hunting for jobs, I took the
subway to the address the woman had given me. I found a small
clinic crowded with people who looked poor and haggard. Drunken
men and women wandered in and out, shouting obscenities, young
children cried incessantly, and old ladies with wrinkled stockings
snoozed in their plastic chairs. Alongside them, a handful of pregnant women, most of them in their teens, carelessly smoked cigarettes that dangled precariously from their painted lips. Across the
room, a man yelled at his woman and made an ugly gesture. As for
the nurses, they sat stone-faced, calling out names and filing papers
with seeming indifference.

How can I let my baby be born in such a place? I thought. My heart
broke for me, for my child, and for all the other mothers and children whom circumstances forced to accept such indignity.

*Will I become like these people, stuck on welfare and trapped in mis-
ery with no way out?* I was so dejected that I didn't even think to
wipe away the tears that were streaming down my face.

Suddenly I felt a tap on my arm. I looked up to see a very black
man with a half dozen gold chains around his neck and a smile
made even more dazzling by the three huge gold caps on his front
teeth. "Why so sad, sweetheart?" he asked.

That was all it took for me to pour out my story in all its de-
pressing detail. When I was finished, he looked me straight in the
eye, smiled his golden smile, and said, "Don't worry, honey. Everything's gonna be all right. Crying isn't good for baby."

I fumbled in a purse for a Kleenex. When I looked up to say thank
you, he was gone. I looked around, but he was nowhere to be seen.

I couldn't help smiling—and I suspected God might be chuck-
ling a little as well. To get me back on track and brighten my spirits, he had sent me one of his special angels, one with a golden
smile and the laid-back optimism of Bob Marley.

"Everything's gonna be all right," the man had said—and it *was*
all right. Within a few weeks, my medical insurance was restored
after I submitted the appropriate paperwork. Also, Philip got a job

at an accounting firm headquartered on Long Island, and I was named director of the Sunday school. Although the part-time job didn't pay anything, the position came with a lovely apartment at an affordable rent in the parish house right in the middle of Manhattan.

I was so happy, I danced and sang in the streets like a fool. Life was wonderful.

Our baby was born in Manhattan a few months later. Early in the morning on May 20, 1988, my water broke. I put on my favorite zebra-striped maternity dress and a pair of pearl earrings that Philip had given me and headed out the door. I was already halfway down the stairs when I stopped and ran back up.

"What now?" said Philip, who was getting more than a little anxious.

"I need to get my rhinestone shoe clips," I said brightly. "I want to look beautiful for our baby!"

Philip just shook his head. Shoes were never far from my mind, even as I was about to give birth! We walked across Stuyvesant Park to Beth Israel Hospital, which was only a block away from our apartment in the parish house. About eight hours later, William Spencer Thien Bao Sawyer made his entrance into the world. His Vietnamese name means "God's treasure," and for Philip and me, he was indeed a treasure, for our marriage and for our spirits. "Lam," as we affectionately called him, became a sign of hope, a living testimony to God's plan for us.

For the next few years in New York, we followed the plan exactly as we believed God was laying it out for us. Philip commuted to his job on Long Island, while I accepted a buyout and left my airline job to stay home with baby Lam. Increasingly I devoted my spare time to running the Sunday school and Vacation Bible School at Saint George's.

But as exhilarating as New York was, Philip and I began to feel God nudging us to leave. We didn't know why or where. In 1989, after nearly a decade in the city, we sensed that there was something out there waiting for us—some exciting new adventure we had yet to discover.

For years, Philip had dreamed of working among the Chinese.

Although the dream seemed impossible from our current vantage point, we thought we heard God calling us somewhere outside New York. So on a sunny summer Saturday in 1989, perhaps somewhat like Abraham and Sarah heading out of Haran toward Canaan, we packed up Lam and all our belongings in our little red car and headed west to a land and a people yet unknown.

25

THE CALL OF EMMAUS

Why did I come to this place? I wondered as I sat next to Philip at the back of the conference room at the Days Inn in Lawrence, Kansas. We had arrived late, and the guest speaker was already in the middle of his pitch. *What's the point?* I thought. *I'll only be more disappointed.*

I had come at the urging of my friend Donna from the Mustard Seed Christian Fellowship in Lawrence, where we had moved toward the end of 1990. More than once, I had gone crying to her in frustration over Philip's endless malaise, and one day she had come up with this as a "solution."

"Go to this meeting," Donna had insisted. "The speaker has a gift for intercessory prayer. It might do you some good."

I couldn't imagine why I would need an "intercessor." My *prayers are as good as anyone's,* I reasoned. *It's just that they aren't working at the moment.*

The truth was, I was tired of praying for Philip and tired of trying to force him to be happy. We had left New York with a new burst of energy and the clear sense that God was calling us away. Secretly I had hoped that with a new start, Philip could begin to feel some release from the cloud of sadness that always seemed to be hanging over him, and for a while it seemed to be happening.

From New York we had gone to Illinois, where we had spent ten months living with Philip's parents while he looked for jobs with corporations or ministries dealing with China. As the weeks went on, I had grown increasingly anxious about his failure to land a job, but I had held my tongue and tried desperately to leave the job search up to God.

As it turned out, the time together with his parents, brother, and five sisters was a period of tremendous growth for Philip, who had seemed to revel in their open hospitality and love. I could tell he was more relaxed around his family, more comfortable with himself than he had ever been before. Any hurtful memories he might have had of the Midwest or of the rejection he had felt at Wheaton College seemed to have been erased by his new appreciation for his roots and his childhood.

Finally he'll be happy, I thought. Then we moved to Kansas, where Philip's brother-in-law had opened the door to a design manager's job at a greeting card display company.

"It's not China," Philip's sister had said. "But the position seems to fit your talents."

It also seemed to be a place where we could thrive as a growing family. By now, Lam was a toddler, and I was pregnant with our second child. With such an abundance of blessings, I was certain that Philip had put his aimless searching behind him.

But as the weeks passed in Kansas, something about him still seemed hurt or wounded, as though some deep scar had yet to be healed. I had no idea what the source of the problem was, and it was beginning to irk me. "Just get on with your life, Philip!" I found myself nagging him. "In Vietnam, bombs were dropping all around us, and yet we had to keep going. There aren't any bombs in Kansas. Whatever is bothering you, get over it!"

None of my exhortations had worked, and as my due date approached I was growing increasingly annoyed at Philip's unceasing woes. I had conquered every problem I had ever faced—except this one—and it was gnawing at me. "I don't know what else to pray anymore," I told God. "I give up."

That's when Donna had suggested that I go hear the man with the so-called gift of intercessory prayer. I had made up my mind *not* to go when, just hours before the meeting was set to start, something nudged me out the door.

"How about it, Philip?" I said. "Want to try it?" I must have surprised him with this unexpected spiritual interest because he just stared at me for a few moments. Then he jumped out of his chair and we drove to the Days Inn, where we found the meeting in full swing. I was so consumed with my anguish over Philip that I barely heard what the speaker had to say. But my ears perked up the minute I heard him say, "If you want to be prayed for, come forward."

Immediately I got out of my seat and walked toward the front of the room, where I stood with a handful of other people and bowed my head.

Then seemingly out of nowhere, I felt a hand on my head and heard a deep voice speaking softly. "I know why you're here," he said. "You want me to pray for a family member."

Before I had a chance to say anything, the intercessor started praying . . . for healing . . . for God to act in a special way with my loved one . . . for an incredible miracle.

I didn't feel a thing. I just walked back to my seat, grabbed Philip, and walked out the door. We picked up Lam at the baby-sitter's, and then, with me driving, we headed home. In the car, Philip dropped his bomb.

"Something incredible happened to me in there," he said. "While you were praying, the Lord gave me a vision of a little boy playing alone at the end of my parents' driveway. Christ was looking down and weeping over him.

"I heard Jesus say to the little boy, 'Come to me and let me cry with you,' " explained Philip. "But the little boy refused to go. He just turned his back and refused to cry with Christ."

As I heard Philip recount his sad little story, tears started flowing down my cheeks. I didn't understand what it was all about, or why God would have put it in his mind, but for once I was speechless.

"Don't you see?" he continued. "I am that little boy. All these years, I've been grieving, and I refused to turn over my grief to Christ. Right then and there, as you were being prayed over, I prayed that God would take my grief. And he did."

I pulled over to the side of the road and hugged him. In a strange way, the story reminded me of the disciples on the road to Emmaus after Jesus' crucifixion. Jesus had come alongside them, yearning to heal their grief, and yet they didn't immediately see who he was or how he could help them in their time of trouble.

Still, I was puzzled. "What do you think it was all about, Philip?" I asked.

He explained that during the service, old feelings of loneliness and abandonment had surfaced as memories flooded back from his childhood to a time when he was eleven months old. Back then, he had been quarantined for several days in the hospital with roseola, and the doctors had refused to let his parents visit because his mother was pregnant with twins. Even after his release from the hospital, he lived for a month or so with his grandmother, until the doctors decreed he was no longer contagious. By then, two new babies were in the house and Philip, who was still a baby himself, had not been able to understand what had happened. He felt like an outsider.

"All these years, and I never understood," he said, shaking his head.

But God had understood, and he had released Philip from his inner torment that very day, all because I had obeyed the inner voice calling me to attend the meeting and walk forward for prayer. Yet oddly enough, the prayer over me had come about because of a mistake.

"I couldn't figure out why you walked up there," Philip said. "The speaker didn't ask everyone to walk forward, only those who had never received Jesus into their lives. Then you stood up and went forward. He prayed over you, and I was healed."

From that day on, our lives exploded with a new sense of possibility and purpose. At the time, we were renting a tiny town house behind Twenty-third Street, which, according to the *Guinness Book of World Records*, has more fast-food joints than any other place on the planet. After Philip went to work each day, Lam and I explored the city, especially the campus of the University of Kansas.

One warm fall day, I had just spread out a blanket on the grass for Lam and me to have a picnic when I saw dozens of foreign students hurrying by. They made me think back to my days as a newly arrived refugee in Illinois, when the Kiefts had taken my family under their wing. I sensed something tugging at my heart. God had used strangers like the Kiefts to bless me; perhaps now I could do the same for these students.

The more I thought about it, the more the idea took flight. I envisioned our home as a place of refuge, where students could feel comfortable visiting or perhaps even staying for periods of time, the way my friend Eddie from People Express had stayed with us in

Brooklyn. When I shared my thoughts with Philip, he was open to the idea, but we recognized two major drawbacks: we didn't know any foreign students, and the town house we were renting was too small to entertain many people. And so we prayed. "If you want this to happen, show us how."

By now, I had seen God's miracles so often in our lives—especially with Philip's miraculous inner healing—that I was growing accustomed to putting things before him with a sense of expectancy, just as I had as a child in Saigon. Day by day, I pushed aside my analytical side and opened myself up "as a child" to the exhilarating mysteries of faith. I relied less and less on *Anh's* will, and more on finding God's will.

On another of my excursions with Lam, we found the house. I was driving around a park one day looking for a parking space when I stumbled upon a cluster of charming Victorian homes on a very short street. I couldn't help stopping to admire them. The setting encompassed red-brick sidewalks, huge trees, old rose hedges, and large front porches big enough to sit on and have a tea party with friends. What was even more appealing was that the neighborhood was within walking distance of the university.

I stepped out of the car with Lam, and as soon as my foot hit the pavement, my nose tickled with the sweet aroma of honeysuckle. Lam and I followed the scent to a magnificent Victorian with gingerbread trim and a "For Sale" sign on the lawn.

Too big, I thought, dismissing the idea as an impossible dream. *It must cost lots of money.*

But I was wrong. It was just the right price, and a month later, with our parents' help, we became first-time homeowners and moved in.

So now we had the ideal house, with a separate "servant's room" upstairs for long-term guests, and a huge library that would be perfect for Bible studies and parties. But where were the foreign students?

Then one day Philip came home with some surprising news. "They're right here!" he said. "The Chinese. They're here."

"Chinese people in Kansas?" I said in astonishment.

"My boss said there are more than five hundred mainland Chinese in Lawrence, at the University of Kansas!"

So Philip and I prayed that God would lead us to some of these

Chinese who were supposed to be multiplying in Kansas—and especially to one who could use a spare room we had fixed up in our big new house. We sensed that he wanted us to make this space available at little or no cost to some needy student.

But God responded in a somewhat different way than we had expected.

⬥⬥⬥⬥⬥

After waiting a month or so for a Chinese student to come knocking, I began to feel a little guilty that the room was sitting empty, and so I took the initiative.

I had heard from a friend that a foreign doctor—a Christian from Nigeria by the name of Ernest—needed a quiet place to live while he studied for his medical boards. So I looked him up and asked, "Would you like to stay at our place while you study?"

When he looked surprised that a stranger would offer such a gift, I explained this way: "God has asked my husband and me to set aside one of our bedrooms for Chinese-speaking students. It isn't occupied right now, and we'd be happy for you to use it."

Ernest still looked a little uncertain, but a few days later I arrived home to find a strange car in front of our house. On the windshield was a poster decorated with droplets of blood and the message: "Covered by the blood of Christ." I walked up the porch steps to find Ernest swinging in the swing.

"Can I *really* be your 'Chinese' student?" he asked with a wide smile.

"Of course. You certainly *look* Chinese," I said, and we both burst into laughter.

Ernest's wife and children were still living in Nigeria while he studied for his medical boards. He moved into our upstairs room and stayed for a year, and it didn't take long before he got addicted to my Vietnamese egg rolls and French *Tintin* comic books.

But if anyone truly got addicted in that relationship, it was Philip and I—to Ernest's exuberant and throw-all-caution-to-the-winds kind of faith, especially when it came to money. He was almost reckless in his belief that God would provide for him and for his little family back home.

When he wasn't studying, he worked part-time as a construction worker so that he could send home one hundred dollars every month to his wife, Joy.

Since financial worries had always been my Achilles' heel, I marveled at Ernest's confidence in God's ability to meet his every need, and I was determined to help him out. By the time Ernest came into our lives, I had already given birth to a second son, James, and was now pregnant with our third child. Needless to say, we didn't have much money to spare. But I started putting aside a little money every month from what I saved with grocery coupons. One evening, Philip popped into the kitchen and gave me a proposition. "I feel that God wants us to give Ernest some money," he said. "I've been feeling the same way, too," I responded. "I've saved about twenty dollars this month. How about it?"

"I believe we are supposed to give him a hundred dollars," said Philip.

I was speechless. But even though I had no idea how Philip was going to come up with a hundred dollars, I quickly agreed. That night, Philip went upstairs and handed Ernest a check.

"I don't know what else to say, but I'm supposed to give you this," said Philip.

Ernest took the check without saying a word, and Philip quickly left the room. The next day, Ernest stuck his head into the kitchen and explained why he hadn't been able to say even so much as a thank-you. It seemed that just moments before Philip had walked into his room, he had been agonizing over his finances.

"I had just discovered that after sending money home to my wife, I would be short one hundred dollars this month for car insurance and gas," Ernest said. "I figured I could do some construction work, but I knew that if I did that I wouldn't have time to study. Then you came with the check, and I was dumbfounded. The Lord provided exactly what I needed!"

We were awestruck by Ernest's story but even more amazed by what came next. A few hours later, the phone rang.

"Is Ernest there?" a man asked. His accent sounded foreign.

"No," I answered. I wrote down his name and number. Later that night, when Ernest got home, I gave him the note.

"Did he tell you why he called?" Ernest asked. He sounded worried.

"No," I replied.

"I don't know this man," said Ernest. By now, he was growing extremely agitated, and he hurried up the stairs to his room.

Could it be something about his family in Africa? I wondered. I knew there was some problem back home, something about relatives who had threatened him because of his Christian faith. But surely the dangers couldn't have reached Kansas. It all seemed too cloak-and-dagger for me, and so I put the notion aside.

The next afternoon, we were sitting at the dining table having Sunday dinner with a few friends from church when Ernest burst through the door and threw several twenty-dollar bills on the table. "Look at that!" Ernest said gleefully.

He was jumping up and down, running back and forth, singing and dancing, all at the same time. "Praise the Lord! Praise the Lord!" he cried, still beaming.

When he was finally able to settle down, he explained that right after cashing the check Philip had given him, he had sensed God telling him to give the hundred dollars to Simon, a Nigerian doctor in Kansas City who was in the same situation as he. "But I didn't want to give the money away," he confessed. "I told the Lord I had just gotten the money. I argued that Philip had given it to me because I needed it."

God didn't let up. As Ernest explained, he kept nudging him until finally Ernest drove fifty miles to Kansas City and handed the money to Simon. "But not all of it," he told us. "Just eighty dollars. I decided to hold back twenty, because Simon insisted he didn't need it all."

On the drive back to Lawrence, Ernest said he had felt no peace. In his mind, he could hear God rebuking him. "I asked you to give him one hundred dollars," God seemed to be saying. "Why did you give him only eighty?"

Ernest admitted that he was so ashamed, he turned the car around, drove back to Kansas City, and gave Simon his last twenty dollars. "That's why I got home so late last night," Ernest told us. "I drove to Kansas City and back."

Ernest's story wasn't finished. As he sat in church earlier that morning, he had felt God pushing him again, this time to call the mystery man who had left the message the night before. The man turned out to be a Nigerian who was visiting Lawrence from another state. He had heard about Ernest and wanted him to stop by.

"When I got to his place," said Ernest, "the man asked if I believed in God. When I said yes, he gave me a handful of bills."

Then Ernest turned to us. "The man said God wanted him to give me *that*," said Ernest. With that, Ernest pointed to the twenty-dollar bills he had thrown on the table. As we watched wide-eyed, he counted them out: "One, two, three, four, five. One hundred dollars!" he said, laughing.

All of us burst into cheers. But mine were the loudest of all. Through this faithful African brother, God was teaching me to listen to his voice and most of all, to be *obedient* to his call—even in seemingly impossible circumstances. Thanks to Ernest, I was beginning to see how truly exhilarating it could be to live a life in the Spirit—especially where money was concerned.

Ernest, by the way, went on to pass his medical boards. Today, he is a successful family physician in Kansas, where he lives happily with his wife and their three children.

❖❖❖❖❖

As soon as Ernest moved out of our house, God seemed to have decided that we were finally ready to deal with some Chinese. Paul Wong, a visiting Chinese scholar, was the next to move into our spare room. Like Ernest, he spent every waking moment either studying or working at the university to earn enough to bring his wife and daughter from mainland China. Paul adopted us as his family right away and often brought over friends, mostly Chinese scholars like himself, to share a meal or a cup of tea.

Eventually, he was able to transport his wife, Mei Ling, and daughter, Wei Wei, from China, and once they had settled into their new apartment, it was their turn to take care of *us*. "Just come anytime," Mei Ling said. "Lunch, dinner—or both."

No matter when we arrived at their apartment, we became active participants in a moveable Chinese feast, where everyone cooked and ate at the same time. Typically, I went straight to the steaming kitchen to join the women, who were stir-frying meat and vegetables and boiling dumplings in a giant pot on the stove.

Philip would head to the living room, where Paul and his men friends were whipping up *jiao zi*, Chinese dumplings.

One afternoon, I peeked out from the kitchen to watch the men at work. Philip was right in the middle of things, taking turns rolling the dough or spooning the ground pork, all the while practicing his Mandarin. He seemed so natural, so confident, as though he had known these people all his life. This was a Philip I had never seen before. As I watched him interacting with the others, I was amazed at how quickly these men warmed to him. They seemed to respond to his gentle spirit and open friendship as though he were part of their family.

"Philip is *ge ge*, older brother," Paul would say. "Anh is sister-in-law!" They seemed to forget that Philip was white and I was "yellow" like them.

"What do you mean?" I'd say, pretending to be offended. "I'm one of you."

"No, *Su Yi* is egg man," someone would retort, using Philip's Chinese name. "He's white outside but Chinese inside!"

In a sense, I felt that description of Philip was a special word from God. Ironically, his very eccentricities, his inability to fit into a traditional American mold, was the very quality that enabled him to move effortlessly into a fraternal relationship with these Asian immigrants—many of whom spoke little or no English.

As our Chinese "family" was growing, so was our own family, with the birth of Kathleen in 1993. When our relatives and friends heard about our "crazy" life, with two little boys, a brand-new baby, and a house full of foreign strangers, they either felt sorry for us or considered us very noble to be "sacrificing for Christ." But we never felt any sense of hardship or sacrifice, not with Ernest or Paul or any of the other students who came after them.

Our Victorian house had become a thoroughfare for students from all over the globe who were looking for a place to feel at home. We found ourselves hosting countless potluck suppers, which infused our cozy strawberry-wallpapered kitchen with tantalizing aromas from Shanghai, Bangkok, Mogadishu, or New Delhi. Philip also taught regular Bible studies for Chinese men while a friend and I taught the women.

My house was always a mess, and we didn't have much extra money, but somehow we always had enough to feed anyone who showed up. Once, after several foreign students were baptized at the Mustard Seed church, I decided on the spur of the moment to invite everyone back to our house for cupcakes, which was all I had in the refrigerator. When we arrived home, the house was already stirring with students and friends, and the table was laden with food. Everyone had brought what they had, and like the miracle of the loaves and the fishes, we ended up with food to spare.

"But where is this leading?" I asked God one night. "I love these students, but do you have something more for us? For them?"

That night, just as students were gathering in our home for a meeting, I ran upstairs to put our three young children to bed. When I went back downstairs, I nearly stumbled over dozens of pairs of shoes and sandals that the students, who were involved in the meeting with Philip, had left scattered all over the floor.

Being an experienced "shoe person," I looked at them a little more closely. Not one boasted a classy designer label like those on the mountains of pairs that still filled my closet, a leftover from my days as a mad shopper at Filene's Basement. But as I looked at the shoes—plastic flipflops, well-worn black pumps, and leather loafers badly in need of a shine—an urge to pray over them gripped me. Perhaps someday, shoes just like these, maybe even these very shoes, would be transformed into God's armor, "the equipment of the gospel of peace," as Paul put it in Ephesians. I also recalled Paul's other words in Romans: "How beautiful are the feet of those who preach good news!"

Tears welled up in my eyes as I prayed, "God, please let us learn to bear your 'good news' not only here in America, but even to the ends of the earth."

I found myself wondering if we should be doing more to communicate the gospel to this potpourri of Asians and other foreign students who were passing through our doors. Certainly God seemed to be revealing his special call to us bit by bit, almost on a daily basis, since we had been in Lawrence.

Again, I thought of the way Jesus had operated on the road to Emmaus in Luke 24. We were learning to listen to others in need and in anguish the way he did. Like him, we were breaking bread with wayfarers. Philip was also communicating his faith directly through the home Bible studies he was conducting. But what was the real impact of what we were doing? Were lives really being changed?

An undergraduate student from Macau, an island just off the Chinese mainland, provided the beginnings of an answer.

▦▦▦▦▦

"I *know* I will go to heaven," I heard Ines telling Philip one evening. "I'm a very good person. I've never harmed anyone and I help as many people as I can. My good deeds will get me into heaven."

Philip and Ines were sitting around the dinner table, deep in conversation, as I was putting dinner on the table. Our visiting foreign students were always plying us with questions about what Americans thought, and I happily left these discussions up to Philip, who could think more logically and philosophically than I. This time, the topic was Christianity and for now, Ines seemed to be having the last word. "It's nice for you," she said, putting the subject to rest. "But I don't need it."

Ines was studying aerospace engineering, and I can't even remember how she came to live with us. But as one of a succession of students who followed Ernest and Paul, she fit into our family as though she had lived with us forever. Wispy thin with straight hair, thick eyeglasses, and a gentle spirit, she captivated everyone who met her.

Like our Chinese friend Paul, Ines loved bringing her friends over to eat my Vietnamese food. She seemed to readily embrace our activities, including going to church for special functions, especially at Christmas or Easter. Still, I knew that from her point of view, these were simply "cultural" experiences that she expected could deepen her understanding of America but would probably mean little else.

Other than occasional visits to church, the only overtly Christian practices we shared with Ines were our prayers. At mealtimes, along with our usual litany of prayers for our family, we never failed to pray for God's blessings on her, her exams, and her family back in Macau.

But that was as far as our efforts at outright evangelism went with her. From the very beginning of our foreign student adventures, Philip and I had agreed that as a matter of family policy, we wouldn't force our spiritual beliefs on anyone who sought shelter in our home. We would encourage them to join us in prayer; and we would conduct regular Bible studies, which they were free to join or not, as they liked. But we would apply no pressure.

Philip had always argued from Matthew that the Bible says to "let your light so shine before men, that they may see your good works and give glory to your Father who is in heaven." He also challenged me to understand that because God is all-powerful, I could trust his Spirit in me to do the work of making his love visible to others through my life.

This approach soon became our byword in our dealings with international students, and I have to admit I liked the policy very much. Since I'm naturally an impulsive, proactive person, it freed me from the pressure of having to perform or make things happen, including "making" people believe.

Over the years, I had come to realize that my spiritual gift—my "light" that God had given me to shine on others—was love, pure and simple. With these students, I could just relax and be myself and enjoy my relationship with them for who they were, and not because of whether or not they agreed with my point of view about Christianity. All I needed to do was let this "light" shine, and I could depend totally on God to work in the hearts of others as he saw fit.

Ines had lived with us for about a year when she happened to go to Chicago one Christmas with a group of Chinese friends. Late Friday night, our phone rang. It was Ines.

"Where are you?" Philip asked. "Are you all right?" I could hear the alarm in Philip's voice. The sound of Ines's crying was so loud it was audible through the phone across the room. My mind started spinning with ways we could get her back from Chicago if she was in trouble.

Philip handed me the phone.

"What's going on, Ines?" I said. "Are you safe?"

"I'm so sorry," she said. "I can't stop crying."

"What happened?"

"I'm so happy," she said, continuing to sob. "I just accepted Jesus into my heart tonight."

"Oh, Ines, I'm so happy too," I said. "I love you." By now, I was laughing and crying at the same time. I hung up the phone and looked at Philip. "How could this happen?" I asked him. "She was so certain that she didn't need God."

When Ines returned, she explained how she had gone to Chicago on a lark, just to see the "Windy City." Once there, something had inspired her to attend a Christian conference with her friends, and she had heard a message about Christ that had touched her heart.

"It all started with you," she said. "I saw how much you love your children and everyone else. That love is so great, it can't come from you—it can only come from God."

Philip and I were flabbergasted. Somehow, God's light had managed to shine through us, even though from our point of view our lives were in a total shambles. At the time, we had our brand-new baby girl, Kathleen, our younger son James, who was still in diapers, and Lam, who was starting preschool. On top of all that, we had just adopted a new puppy, who chewed everything in sight and drove me crazy.

"I don't get it," said Philip. "When Ines lived here, every day when I got home from a frustrating day at work, you would be waiting at the door ready to hand me a child and complain about what the dog had just destroyed. The house was in complete chaos. I often wondered if I should kill the dog and then myself. How could Ines have seen anything good in our lives?"

But she *had* seen something good, not because of anything special we did or said, but by the Spirit in us. That was something to rejoice over.

Soon the former agnostic became so "on fire" for God that one by one, in a domino effect, her friends in the engineering department became believers too. Her fervor was so intense it touched even the parents of one of her converts, who on a trip to Lawrence from Beijing turned their lives over to Christ. When the couple returned home to China, they began witnessing to their friends.

As for Ines, several years later, after we left Kansas, she married a Chinese student who quit engineering in order to go to seminary. At their wedding, she asked all the students who had frequented the Sawyers' house to come up for a picture. Sixty familiar faces gathered around the smiling couple. Many of them had come to Christ since they had been at our house.

I marveled as I looked at the picture and at the joyous faces of Ines, her husband, and their friends. One of the students had become a campus missionary. Another is actively involved in her church as a Sunday school director. Ines's husband will become a pastor, and the two of them are now in ministry in the Midwest.

Yet all we did was invite them to our home, love them, break bread with them, and include them in our lives. The Spirit had done the rest.

✦✦✦✦✦

Despite our booming house-church ministry, I could tell Philip was growing restless. We had been in Kansas for nearly five years, and although our life was enormously rewarding, a hunger remained in his heart for something more. By now I was able to recognize the signs as God's gentle leading, but again, we weren't sure where. The idea of China was still paramount in Philip's mind, and we were even considering Mongolia when a missionary couple from Taiwan stopped by to visit. "What do you think about working in Vietnam?" they asked us.

"I don't know," said Philip.

Forget about it! I thought. But out of politeness, I kept quiet.

God wouldn't let go of us. Soon the phone was ringing incessantly with calls from Colorado Springs, where an organization called REI-Vietnam was based. The organization, staffed with many committed Christians, was involved in providing teams of doctors, teachers, and other professionals to Vietnam to help develop the country's badly needed infrastructure, and the work piqued Philip's interest.

After a trip to Colorado, where we met the staff and learned more about their work, Philip was sold. Their philosophy dovetailed with the approach God had shown us in our work with foreign students, and it seemed that the way was clear for us to go.

But something held me back. In spite of what I had learned from our Nigerian doctor friend, Ernest, about the spiritual joys of living on the edge financially, I still hadn't completely shed my self-image as the "material girl" who loved to socialize and shop. Besides, I had heard there wasn't much money in this new venture. In fact, there was *no* money in it. If we wanted to join the organization, we would have to raise our own salaries!

"Are you kidding?" I said to Philip. "Do you mean we won't get a regular paycheck? Why don't you just work for a couple more years so that we have some money stashed away, and then we can do it?"

But if I were honest with myself, the lack of money wasn't my biggest fear. Vietnam was what really worried me. If I had been single or childless, I *might* have considered going back. But I was a mother with three small children. Not only that, I was a *Vietnamese* mother who had escaped from Saigon just as South Vietnam fell to the Communists. That meant the current regime might choose not to recognize me as an American citizen when I entered the country. The whole idea seemed more than just reckless; it might be suicide. *I will not take my children back to that hellhole,* I thought.

Memories of the war flooded back into my consciousness, along with the paralyzing fear that had gripped us after the *Viet Cong* had moved into Saigon during the 1968 *Têt.* Images of Hoa Lo prison, where hundreds of American pilots had been brutalized, haunted me. I remembered our escape—and the incredible joy and relief we had felt when we reached the U.S.S. *Midway* and realized that at long last, against all odds, we were free.

"*Tu biet,*" I had said in the helicopter that lifted us out of the American Embassy compound in Saigon. "Farewell forever." And I had *meant* those words. Yet now we were thinking of going back?

Desperately I bargained with God. "I'll go anywhere in the world you send us, but not Vietnam," I told him.

God didn't seem to be listening. Philip was growing more and more enthusiastic, and I could tell that he felt called to this mission in Vietnam with a passion he had never shown before. Still, I needed a concrete sign.

We had the encouragement of Philip's parents, along with our first "support" check from my former prayer partner who had preceded me as director of Saint George's Sunday school in New York. What other signs did I need?

Like Gideon with his fleece, we sent out letters to various friends and churches, asking for financial support. Within days, we heard back from Christ Church in Oak Brook, Illinois, the very church that had sponsored my family and me as refugees. They were eager to get behind us, but first they wanted us to attend a mission conference.

As we drove north to Illinois that April, I was still wrestling with God in the car. "I need a sign," I pleaded. "I need to know if this is your will, and not just Philip's. I'm scared to take my children back to the place that is filled with so many terrifying memories."

The church was already bustling with people for the mission conference when we arrived. I hadn't been back to Oak Brook for twenty years and in the interim, the church had grown much larger and more intimidating. When I didn't see any familiar faces, I started to get nervous. *We're not supposed to be here*, I thought. *This is all a big mistake.*

Then one of the pastors came running toward me, along with a lady I recognized as Mrs. Conway. "You've got to look for Mrs. Fitzstevens," Mrs. Conway said. "She was in Vietnam for many years as a missionary, and I know you'll want to get acquainted."

As if on cue, a tall, handsome woman who looked to be in her early seventies walked up to me. *"Chao co, co khoe khong?"* she said in impeccable Vietnamese. "Good morning, young miss, how are you?"

"Chao ba, cam on," I replied. "Good morning, Madam, thank you."

"When did you hear the Good News and become a Christian?" she asked.

I was a little startled by the directness of her question, but automatically I answered, "Before I was born."

"That's impossible," she said. "You have to believe in Jesus in order to be a Christian."

"I know," I said. "But I believe that when my grandfather accepted Jesus many years ago, God set me aside for him." As I heard myself speaking these words, my heart felt lighter, as though God himself was speaking through me. When the lady pressed me to explain, I told her about my Grandfather Tieu's opium addiction, and about the missionaries who had given him the Bible tract that had led to his conversion. Before I could finish, she cut me off.

"My father must have known your grandfather," she said excitedly. "I was very young at the time, but my parents sometimes talked about an opium addict who became one of the elders of the church in Hanoi."

It was hard for me to process what she was telling me. Her parents knew my grandfather? How was that possible? "I'll have to ask my mother," I said, reeling from the apparent coincidence. Later that night, I called my mother. "Ask her if her name is Esther," my mother said. "Esther Van Hine. Her father was a missionary who sometimes gave Bible lessons to your Grandfather Tieu. Her mother was often sick, and her father would bring her to our house to stay."

The next day, I couldn't wait to get back with Mrs. Fitzstevens. "Is your name Esther Van Hine?" I asked her.

"Yes," she said. "It was my maiden name. I'm married to John Fitzstevens. It all started coming back to me last night. Your grandfather must be Mr. Tieu."

"Yes, he is!" I said, practically screaming. "You are my sign!" I said, giving her a big, uncharacteristic Vietnamese hug. "You are the sign I prayed for because I had so little faith."

The next morning, the congregation of Christ Church, led by Rev. DeKruyter, the pastor who had opened his arms to my family twenty years earlier, gave their official endorsement to our work in Vietnam. Then one of the pastors began to pray: "Twenty years ago to this day, Vietnam was falling. Our history, Vietnam's history, Anh and Philip Sawyer's history, and your history, Lord, are intimately connected."

As I stood in front of the church with Philip, Lam, James, and Kathleen, I couldn't stop the tears from flooding my eyes. Although I hadn't fully realized the scope of its role, this church had been part of God's plan for me from the very beginning. Through these people, God had rescued me from Mr. Billings and brought me and my family out of the refugee camp as a young woman to begin a new life of joy and freedom. During the year in Illinois, which this church had made possible, God had given me my soul mate. Now the church was entering my life again as I prepared to respond to our new call, the call of Emmaus.

In the recesses of my mind and spirit, I could hear the celestial song that must have also resonated in the hearts of those travelers on that road just outside Jerusalem in the early first century. A peaceful, gentle melody urging love and service to others in distant lands whispered in my heart. I also realized that this was the mature version of a song I had known "from before I was born," as I had told Esther, a prayer that had been on my lips from the moment I entered the world as Ngoc Anh, only steps from the *Song Saigon*, the great river of my birthplace.

No one had taught me the lyrics of this inner hymn, but now I knew them by heart: "Lord, make me the instrument of your peace. Let me love the Vietnamese the way you have always loved me. Let me walk alongside them . . . listen to them . . . break bread with them . . . and do all I can to open their eyes to your Spirit."

26

HOMECOMING

In 1995, we moved to Colorado to work at the headquarters of REI-Vietnam, and in October 1998, I found myself with Philip on a plane returning to Vietnam. Philip had been there many times leading short-term projects, but for me, the trip was a first. In my head, or "in my stomach" as we Vietnamese say, I felt it was a crazy plan for me to go at all. But my friend Carol had moved into my house with her family to take care of my children, and everything had seemed safe and secure, until the Vietnam Air jet made its approach to Hanoi's Noi Bai Airport.

I was so jumpy I couldn't relax, and so I opened my Bible randomly, hoping for some words of comfort. A few verses in Luke leaped off the page: "But before all this they will lay their hands on you and persecute you, delivering you up to the synagogues and prisons, and you will be brought before kings and governors for my name's sake."

I could feel the fear returning. The old unwelcome acquaintance was back. I remembered the feeling too well. My heart weakened. "Please protect me, God," I prayed. "If it's your will for me to be in prison in Vietnam, please take good care of Philip, Lam, James, and Kathleen. If it is your will for me to die, please give Philip a good wife."

I gripped Philip's hand so hard my knuckles were white. We landed at Noi Bai Airport late in the evening and parked on the tarmac, where buses waited to take us to the terminal. I could feel the fear spreading in my soul. The dark night outside—the hot, damp air, the officials with olive-green Communist uniforms and hats with gold stars—brought back terror that I thought was gone forever. I clung to Philip.

"Don't worry," he said, sensing my tension. "I have your passport."

Why did I come here? I thought. *I'm not wanted here. The people hate me.* The thought kept playing in my mind like a broken recorder.

As we followed the crowd to the bus, I held Philip's hand tight. The bus started moving and before long, I could see the terminal. My heart sank. The sight of the dim yellow lights inside reminded me of Saigon during the war. I had forgotten—or maybe I had tried to forget—how old and poor things looked.

Inside the terminal, we lined up in front of a row of podiums, where police and customs agents were checking passports. When it was our turn, a policeman waved Philip through, and then he gestured to me to come alone to his station.

I remembered the face, haggard and cold, a face I had seen in the newspapers of *Viet Cong* who had shot and killed my people. Fear controlled me entirely now.

"Where is your passport?" the official demanded.

"Philip! Philip!" I screamed. "My passport!"

Philip came over to the podium, handed me my passport, and waited. Again, the official motioned him through.

The man scrutinized my passport and examined it for what seemed like a very long time. I couldn't see what he was doing, since the front of the podium was higher than his desk. "You don't have extra pictures," he said, fixing his eyes on me coldly.

I didn't know what he was talking about. Everything should have been in order. The Vietnamese Consulate in Washington had stapled my visa and extra photographs right onto the passport, and I had seen them with my own eyes. What could possibly have happened to them?

"You can't go through!" he said sternly. "You don't have pictures."

My knees felt weak, and I could feel the blood draining out of my face. "Lord, show me your kindness," I prayed.

Out of nowhere, another official appeared. "Let her go," the man ordered the customs official.

I grabbed my passport and walked through the crowd as though

I were in slow motion. I had no feelings. All my nerve endings were shot. I was too scared to think, to feel, to care. Philip caught me wandering around in a daze and led me back toward our luggage.

Outside, a colleague from REI-Vietnam was waiting for us with a van. Philip loaded it with our luggage and several huge boxes of donated medical equipment and materials needed by hospitals throughout the country. This was Hanoi. It still hadn't sunk in.

On the drive to the city, I was only vaguely aware of my surroundings. It was so dark outside that I could only imagine the scene that Philip was describing for me: rice paddies along the highway . . . Long Bien Bridge over the Red River, the *Song Hong* . . . Bach Mai Hospital, which an American bomb had damaged during the war.

I listened to him without really hearing. I was still in a dream, or was it a parallel reality? Only a few hours before, I had been in America, free to do whatever I pleased. Now I was paralyzed with fear, afraid of what to say or do.

Once we were rumbling through the heart of the city, the generous streetlights and still-busy streets started to make me feel safe and welcome. Even though it was late at night, bicycles and motorcycles rushed by in every direction. Horns were honking everywhere. Cafés and sidewalks were alive with people.

"It is so hot that people take to the streets," said our colleague, who seemed to understand what I was thinking.

A few minutes later, we pulled up in front of the house rented by an REI staff member from the States, where we would stay during our visit. I was so exhausted that as soon as I hit the bed, I collapsed into a deep sleep. Early the next morning, I was the first one up. Philip was still asleep and the whole house was quiet. Trying not to make a sound, I tiptoed to the dining room with my Bible. As I sat at the table alone with God, I willed myself to thank him for bringing me back to this place. Nobody in my immediate family had returned to Hanoi since my parents had left the north in 1954. But it was the place of their beginnings, my beginnings, a place my mother had described to me lovingly in stories of her childhood.

For me, though, it was also "enemy territory," and before I let fear take me any further, I took shelter in my prayers. "Lord," I prayed, "This is the day that you have made. Let me rejoice and be glad in it."

"*Xoi nong day!*"

The song of the sweet rice vendor! My heart leaped with joy as I ran to the window. Out on the street, a barefooted woman wearing a cone hat appeared, balancing a long bamboo pole on her shoulder. On each end of the pole, a flat basket brimming with rice balls swung back and forth.

I wanted to dash onto the street to buy some of her sweet rice, but then I remembered I didn't have any Vietnamese money.

From then on, every morning at daybreak, I awoke and sat by the window, partaking of the sensual feast that is Hanoi coming to life. I reveled in the smell of the wet earth from the previous night's rain, the sound of metal gates opening and closing, the songs of the squid vendor and the noodle man, the sweet and pungent aroma of incense being offered at an ancestral altar, and the call, "*Chi oi, em oi!*" of a mother waking up her children. These sights and smells and sounds drew me closer to the heart of Hanoi, and I began to feel at peace.

Before I left Colorado, God had given me a simple vision of him and me for this trip, and I remembered it now. In my vision, I had pictured myself as a child, just going to work with my "dad." He wanted me to see him at work, not because I could be of any great help—more likely I would get in the way—but because he loved me and wanted me to feel his heart for his people.

As I looked out the window onto the streets of Hanoi, I thought of my "dad" and his work, and I was humbled. *What, exactly, had I been afraid of?* All my fears seemed to have disappeared.

❖❖❖❖❖

"Jump on," Kathie told me, motioning to the back of her motorcycle. The beautiful redheaded nurse, who taught English as a second language to medical doctors as part of her work for REI-Vietnam, had invited me to visit her English class, and happily, I had obliged—until I saw the motorcycle.

I straddled the seat behind her, clutching her waist and resting my chin on her shoulder as she roared down the street fearlessly into the chaotic traffic. There were no traffic lights. Motorcycles, bicycles, cars, and pedestrians seemed to be in constant motion, going in all directions. Horns honked incessantly. A car swooped close, *too* close, I thought, and instinctively I shifted my body weight to the other side of the cycle.

"Relax, Anh," said Kathie. "You'll get used to it."

I didn't breathe easy until Kathie turned into the parking lot of the hospital where she taught her class. I followed her through a shady outdoor courtyard, the Vietnamese equivalent of a hospital waiting room, and saw relatives of the patients squatting on the ground, waiting for word about their loved ones. Here and there I could see a nurse helping a patient with walking exercises, or hear the concerned voice of a family member talking with a doctor. The chattering in Vietnamese reminded me of my new reality.

Kathie's students were already waiting for us in the stifling hot classroom. Even the ceiling fans whirring in a fast mode didn't make a dent in the thick humidity. "Good morning, everyone," Kathie said brightly.

"Good morning, teacher," the class responded in unison.

The words triggered memories of Saigon and my years in high school and Minh Duc Medical School, and I could feel myself being carried back to another place, another life. Nothing had changed. The north. The south. They were so alike. Kathie's voice broke through my reveries.

"I'd like to introduce our special guest, Anh Vu Sawyer."

All eyes were upon me, and I started to feel a bit edgy.

"Anh lives in America with her husband and three children," Kathie continued. "Her husband works with my organization here in Vietnam. Feel free to ask her any questions."

With that, she turned the class over to me. I looked out at a sea of faces, all doctors and nurses in their late twenties and early thirties. They looked just like me. I was one of them, and yet a gap stretched between us.

On the spot, I prayed: "Dear God, I don't know how to start. Give me the grace to make a good impression."

"Why don't we begin by your telling me your name and what you do in the hospital, and then you can ask me some questions?" I said, trying to deflect attention from myself.

The students started to introduce themselves, giggling self-consciously as they attempted to speak. I remembered how awkward it had been for me trying to speak English with strangers when I first arrived in the States as a refugee.

"What state of America do you live in?" someone asked. The questions had started.

"What do you think about Hanoi?" asked another.

"It is a very beautiful city," I answered. "I read about it in Vietnamese novels when I was young and heard about it from my mother. It is just as she described it." *So far, so good,* I thought.

"When did you leave Vietnam?" asked a young man in front.

"I left in 1975," I said.

"Why did you leave when your country was finally united?" asked a young doctor sitting by the window. His tone had a sharp edge, and I could tell that the questions were beginning to heat up.

"If you were in my position, you would have wanted to leave too," I said. "As I was growing up, I never knew a moment of peace. Every night, I went to bed expecting that I wouldn't wake up the next morning. The shelling always came at night. My younger sister was afraid, and I told her that if we died, the next morning when we awoke we would be in heaven with God."

The words flowed effortlessly out of my mouth. I could see some of the students looking at each other and nodding. They had lived through it, too.

"I know what you mean," said one young woman. "I was frightened when the sirens went off, warning us of American planes approaching the city. Although I was very young, I still remember the explosions."

"You were a child, but I wasn't," piped up an older doctor, who was the leader of the group. "I was working at Bach Mai Hospital one Christmas. Normally we had surgery in the basement, but because it was a big American holiday, we assumed the planes wouldn't come and that it was safe to operate upstairs. But they did come, and my best friend was killed. She was going to be married the next day."

I could hear the hurt and anger in her voice. The wounds of the war were still fresh, and soon, other, more pointed questions flooded forth from my listeners.

"How could you live among our oppressors?" a young woman

doctor asked incredulously. "We didn't start the war with the Americans. They came to destroy our country and kill our people!"

I could hear a buzz sweeping around the room. "Why do you ask her these questions?" someone whispered to the woman, trying to quell the tension.

Again, the words flowed out of my mouth. "Many Americans did not and still do not approve of the Vietnam War," I told her. "It was the American people who demanded to have the war stopped and the troops recalled.

"Today, many Americans care deeply for the Vietnamese and want to help," I explained. I cited Kathie, who had left her family and a good job to work in Hanoi, and the volunteer doctors who came regularly to Vietnam to work on health projects with REI-Vietnam. I mentioned how my trip and Philip's work were supported by hundreds of Americans across the country who wanted to see the Vietnamese people flourish. "These Americans don't think of Vietnam as the enemy," I insisted.

I could see that the young woman still wasn't satisfied. Her eyes flared angrily, and she was sitting on the edge of her seat, poised to attack. "So do the Americans admit that they lost the war?" she said.

By now, I could see that many people in the room were growing annoyed at her aggressiveness. They waved their hands at me as if to tell me to ignore her. But again, the right words came to me.

"I'm a great reader," I said. "One of the books I remember most was *All Quiet on the Western Front*, a novel by Erich Maria Remarque. It was about World War I, but it applies to every one of us. The message of his book is that the victory of all wars is the end of them.

"Many American mothers lost their sons, young wives lost their husbands, and children lost their fathers. I think Americans were very glad the war was over. And I was too. I came back because I love my country and I want to see peace reign here."

As I finished, I noticed a young doctor in the back row raising his hand. During the entire interchange, he hadn't said a word. He had just sat quietly, watching me with eyes so intense they seemed to pierce right through me. I had dreaded hearing from him because I sensed he might be the toughest of all to handle. Now that he was about to speak, I didn't think I had the power or presence of mind to respond effectively. The heat had sapped my energy, and I was spent emotionally.

"Excuse me," he said. "I have to leave because I'm scheduled to do an operation. But I have something to say."

As all heads turned toward him, I held my breath and braced myself for another attack.

"You are a very rich person," he said quietly.

I quickly shook my head to deny the charge, remembering how my father's mother had been persecuted by a people's court for being a *dia chu*, a landowner. "No, no," I said. "In America, we are considered lower middle class . . ."

The young doctor interrupted me and looked agitated. "I don't mean that," he said, with his eyes flashing. "I mean you are very rich in your *heart*. You have the same heartbeat as the Vietnamese people." Then he rushed out of the room.

I sat down in a chair and in front of everyone, I started to cry. *How I love you all!* I wanted to call out to them. God had used my fiery ordeal to break my heart for these people, and now I found myself wanting to share my life with them.

By now, Kathie had taken over the class and dismissed them. Soon students were pressing around me to say thank you. "Can we have a picture together?" I asked, when I pulled myself together.

As the students crowded around, there was one who pushed through her colleagues to stand right next to me. It was the young doctor who had come on the attack. She put her arm through mine and said, "Can I stand next to you?"

"Please do," I said. I grabbed her free hand and gave it a squeeze.

Later, when I looked up the Bible verses in Luke that God had given to me on the plane, the meaning finally dawned on me. In a way, I had been brought before "kings and governors," or at least the elite of Vietnamese society. Some had sought to "persecute" me, as the Bible had said they would.

But the verses hadn't ended with defeat. On the plane, I had been so consumed by fear over what I was reading that I had failed to read the verses that came afterward:

This will be a time for you to bear testimony. Settle it therefore in your minds, not to meditate beforehand how to answer; for I will give you a mouth and wisdom, which none of your adversaries will be able to withstand or contradict.

I will give you wisdom! That is exactly what had happened to me in front of the students. If I had been told the students' questions ahead of time, I would not have been able to come up with the answers. Perhaps I might have canceled the trip altogether. But at the right time, the Spirit had given me the words to say, and even the most hardened of my listeners had been touched.

Emboldened by the Spirit, I ventured forth to explore Hanoi further. Fear was forgotten—buried forever, I was sure. I felt so sure of myself that even though I had been warned against it, I decided to visit the Hanoi Protestant Church, where my grandfather had been an elder, in search of my spiritual roots.

I wasn't prepared for what I would find.

27

CLOUD OF WITNESSES

I knew I had to visit the Hanoi Protestant Chruch. In a way, it was my spiritual home, the place where Grandfather Tieu's fervent witness for Christ had sown the seeds of faith that had bloomed through three generations and now continued with my children.

But the message I had received from colleagues was, "Don't go."

My mother had fled to the south in part because of her faith, and I knew that believers were still suspect. Yet I couldn't help myself. I wanted to see for myself the piece of real estate that had become hallowed in my imagination. I wanted to walk where Grandfather Tieu had walked, visit the apartment where *Giao Si* Cadman and later my Grandmother Nhu had lived, and hear the footsteps of my mother and Esther Van Hine in the courtyard where they had played as children.

But it wasn't just the prospect of exploring the buildings that drew me. I had heard that an old couple who had known my grandfather was still living in the church compound. From time to time, people had seen them sitting on a bench in the courtyard, under the shade trees. The idea of making a flesh-and-blood connection with people who were peers of Grandfather Tieu, and who were said to love the Lord as he had, was too enticing to pass up. I needed to see them for myself and hear their testimony from their own lips, to confirm that the reports I had heard from my childhood were true.

At first, I wasn't the least bit afraid. After my experience with the English class, I had a new sense of God's power. I was confident that wherever I went, even in the midst of a fiery furnace, he would prepare the way for me and protect me as he did Shadrach, Me-shach, and Abednego. And so, the day before I was scheduled to leave Hanoi, I decided to look them up.

I hopped a *xe om*, the ubiquitous motorcycle taxi that went al-most anywhere for a dollar, and asked to be dropped off in front of the Leather Market, which was right near the church. By now I had gotten used to the death-defying motorcyclists, and instead of grip-ping the driver's waist with my hands in terror as I had done on the way to the English class with Kathie, I held them loosely by the driver's side and balanced myself naturally.

The *xe om* dropped me off at the market, and I went inside. Just as my father, Phuong, had done many years before, when he was on the run from the Japanese, I walked through the market and walked up and down the rows, one by one. I saw the chicken stall, with its cutting board and woven baskets with live chickens and ducks; the smoking stall where someone was selling tobacco products and bamboo opium pipes; and the flower stall, ablaze with chrysanthe-mums, roses, and lotus flowers. When I came to a stand selling *pho*, I couldn't resist stopping to eat a bowl of my favorite soup, with raw beef and tripe thrown in for good measure. I pulled up a seat and slurped down the noodles, savoring the delicious aroma of mint, basil, and cinnamon that filled my nostrils.

When I was finished, I left the market and found the street that led to the church compound. Now, unexpectedly, I found myself moving deeper and deeper into a different, more threatening world. When I finally reached the church, I took one look at it and cringed. I sensed someone, something was watching me, waiting for me to make one wrong move. The old fear was back.

I thought I was beyond it—that God had given me the strength to overcome it. But at the sight of the little church, with its gate open wide in welcome, I blanched. *I can't stop now,* I thought. *I've got to find the old couple. I must find them.*

I put my head down and started walking as fast as I could through the gate. I knew that if I looked up, or hesitated for even a moment, I would turn around and never come back. It took only a minute to reach the front door of a two-story building that I assumed was the church office. "Hello," I said, poking my head in the door.

A woman was seated at the desk. "Can I help you?" she asked, smiling sweetly.

I explained that I was looking for an elderly couple who were supposed to be living on the church grounds. "I believe they knew my grandfather," I said. "I'm Mr. Tieu's granddaughter."

"Oh, you mean Mr. and Mrs. Hoang," the young woman said. "Their grandson is the pastor. They're right upstairs."

She went to announce my arrival and then beckoned me to come up. I hurried up the steps and followed her into the living room, which was cluttered with children's toys and books. In the corner, a little girl sat practicing the piano.

"They're in here," the young woman said, pointing to a tiny room adjacent to the living room.

The room was dark, but there, sitting on a small bed made from a raised cement platform that nearly filled the room, was the old couple. Age spots peppered the man's ancient face and a wispy beard graced his chin. But his clothes were à la mode: at age ninety-seven, he was wearing a white T-shirt with the picture of a Chihuahua and the words, "I'm the boss."

As for his wife, "the second of Mr. Hoang's two wives," as she was quick to point out, her ninety-eight-year-old face was wrinkled as a prune. Dark cotton pajamas, the everyday clothes that people had worn in Vietnam from time immemorial, draped her bone-thin frame.

I noticed two well-worn Bibles by the side of the bed and a black velvet wall hanging with a picture of Jesus as the Good Shepherd. The words *Thi Thien* 23:1, Psalm 23:1, were inscribed underneath.

From the looks of it, I had apparently awakened them from a nap. "How do you do?" I said. "I am Mr. Tieu's granddaughter."

"What did you say?" the man asked.

I leaned closer. "Mr. Tieu's granddaughter," I shouted in his ear.

His eyes lit up in recognition. "Ah, Tieu," he said. "I knew him from his days in Vinh," he said. "He and I were both *lac loai*, 'lost.' But then Tieu was freed from his opium addiction, and I knew that through Jesus, I could be too. When I came to Hanoi, he led me to this church."

Mrs. Hoang seemed to be nodding. Her eyes were closed, and at first I thought she was falling asleep, until she started mumbling something under her breath. "The good news will be spread to many," she said, as if in a trance.

"Life was difficult for us sometimes," Hoang confessed. "My son was the pastor, and he died when he was thirty-six. Now my grandson is pastor."

"The Lord's faithfulness is forever," intoned his wife, paraphrasing Psalm 119.

"When your grandfather was dying, he called me to his bed and told me that he was going to be with Jesus," Mr. Hoang remembered. His eyes filled up with tears. "*Bo chet de da. Nguoi chet de tieng,*" he said, recalling an old Vietnamese saying. "When the cow dies, it leaves behind its hide. When people die, they leave behind their reputation." He added, "Your grandfather was very risky, very courageous."

But as I looked at them, I realized that they were the courageous ones. For nearly a century, they had lived through wars, poverty, death, and fear, and yet they had remained faithful. Their faces might be wrinkly and old, they might be tired and worn out, and their memory might be a little shaky, but they hadn't forgotten the promise of Scripture.

"The Lord never forgets those who love him," Mrs. Hoang said.

It was true. The Lord has not forgotten my people. Through these two dear believers I was witnessing firsthand his love for the Vietnamese for an entire century, and much longer, far into the distant mists of the past. And what he had done for my forebears, he would do for me.

This confidence in Christ's unswerving love and faithfulness was my inheritance. It was the legacy that had passed from my grandfather to my mother to me, and to my children.

With tears in my eyes, I said my good-bye to Mr. and Mrs. Hoang. But as I looked over my shoulder, I sensed that they were not alone. Standing with them in their tiny room was a crowd of familiar people.

Grandfather Tieu.

Grandmother Nhu.

Giao Si Cadman.

Giao Si Van Hine.

Giao Si Jackson.

They were gone, but somehow they were also all there, a "cloud of witnesses" watching over me, bidding me good-bye.

"*Tam biet*," they seemed to be saying.

The next day, when my plane lifted off the ground to take us back to the States, I looked out the window to see the peaceful countryside stretching out below me. This time, no bullets were flying by my window, as there had been on my first departure from Vietnam more than twenty years before. Instead I saw golden yellow rice paddies, ready for harvest.

When I had fled Saigon, I had said, "*Tu biet*," "Good-bye forever," vowing never to return. But this time my heart was singing. "*Tam biet*," I said. "Farewell, but only for now."

GLOSSARY

ao dai A form-fitting, silky, two-paneled dress, slit from the ankles to the waist, and worn with pants.

banh cuon A crepe made with steamed rice and filled with diced pork, mushrooms, onion, garlic, and fish sauce. The crepes, which are rolled up tight like tiny cigarettes, are eaten with *nuoc cham*, a spicy sauce made with anchovy extract, lime juice, sugar, water, and hot pepper.

Be Tu "Little Number Four," a diminutive name bestowed on the third child in a family.

Chi An honorific title meaning "elder sister," which, in conjunction with a person's first name, is used familiarly to refer to a nanny or any older woman. Anh's nanny, whose first name was Huong, was known as *Chi* Huong, or "elder sister Huong." Other terms commonly used for nanny are *ba* (Mrs.), or *co* (auntie).

cyclo A pedal driven, open-air "taxi," which features a passenger seat in front, and a bike, pedaled by a driver, in back.

dong Vietnamese dollars.

Me Mother.

pho A soup that is a staple of the Vietnamese diet, made with rice noodles, thinly sliced beef, and clear beef broth, and seasoned with ginger, star anise, garlic, onion, and cinnamon. Before being eaten, the soup is topped with fresh cilantro, sliced onion, and a squeeze of lime, along with fresh basil and bean sprouts.

tam biet Farewell for now. This temporary good-bye implies a return at some time in the future.

tu biet Farewell forever. The speaker of these words expects never again to return to the person or place she is leaving.

SELECTED REFERENCES

Booth, Martin. *Opium: A History*. New York: St. Martin's Press, 1996.

Cartwright, David. *Dark Paradise*. Cambridge: Harvard University Press, 1982.

Cowles, H. Robert, ed. *Operation Heartbeat*. Harrisburg, Pennsylvania: Christian Publications, Inc., 1976.

Dareff, Hal. *The Story of Vietnam*. New York: Avon Books, 1966.

Diem, Bui and Chanoff, David. *In the Jaws of History*. Boston: Houghton Mifflin, 1987.

Duiker, William J. *Ho Chi Minh*. New York: Hyperion, 2000.

Elders of the Hanoi Protestant Church, eds. *Memorial of the 85th Year of the Building of the Protestant Church in Hanoi*. Hanoi, December 2000.

Elliott, Duong Van Mai. *The Sacred Willow*. New York: Oxford University Press, 1999.

Evearitt, Daniel J. *Body & Soul*. Camp Hill, Pennsylvania: Christian Publications, 1994.

Greene, Graham. *The Quiet American*. New York: The Viking Press, 1956.

Hartzfeld, David F., and Nienkirchen, Charles, eds. *The Birth of a Vision*. Saskatchewan, Canada: His Dominion, 1986. Produced by Buena Book Services, Alberta, Canada.

Hefley, James C. *By Life or by Death*. Grand Rapids: Zondervan, 1969.

Hubbell, John G. *P.O.W.* New York: Reader's Digest Press, 1976.

Irwin, E. F. *With Christ in Indo-China*. Harrisburg, Pennsylvania: Christian Publications, Inc., 1937.

"I Will Say 'Yes' to Jesus," in *Hymns of the Christian Life Nos. 1, 2, and*

3 Combined. New York: Alliance Press Co., copyright A. B. Simpson, 1908.

Jackson, Hazel, *Thirty-Five Years in Vietnam*. Unpublished Manuscript, Courtesy of Victor Jackson.

Karnow, Stanley. *Vietnam*. New York: The Viking Press, 1983.

Kolko, Gabriel. *Anatomy of a War*. New York: Pantheon Books, 1985.

Niklaus, Robert L., Sawin, John S., and Stoesz, Samuel J. *All for Jesus*. Camp Hill, Pennsylvania: Christian Publications, Inc., 1986.

Sheehan, Neil. *A Bright Shining Lie*. New York: Random House, 1988.

Smith, Gordon Hedderly. *The Blood Hunters*. Chicago: Moody Press, 1942.

Tang, Truong Nhu, with Chanoff, David, and Toai, Doan Van. *Viet Cong Memoir*. New York: Harcourt Brace Jovanovich, 1985.

Thompson, A. E. *A. B. Simpson: His Life and Work*. Harrisburg, Pennsylvania: Christian Publications, Inc., Revised Edition, 1960.

Tozer, A. W. *Let My People Go!* Harrisburg, Pennsylvania: Christian Publications, Inc., 1947.